Praise for *Awaken*

"A human being is not an entirely solid object. We are built out of layers of energy, light, and consciousness, held together by a universal force. To be awakened is to get in touch with the subtleties of this force, and to use it wisely and productively. This is the extraordinary accomplishment of *Awakening the Holographic Human*."

—Janet Iris Sussman, author, musician, intuitive counselor, and developer of the Sunpoint™ subtle energy healing system

"A great deal has been written about ancient healing traditions, botanical therapies, astrology, chakras, and sacred geometry. In *Awakening the Holographic Human*, Dr. Botchis brings her deep experiential understanding of these topics to guide the user to weave his or her own unique tapestry of life into a soulful wholeness. Based on the interconnectedness of Nature and the human being, this book combines the practical with the mystical to create a universal handbook for living well. It is my pleasure to recommend this book to her readers."

—Dr. Rosemary Bourne, MA, Dipl. Acu., director, Institute for Esogetic Colorpuncture, USA

"In the twenty-first century, what is becoming humanly possible is beyond what we ever could have imagined—until now. *Awakening the Holographic Human* addresses the need of our time, bridging ancient and modern paradigms—from earth-based therapies to techno-intelligence—to bring us to the cutting edge of healing and higher consciousness. Dr. Botchis is an extraordinary emissary of the natural world!"

—Juliana Swanson, holistic Vedic astrologer and wellness coach

"Here we embark on a multidimensional journey through a deep trove of earth wisdom, guided by the direct cognitive experience and penetrating intellect of the author. With its broad scope, encompassing plants, gems, subtle body, symbolic systems, and higher consciousness technology, this book is an inspiring vision of wholeness. The reader will encounter a plethora of practical modalities for living in harmony with body and mind, suffused with a bold integrating intelligence."

—Douglas A. Mackey, PhD, author of *The Dance of Consciousness* and *Philip K. Dick*

"Lilli Botchis is one of the most important herbal and natural healing experts I know, and her new book, *Awakening the Holographic Human*, shares the wealth of her wisdom. She uses her understanding of gems and flower essences like an art form, revealing the inner workings of nature in beautifully crafted language. Her understanding of the wisdom of nature to heal is a gift to all of us. The subtlety and depth of her perception is astounding. I am joyful that this book is in the world."

—Diane Frank, author of *Blackberries in the Dream House* and *Yoga of the Impossible*

Dr. Lilli Botchis is a brilliant researcher in the field of consciousness. In *Awakening the Holographic Human*, she speaks with deep understanding born of years of study in the ever expanding world of esoteric knowledge, providing an essential service to professionals and lay people alike: synthesis. Her personal exploration of consciousness allows her to express the unifying principles in this important, relevant, and transformational perspective on health, human life, and spiritual awakening. I highly recommend this book and the world of deeper insight and understanding that it opens up at this critical time in our human journey on Earth.

—Jennifer Hamilton, RN, BSN, certified Sunpoint practitioner, Thresholding death midwife and celebrant

"*Awakening the Holographic Human* is an invaluable resource for health practitioners and for anyone passionately committed to self-discovery. It's filled with practical wisdom about how to make the best use of gems, flowers, color, the chakra system, and the astrological zodiac. Dr. Botchis's deep connection with the natural world and her exquisite sensitivity enable her to masterfully guide you in creating profound shifts in your consciousness. An extraordinarily transformational book!"

—Marci Shimoff, #1 *New York Times* best-selling author of *Happy for No Reason*; featured teacher in *The Secret*

"Lilli Botchis is a deeply caring, fully present human being committed to ameliorating the pain and confusion of our times. Her profound understanding of consciousness as the creative force in life is offered in her book *Awakening the Holographic Human*. Lilli's intelligent, compassionate presentation allows us to perceive our internal and external reality more directly, and we realize the most important lesson we are here to learn is how to love."

—Sallie Morgan, RN, BA, Ayurveda natural health therapist

AWAKENING *the* HOLOGRAPHIC HUMAN

Nature's Path to Healing & Higher Consciousness

Also by Elizabeth E. Botchis, PhD

Plants in the Light of Healing

A Practical & Spiritual Guidebook to Herbal/Flower Essence Blends

Planetary Gem Elixirs: Unlocking the Holographic Psyche

A Universal Healing System Founded on
Vedic Astrology and Geo-Chromatic Gem Therapy

AWAKENING the HOLOGRAPHIC HUMAN

Nature's Path to Healing & Higher Consciousness

Elizabeth E. Botchis, PhD

Published by 1st World Publishing
P.O. Box 2211, Fairfield, Iowa 52556
tel: 641-209-5000 • fax: 866-440-5234
web: www.1stworldpublishing.com

Cover design by Joma Sipe
www.jomasipe.com

First Edition

LCCN: 2017901687

Softcover ISBN: 978-1-4218-3766-6

Hardcover ISBN: 978-1-4218-3767-3

eBook ISBN: 978-1-4218-3768-0

The information included in this book is for educational purposes only. It is not intended to be used as a basis for self-treatment or as a substitute for professional medical care, nor is it intended to diagnose, treat, cure, or mitigate any disease, illness, or symptom. The reader should consult with a qualified health professional with regard to all symptoms, treatments, and dosage recommendations. Any reader taking prescription medication must be especially careful to seek professional medical attention before using any formulas or substances described in this book. The author and publisher shall have neither liability nor responsibility to any person or entity with respect to any loss, damage, or injury caused or alleged to be caused, directly or indirectly, by the information contained in this book. Any application of the information contained in this book is at the reader's own discretion and risk.

To the devic intelligence
of the natural world,
which has graced me with insight,
understanding, and transformation

The staircase to Heaven is inside your heart;

you enter through the door of your soul.

Our whole life is but an attempt to find this miraculous entrance.

—Vladimir Martynov

CONTENTS

PREFACE

I learned early on that I was not from this world. I was five years old, outstretched, belly to the ground, and gazing into a blade of grass—when an instant opened and infinity rushed in, taking me into a wakeful state of memory: I had been intentionally planted here on Earth. An unshakable certainty rooted me to this planet, for which I felt immense reverence and responsibility. The moment stretched into a suspended, all-encompassing state of awe. I clearly was here on purpose.

I witnessed this incident both in the moment and from outside it. There was no differentiation between myself and the realization. This knowing happened, and the imprint remains: I was here to tell the truth about what I saw, felt, and would come to know. It was an unquestionable state of reality that I continue to this day to carry quietly and respectfully.

Knowing on a prelinguistic level that my soul's origin was from other worlds, I was made aware that I had come to deposit information of a different kind and to act on behalf of the collective cosmos of beings, not just the collective consciousness of this planet.

Knowing I had been purposefully planted on Earth gave me a sense of belonging, a home, and a spiritual destination in time that I wasn't able to articulate to others early on. This knowledge caused me to go deeper into a space of creative power and imagination, of archetypical and mythological living that expressed itself in childhood theatrics that were odd, unusual, wild, and outside definitions of gender. I felt like a spiritual pioneer with a human space suit on, looking for adventures that would allow me to enact the realities I was living on the inner landscape of my soul—the same realities that churned in the collective unconscious of humanity.

I turned to Nature to delve into the mysteries of life. I would pick a flower, drink in its smell and color, and wonder, *How is it that this flower can increase my capacity to experience love and feel happy?*

I found myself feeling and seeing into the fabric of other people. This penetrating insight (some people thought I was staring into them) went beyond empathically feeling their feelings and telepathically hearing their thoughts: it was clear to me on a primordial, knowing level that the person before me was more than a collection of his or her surface-level emotions and thoughts. When I gazed at another human being, I entered into the secret hidden territory of his or her innermost nature, a nature that we shared. I recognized a luminous quality of essence radiating from within. Over time, my ability to access and process internal psychic information became the most natural, real, and dominant way to know life, often pushing the external aside. My natural mode of learning, communicating, and exchanging information clearly emerged: I would enter into a field of resonance with people, plants, and other objects that captured my curiosity, so I could learn directly from, through, and with them.

I saw light in everything, particularly in the forests and sky that surrounded my home in Massachusetts. I thrived, ecstatic as I witnessed wild animals, birds, plants, and flowers that lived near and around my home. Not only could I converse with them through resonance, I could also understand that they were conversing and imparting information and sensory feeling to me—an interaction I enjoyed as much as, if not more than, interacting with people.

This all transpired on a nonverbal, prelinguistic level. Like the wordless prayer of plant, gem, and color, it is the naked reality I have lived and loved in all the years of my life. As with many indigenous peoples, it is the way of the shaman.

ARCHETYPES AND PARALLEL REALITIES

As I child, I lived my life playing and enacting all that my psyche could imagine. Physically, I was vital, strong, fast, and agile—a daring soul. I excelled at sports and loved to engage in dramatizations of past-life imprints—

dominant themes were priest, medicine man, and Native American warrior.

I was also gifted with the creative powers of the dyslexic child. I loved the thrill of imagination, color, forms, and scents—the rush of new adventures. Alongside this vivacious nature was a deep, contemplative, and philosophically inquisitive mind.

My immigrant Greek parents, who lived an Old World lifestyle, had an intuitive and innocent sense of my unconventional behavior. I had the psychic sensitivity of the feminine—in love with nature and flowers—and the dynamic power, spirit, and willfulness of the masculine. This so-called dual subtle-body configuration gave me a very full range of motion on all levels—emotional, intellectual, physical, and spiritual. I was what we would call today a star child.

But the 1950s school system did not yet know about star people (just as today's school system doesn't know about the indigo- and crystal-frequency beings now populating our planet). I was naturally lively, steeped in the inner world of unbounded spaciousness, imagination, and dynamic creativity. But when I started school, the expectations of me to perform within systematized parameters of memorization saddened my heart and dampened my spirit. For my dyslexic brain, it was all too plain, boring, artificial, and pointless.

Being required to speak exclusively in the English tongue further imposed a rigid feeling of conformity, inhibited my ethnic freedom of expression, forced gender identification upon me, and drove irrational formality onto my plate. My rich inner life, creativity, and imagination were forced to go underground. But while I silently observed the demands for illogical conformity, inwardly—ever the rebel and revolutionary warrior—I never surrendered.

My ability to imagine was the gateway into seeing the composites of my psyche. The collective pool of bio-human consciousness was vivid and potent in my psyche, and I spent my early years living and integrating the multiple and dynamic forces of energy inherent in the archetypal world of my psyche.

From a very young age, I had bleed-throughs of simultaneous past lives (which I see now as ongoing parallel realities). My awareness of myself contained clear experiences of a composite of archetypes that lived as "I," with detailed memory, as if it were all happening in the present on some level.

My soul/psyche was deeply involved in resolving and integrating the sub-routines and imprints from these past lives. I found that I could and would shapeshift and explore the primal energies of these archetypes, which to this day I share a sacred space/time with: the warrior from Native American soul experiences, the soldier from World War II, the Spartan Greco warrior, the high priest who created and performed rituals of initiation and rites of passage, the doctor/healer who created brews and elixirs, the Egyptian alchemist who soul-journeyed into the afterworld, the merchant who loved to sell and barter for exchange of goods, the philosopher, the clown, the court jester, the contemplative stoic, the prostitute, the pirate, the doctor, the magician, the mad professor, the inventor, and the alien intelligence that spoke without words and saw with one eye—these soul-level realities all dwelled within as the I.

I was able to see all of these archetypal expressions of my psyche in others as well, whether they were conscious of them or not. In time, I developed a means of knowing others and knowing myself that was enriched by self-contemplation and the desire to see even deeper into the essential nature of everything. The light of soul was permeating life, and it led to the serious and dedicated practice of meditation. I engaged in contemplative practices and philosophical inquiries that allowed me to know and experience the essence and potency of my nature, like the blade of grass that once lifted a veil and continues in each moment to hold the window open.

Some of my own subroutines and archetypes were stronger and more prominent than others and have required greater time to transmute, manage, incorporate, and synthesize into my soul's reservoir of talents, traits, and characteristics. Yet always there was a non-localized space within my being that was beyond all this and lived as an impersonal expression of nature—which I recognize today as the "transpersonal Self."

CRISIS AND THE CALL TO HEALING

Despite my challenges with learning, until the age of twenty, I was vital, dynamic, strong, creative, healthy, and happy. Then one day I began experiencing shortness of breath. My heart started to feel contracted, and I began to lose weight despite eating huge amounts of food. I began having severe cardiac arrhythmias and excruciating, crippling muscle spasms. My tremors were so bad that I couldn't hold a pencil. I was losing hair, I couldn't tolerate light, and my anxiety and irritability were increasing. Every level of my being was affected, and I felt completely lost as to what was going on within me.

Believing that I was going to die, I drove myself to the hospital and walked into the emergency room. I was immediately hospitalized; tests revealed that I had pneumonia and Graves' disease—a progressive neurodegenerative and immune disorder considered life-threatening and incurable.

Over time, the doctors were able to stabilize me through the use of multiple medications and nuclear medicine. However, within two months, the changes to my system from the prescribed medications caused me to go from 120 to 170 pounds. My doctors told me I would need to be on medication for the rest of my life.

Fortunately, this reality just didn't feel true to me. It wasn't in alignment with my nature and how I wanted to live my life. My soul guided me to seek and explore natural cures—and I was catapulted into the world of natural healing and the exploration of higher states of consciousness that led me to where I am today, both personally and professionally. I learned how to use herbs as agents of healing to regenerate and balance my body. I learned how to use flower essences to manage my dyslexia and heal the emotional challenges I had, resulting from self-consciousness, lack of confidence, and low self-esteem. I began to experience and understand these gifts of Nature as celestial material, packets of intelligence that spoke the language of healing to my body, my emotions, my mind—even my soul. I learned how to apply these gifts within the universal templates of the zodiacal archetypes and the chakra system, which gave me entry into my own holographic nature.

Today, there is no trace of Graves' in my body. I take no medication, and I attribute my health and state of well-being to the power and intelligence of Nature available to us all. *Awakening the Holographic Human* is an attempt to capture the wisdom that I have gained through my journey from crisis to healing and beyond. It is about the therapeutic and magical elements of Nature that God has given us: flowers, herbs, gems, and the healing energies of our planet—an offering of the sacred tools of the Earth, for which I am eternally grateful.

ACKNOWLEDGMENTS

With gratitude and honor, I thank the devic intelligence of the natural world, which has so graced me in this lifetime with insight, understanding, transformation, and revelation, that I may share what I have come to know as visible and true with all those whom this body of knowledge touches.

I remain in reverence for and gratitude to my Master teacher, Maharishi Mahesh Yogi.

I give soulful gratitude, honor, and love to my spiritual companion and enlightened editor Jennifer Read Hawthorne, for her light of consciousness and ability to see into the organizing structure of this book. With linguistic mastery, Jennifer guided the healing vibrations of this book to radiate and bless readers in their use and enjoyment of the knowledge contained herein.

Deepest gratitude also goes to my dear lifelong spiritual friend and guiding light, Janet Iris Sussman, for her patience, full-heartedness, devotion, and eye of illumination, which supported the awakening of my heart and soul to make this book possible.

I also wish to acknowledge Doug Mackey with great gratitude for his unconditional heart, shining the light of consciousness and providing practical and spiritual insight on the many diverse aspects of this body of knowledge. His illuminated feedback provided a steady grounding force along the path towards bring this book into manifestation.

Thanks to Suzanne Lawlor for her lifelong inspiration and soulful recognition and encouragement, always seeing into the deepest nature of the sublime and thus holding an inner space for cognition and grace to flow.

I also wish to acknowledge Patricia Kaminski and Richard Katz, founders of the Flower Essence Society, for their lifelong contribution to the planet, awakening the majestic healing powers of plants in the hearts of hundreds of thousands of people. They personally set the stage for me to delve into the spirit and consciousness of nature as who I Am.

I give gratitude to Jay Boyle for his generosity in providing me with the highest quality, most luminescent astrological gemstones utilized in the creation of Planetary Gem Elixirs.

A final acknowledgment to Lucile Portwood, a mentor and friend who paved the way for my education and initiations, both professionally and spiritually.

INTRODUCTION
An Invitation to the Sublime

Knowing yourself is the beginning
of all wisdom.
　　　　　　　　—Aristotle

The human race is at the tipping point of disaster, desperate for transformation. Crises of every kind—social, economic, political, ecological, and spiritual—pose seemingly insurmountable challenges to mankind. And as if the stress of watching the evening news weren't enough, we're all forced daily to deal with our own social, economic, and spiritual crises.

Overwhelmed by everything from the pace of technology to too much to do in too little time to expenses that exceed our income, we long to reconnect—with sanity, with nature, with ourselves. We're turning by the millions to spiritual practices, such as meditation, yoga, and mindfulness. We're choosing alternative medicine, such as mind-body and energy medicine. And we're realizing that the madness within humanity—which is both accelerating and intensifying—can be transmuted by only one thing: a shift in consciousness.

Such a shift in consciousness is the topic of *Awakening the Holographic Human: Nature's Path to Healing and Higher Consciousness*. In this book, I have attempted to articulate the state of beauty that resides in every human being, the state that can be lived by anyone as limitations are cleared. This infinite, supernatural state is a state of higher consciousness capable of anything—cognizing, healing, manifesting, understanding, and compassion—all beyond our ordinary comprehension of what it means to be human.

The true glory of this supernatural state is that it allows us to shift from a personal state of reference to a transpersonal experience of living, one that is not limited by the conditions of our personal reality. Transpersonal living allows us to view our lives from a more objective perspective; as we grow in the ability to allow and accept, we are no longer bogged down by our personal "stories." We no longer fall victim to our beliefs, thoughts, and reactions—are no longer enslaved by them.

To go beyond the personal is to go deep into the Mystery, the Sacred, the Sublime. This state has been revealed to me over the years through Nature, through experiences of intimate communion with what I call "the personal cosmos." Mother Earth is generous in the tools she offers us humans, and my own revelations have been well served through the experience of flowers, herbs, gems, colors, and energy when applied within the universal templates of the chakras and the stars—blueprints of Nature that contain codes for us to enliven and elevate our consciousness to that of the "holographic human." I joyfully share my experience and knowledge of these blueprints and gifts with you in this book.

Every flower essence I ever made or imbibed revealed to me more of my own nature. Every gem elixir I created revealed the mechanics of creation and the possibilities for manifesting the fullness of life on earth. Taking a flower essence or gem elixir provided an inner journey, initiating me as I walked through the passageways of my own psyche into something I never imagined myself to be. Herbs, colors, and the subtle energies of breath work, yoga, meditation, and bio-resonant technologies propelled me further into the limitless possibilities of human potential.

My self-inquiry into the holographic human revealed a composite of universal templates in the zodiac and chakra systems. Early on my life's path, as I began an in-depth study of the mystery teachings and esoteric sciences, **I discovered that these subtle and celestial templates resonated harmonically with earth-based materials and energy forms—plants, herbs, gems, light, and color.** These templates—composites of our own psyche, or soul potential—form the basis of all human experience and of an awakening of consciousness that is beyond our ability to imagine.

At first, I identified strongly with the primary archetypal template that my own astrological chart defined. It was invaluable in understanding the makeup of my personality—its strengths, weaknesses, soul gifts, and challenges—as well as the forces of Nature embodied by my particular archetype, innate to its signature. However, over time, I came to experience and understand that I was a holographic human—that all these cosmological templates were active within me. I realized that the unlocked potential within every template was waiting to be brought forward in self-mastery.

Through my study, training, and spiritual practices with the chakra system, I came to vividly experience that these energy portals were a means to connect me to the living cosmos; each one had a theme, a governing principle universal to all humans on the path to awakening our holographic self.

This journey through my personal cosmos has allowed me to see the world through Nature's heart and eyes, to understand the forces that shape our destinies, and to be a part of the larger ongoing shift I've witnessed over the years—the shift from a personal, reference-based reality into a growing awareness of a transpersonal, holistic, and multilayered reality. With the rising popularity of modern and ancient cosmological systems, healing traditions, and spiritual sciences, human consciousness has begun turning an eye both inward and toward the heavens to more fully examine and understand the nature of personal reality and how to expand beyond it into something greater: the holographic human.

The result is nothing less than a lifting free of our concave cosmological heredity—a self-centered, limited view of ourselves—to embrace the totality of the universal psyche. This cosmic mind is fluid and alive, and it has at its disposal a holographic framework out of which it can understand the personal/transpersonal reality and all the myriad diversity of human nature.

This book is a guide that can illumine the personal pathway as the veils are lifted and one merges into a fluid, holographic field.

WHO SHOULD READ THIS BOOK

If you're interested in psycho-spiritual and emotional healing, the sacred mechanics of creation, transformation, the development of higher states of consciousness, or understanding and actualizing the human spirit and its potential—then this book is for you. It it equally useful to the health professional and the individual passionately committed to self-discovery.

Each human psyche is capable of stretching the fabric of what it means to be human—man; woman; child; professional; layperson; or person of a certain color, race, culture, or tradition—all the way into a transpersonal reality based on pure states of divine expression. Such a transformation is to step into the presence of the future now.

As humans awaken simultaneously and in concert with the awakening of our planet, we are asked to respond to this call, which transcends both ancient and modern reference points and definition. This shift in identity, from form to formlessness, from the physical to the subtle structures of light and energy that uphold form, requires living inside the skin of all forms to master the governing principles, energies, and characteristics of nature within us—that is, to become an earth-based cosmological being. This means being able to feel the reality of all forms—a flower, a tree, a stone, another human being, a country, a planet—and to be in presence with them, to feel their aliveness.

The implications of such a shift are staggering. As each individual recognizes himself or herself as part of the whole of Nature, it becomes impossible for him or her to destroy. We cannot cut down the trees in the Amazon if we can feel the significance of its ecology and its role in our well-being on planet Earth. We cannot butcher elephants for their ivory if we can feel the spirit of these magnificent animals. We cannot use the oceans as our dumping grounds if we can feel the cry of their life force dwindling. **Every individual shifting from the personal to the transpersonal contributes to a shift in collective consciousness.**

As a writer, I have attempted to articulate and describe the supernatural state of being, that potential that resides in all humans, given the opportunities that silence, stillness, and reverence for creation offer humanity. It is my desire with this book to introduce you to these realms and to awaken and enliven this reality within your awareness.

WHAT YOU'LL FIND IN THIS BOOK

Awakening the Holographic Human attempts to describe the relationship between our corporeal, heartfelt sense of identity and the cosmic, indefinable source of divinity that resides within the human heart and soul. We are children of the Universe, and as such, every part of the pattern of creation, every sacred element is related to and through us.

A hologram is an image or system with different aspects, each of which can be seen to represent the whole. *Awakening the Holographic Human* offers a synthesis of many time-honored systems of healing—including the sciences of light and color, Eastern and Western astrology, planetary gem therapies, alchemy, and botanical therapies—into which I have delved deeply to gain a greater understanding of myself. This book is designed to bring universal perspective through my own journey into these realms, offering insights into these traditions based on direct knowledge and experience of the forces of Nature expressed through planetary bodies, plants, gems, herbs, color, and subtle energy. As a result, readers are given access to an in-depth understanding of themselves and their relationship to the world at large.

The language of Nature and the language of the body are cryptographic; to apply their knowledge practically, they each require sensitive translation. The interpreter must decode sacred messages, embedded in the symbolic knowledge of the psyche, that are reflected in the pictorial imprint of Nature. The petals of a rose, a pinecone, and a seashell tell the story of the spiral configuration of Nature that presents itself in the template of the body.

In *Awakening the Holographic Human*, the reader will learn how to select and/or create unique bio-resonant formulas that heighten awareness and provide insight into the prismatic fragments of the psyche as it morphs towards new pictures of holographic design. **This book is a vehicle to empower the soul to actualize new dimensions of life.**

Chapter 1, "The Holographic Psyche: A Transpersonal View of the All-Possible Human," explores how the transpersonal path brings one into the essence of what it means to be human. To be true to our natures, we must use healing approaches and therapies that follow the basic human architectural principles found throughout Nature—including the human physical and subtle bodies—that create, maintain, and sustain life. The psyche, or soul, is the gateway to accessing Nature's blueprints for health and higher consciousness—the gateway to becoming the holographic human. The holographic psyche is a transpersonal state—a state beyond the personal three-dimensional reality that we experience conditionally on Earth. The shift from a personal toward a transpersonal, non-referential identity brings one into a life-path trajectory that aligns with the highest levels of human destiny. Chapter 1 looks at the holographic psyche in terms of the "all-possible human" and how the transpersonal path brings one into the essence of what it means to be a cosmic human. It explores deeply the nature of the holographic psyche and the significance of the mathematical heart, which infinitely attunes us to the transpersonal nature of our cosmic being. It makes the connection between our physical form—especially the heart—and the mystical blueprints that form the basis of creation.

Chapter 2, "The Mythic Landscape of Healing: A Multicultural Perspective," shows how the natural world reflects the movement of mind and spirit. It describes six traditional systems of healing that recognize spirit as the predominant influence in healing and well-being.

Chapter 3, "Plants in the Light of Healing: Aligning Mind/Body/Soul," explores one of the key tools Nature gives us to apply within the universal templates of the chakras and the zodiac. All plants are visionary teachers and healers whose role is to act as an inner guide, speaking directly to the soul in the language of light, sound, kinesthetic experience, smell, and taste. In this chapter, the reader journeys into the mystical nature of plants—how they heal and speak to the human mind/body/soul. The chapter also highlights practical plant preparations for maintaining health and wellness in life.

Chapter 4, "Gems in the Light of Healing: Accessing Cosmic Intelligence," describes another major tool that can be used in concert with the chakras and the zodiacal archetypes for healing and expanding consciousness. Though gems are created on Earth, they resonate with stellar points of origin throughout the galaxy, interfacing with energies that empower their healing properties. The gem is part of an extended influence of stellar light that forms the pathways for specific waves of creative intelligence to bring each celestial pattern into form. This chapter describes how gem elixirs work through the chakra system and subtle bodies, how gems enhance the light within our electromagnetic body, how they're made, and how to apply gems as color/light therapy. We'll also look at the use of gems and gem elixirs as astrological remediation.

Chapter 5 is "Sacred Geometry and the Mystical Power of Gems." Sacred geometry is a mathematical language that reveals information about how creation unfolds. It was understood by the ancients to be the "language of the Godhead." Gems are composed of minerals that organize themselves using this language of geometry. They are precise mathematical formulations that reveal a profound depth of meaning about the creative forces that govern life and our universe. This chapter looks at the primary organizing patterns of the manifest world known as the Platonic solids and how each of these evolutionary mathematical progressions is directly expressed through gems.

Chapter 6, "The Twelve Zodiacal Archetypes: Nature's Blueprint of Our Holographic Psyche," explores one of the two primary universal templates described in this book, divulging the deep, primordial metamorphosis of the idea of human into the concrete mechanism of human. The astrological archetypes form the energies upon which all mystical gnosis is built—from the runes, to astrology, to tarot, to aspects of Vedic science. Knowledge and mastery of these archetypes form the foundation of all our aspirations, the place of residence for all our potential. Flower essences and gem elixirs associated with each archetype are provided to help the user embody the higher-dimensional attributes and forces of Nature.

The chakra system is described in Chapter 7, "The Seven Chakras: Dimensional Bridges." The chakra system is the second major template we explore. This chapter ties together our physiology with the psycho/spiritual constructs that form the basis of physical form. The foundation of both our humanity and our divinity, the chakra system clothes us in light. It gives us the fundamental tools of reckoning between our environment and ourselves. Flower essences and gem elixirs associated with each chakra are offered as illustration and vehicles for entry into the sacred fields of the chakras.

Chapter 8, "Higher Technology for Higher Consciousness: The Birth of Bioactive Techno-Intelligence," looks at the extension of the natural world into the world of technology for higher consciousness: specifically, the birth of techno-intelligence. Systems of technological organization are now being inescapably woven into human reality; technology has become an extension of human functioning. The impulse of a thought can move an artificial limb or command a remote device such as a television. It is no longer a matter of technology being seen as something foreign to our human identity; the question for humanity is, How do we live in harmony with technology and preserve our humanity? This chapter explores this question and looks at how the functioning of human beings is changing to equip us to handle the speed, efficacy, and neural challenge of modern technology.

Color, a category unto itself, is the backbone of our experience of nature and of everything we know as real. More than a vibration, color is a tool that the Creator manifested to explain diversity in the midst of unity. Color is the window to our own souls, as well as to the delicate refinement of the exterior world. When the knowledge of the chakras, the knowledge of the archetypes, and the knowledge of color are blended with our experience of the *Atman*, the Self—the essential, colorless, odorless, infinite Knower— there is a marriage of heaven and earth that speaks volumes about who we are meant to become. You will find color mentioned in every chapter in this book as it relates to plants, gems, planets, and chakras.

HOW TO USE THIS BOOK

I invite you to enter into the knowledge held in this book as if it were a holographic reflection of yourself. It can best be utilized as a living divination tool that can give insight into your personal reality and provide you with colors, gems, flower essences, botanical formulations, and healing tools that can be of support relative to your asking and quest for assistance.

The most systematic way to utilize the information set forth in this book would be to work within any one system or multiple systems described herein: archetypes, chakras, color/light therapy, gem elixirs, flower essences, or botanical formulations. Let's say, for example, you choose to start with the archetypes. Start with Aries, the first archetype, and take the prescribed remedies for one month. Then move to the next archetype, Taurus, for a month—and so on. Or you could use the chakra system as a starting point, using formulas/remedies for the base root chakra for a month, then ascending chakra by chakra each month to the crown. These systematic approaches will allow you to gain deep insight into your own nature and the processes of self-mastery described in this book. The lifelong journey is ever shapeshifting, and ultimately, a path well taken becomes invisible. In other words, eventually, you will outgrow the boundaries of whatever system you use.

A more intuitive and organic approach is equally honored: with sincerity and openness, hold the book between the palms of your hands, ask a question, wait for the feeling of Presence, and open the book with reverence. Reflect on the information found on those specific pages. Although this is a nonlinear process, the innate intelligence of the soul will guide you in the random order that is implicit and explicit in Nature. As the ancient law of Nature says: as above, so below; as within, so without. And so it is.

As you follow this trail, you will be vested in a sacred perception of truth. This is not a new knowledge, as much as it is a special vessel of indigenous knowing passed down through the ages; it is a tale told to humanity in a form that is fitting for this age and time.

Since we are human souls seeking a home for ourselves on a planet that is still at times full of hostility, fear, and hopelessness, the sacred medicines that the Creator has established for us are harbingers of a world in which all fear will someday be eradicated and all creatures will live in peace and goodwill. We are dualistic creatures, split from the house of the infinite but seeking our way back to the magical castle of divine union.

The healing substances, modalities, and systems described in this book are among the most potent and practical tools for accessing Nature's blueprints for healing and higher consciousness—to help us find our way home. Life is a spiritual journey, and like H. Spencer Lewis, founder of the Rosicrucian Order, I believe that "there is nothing so inspiring, so filled with peace, happiness, perfect health, joy, and contentment as the development of the spiritual nature."

May this book bring you untold blessings.

THE HOLOGRAPHIC PSYCHE

A Transpersonal View of the All-Possible Human

The goal of life is to make your
heartbeat match the beat of the universe,
to match your nature with Nature.
—Joseph Campbell

Every human being is holographic in nature. The most commonly understood definition of *holographic* is that "the whole is contained in all the parts." Applied to the human being, this means that every individual is a composite of the entire cosmos.

Every individual is capable of functioning as a seamless and integrated exponent of the wholeness of life, a psycho-physiological bliss state that encompasses contentment, happiness, compassion, kindness, and advanced states of cognitive functioning and knowingness.

Psychic/spiritual expressions of the holographic human include advanced human functioning like telepathy, felt mathematics, time travel, and unbounded non-referential awareness. Every individual also carries the blueprints for perfect physical and mental health. Yet good health is an illusive state in the human race, defined mostly by an ill-health system that masks and deranges our blueprints for health.

The psyche, or soul, is the gateway to accessing Nature's blueprints for health and higher consciousness—the gateway to becoming the holographic human. **The holographic psyche is the inner light of consciousness that** shines through the unique prism of the individual's soul and is expressed on the canvas of life.

The holographic psyche is a transpersonal state—a state beyond the personal three-dimensional reality that we experience conditionally on Earth. The transpersonal state implies the use of holographic awareness; the holographic psyche is the platform, the mechanism for becoming a transpersonal being cosmologically integrated into the oneness and fabric of galactic life.

This chapter looks at the holographic psyche in terms of the "all-possible human," meaning in terms of how the transpersonal path brings one into the essence of what it means to be a cosmic human. It explores deeply the nature of the holographic psyche and the significance of the mathematical heart, which infinitely attunes us to the transpersonal nature of our cosmic being. This chapter makes the connection between our physical form—especially the heart—and the mystical blueprints that form the basis of creation.

Ancient and modern seers, healers, shamans, and metaphysicians view the transpersonal journey as a transdimensional process linking many realms of awareness. Lucid dream states, heightened sensory awareness, zero-point energy (an integrated field of infinite correlation), the scalar-wave coherent field phenomenon (a nonlinear, self-regenerating energy wave), and near-death awakenings tap into the archetypal templates of our collective psyche. Through such peak experiences—in combination with meditative, contemplative, and devotional practices—one grows in transparency and becomes able to view life beyond the perimeters of the ego. The shift from a personal towards a transpersonal, non-referential identity brings one into a life path trajectory that aligns with the highest levels of human destiny.

BRIDGING THE GAP BETWEEN THE HUMAN AND THE COSMIC SOUL

The holographic psyche is the bridge between our cosmic soul and everything it means to be human. It is a holographic map, a blueprint of the historical and future aspects of one's body/mind complex. The individual human psyche is a microcosm of collective consciousness played out through one's body, mind, and emotions.

Through this blueprint of the body/mind, one is bonded to the condition of universal interdependence. As one's holographic psyche emerges as the template between inner and outer reality, one gains access to the innate ability to walk through life in Oneness as an infinite, interconnected, interdependent, galactic human.

In the initial stages of the psycho-spiritual shifts toward the transpersonal self—which this book seeks to facilitate—the individual soul most often confronts the personal, psycho-emotional realms. There is an inherent identification with ancestral patterns that calls for the journeyer to traverse his or her ancestral lineage, clearing inherited karmic imprints from the psyche.

During the transition into the transpersonal state, the individual begins to embody a level of subtle vibration that widens the universal flow of energy and information. Through his or her insight and the vigilance of self-examination, the rigid domain of the ego and shadow self becomes infused with the transpersonal perspective of expanded awareness. This expansion opens a space for the clearing of the distortions in the psychological matrices that limit human creativity and potential.

The healing journey into holographic functioning is unbounded in its creative intelligence; through the realignment of psyche with Source, one can undergo vast changes in cellular and neurological function. The transpersonal path is a synergistic relationship between our corporeal, heartfelt sense of identity and the cosmic, indefinable source of divinity that resides within.

A HOLOGRAPHIC PHILOSOPHY

The templates of human-based archetypal and cosmological mapping—such as astrology, the I-Ching, runes, the enneagram, and the tarot—can accurately reveal how personal trajectories of consciousness open out into the panoramic view of a wider transpersonal destiny. These ancient and modern space/time maps serve both individual and sociocultural psychologies. When applied with deep knowledge and heartfelt desire, these maps serve to invoke soul memory of the nature of personal reality as it unfolds on its cosmic journey towards full recognition of the Self.

In the healing process, it is vital to address the transformation of ancestral roots and prenatal patterns. By identifying familial imprinting in the psyche, one is able to discern how certain genetic predispositions express themselves in the individual psyche. These imprints provide clues to the present-day markers that can lead to problematic or painful outcomes in one's life.

Holographic functioning liberates the inner, personal point of reference so one can enter higher-dimensional space. This freedom produces coherent, synchronous, highly intelligent constructs of reality that are beyond the boundaries delineated by fixed psychological anchors or collective reasoning.

The forces of life on this planet are precipitating a breakthrough awakening to new depths of perception. A visionary typography of the psyche is now emerging that includes light, color, sound, sacred geometry, and more. The subtle senses are a means of accessing higher cognitive knowledge. A geometry of light, sound, and color maps the realms of the holographic psyche. A multidimensional world is laid open to awareness.

From these domains, we can begin to construct a new map of the psyche, which encompasses a primordial visual memory that includes biological, psychological, mythological, and spiritual dimensions. This new map of the psyche will enable us to directly understand phenomena such as the unconscious as a repository for re-experiences of birth and encounters with death,[1] the collective unconscious as described by Jung, the Bardo realms of Tibetan Buddhism, and the Dreamtime of Australian aborigines.

We are destined to embrace an informed mysticism that will cause a collective migration into the most sensitive lenses of individual and global psyche. A new living model of humanity can transform the archaic landscape of a deadened awareness into a thriving species that lives and works in realms beyond current collective boundaries. Living the life of the soul produces a quickening that transcends the fixed personal parameters of the mind and reweaves the psychological structures that hold one to the precepts of social normalcy.

THE TRANSPERSONAL NATURE OF THE PSYCHE

The transpersonal path brings one into the essence of being human. It guides perception into the substructures of consciousness, bringing light to the not-yet-conscious mind and thus tapping into the well of the universe.

Transpersonal therapies can be defined in terms of three worlds: a "middle world" (our everyday temporal reality) and the "upper" and "lower" worlds (internal dimensions entered via heightened states of consciousness). These transpersonal inner spaces have been accessed by common and cultural methodologies, such as holotropic breathwork, lucid dreaming, meditation, entheogenic plants, bio-spirit elixirs, flower essences, and kundalini yoga. All of these practices lead to the reconstruction of what is understood as the psyche.[2]

The human psyche transcends corporeal existence, giving rise to the landscapes of multidimensional reality in which we actually live.[3] In these transpersonal realms, it is possible for individuals to experience the world of plants, animals, devic intelligence, angelic beings, future selves, and other elevated spiritual beings communicating directly to individuals within their own psyche.

Nature's organic blueprints, like the Golden Mean Spiral and others explored in this book, serve as coded pathways into the realms of the transpersonal holographic psyche. Present and future therapeutic and healing models must be sourced from within the transpersonal holographic dimensions of being in order for the evolutionary human codes to awaken. We are now being invited to enter into a consensus reality that is based on the holographic nature of life.

HEART AND MIND: KEYS TO THE HOLOGRAPHIC PSYCHE

Holographic psychology rests upon a deep cognitive change in the understanding of the nature of the mind and the role of the spiritual heart. The heart is the key to unlocking the pathways into the transpersonal, luminescent dimensions of our human psyche. The transpersonal path is a journey into the deepest realms of human awareness, into the essence of being human; the heart leads the mind to perception of the substructures of consciousness. These transpersonal realms bring the light of awareness into the common mind.

The interplay and ultimate fusion of the mind with the heart elicits a direct experience of what East Indian spirituality refers to as the *Atman*, or essential Self. The higher-functioning mind has the capacity to interact with the field of cognition to process information and feed it to the psyche. Within this field lies insight into temporal processes of past, present, and future, which fundamentally lend knowledge to the newly unfolding life trajectory. The feeling level of the heart is silently and intimately calibrated to reflect the elevated spiritual capacities of the mind.

The heart is the seat of the soul. The resonance of the heart activates sonic superconductors in the brain, releasing psychoactive chemicals that catalyze higher levels of functioning and intelligence. This suggests that a unified consciousness is chemically, emotionally, mentally, and spiritually based and is not only dependent on the physical capacities of the individual. For example, the fact that the renowned scientist Stephen Hawking is confined to a wheelchair due to ALS (amyotrophic lateral sclerosis) is an example of consciousness functioning at a very high level within an unconventional physical nervous system.

When the heart resonates love, or coherent emotion, the physical body becomes resonant with impulse signals sent out from the heart. The whole body can be understood as a thinking body in which each cell is capable of producing chemicals known as neuropeptides, which correspond to the mind and heart. This is seen in brain/body research and is referred to as the *biology of belief,* a concept from developmental biologist Bruce Lipton.

When one experiences coherent emotion, or love, intelligence crystallizes itself into thought and reconstructs molecules into new chemical patterns that cultivate a cosmic, transpersonal perspective. This higher crystalline intelligence of the human psyche has the capacity to unite with the archetypal forces of Nature. These forces are then integrated into the psyche and are capable of repackaging information to reflect the changing neural networking associated with creative processing and higher states of functioning.

Due to this holographic functioning within it, the mind/brain can "re-net," or create, a new typography of the psyche through spiral matrices of intelligence that loop in and out of the repositories of the brain like bees in a hive.

Coherent emotion, or love, crystallizes at various points to maintain a density of coherence that draws consciousness to itself and activates creative intelligence where consciousness was once dormant. This love frequency can also increase the capacity of neuropeptides to be superconductors for vibrational activity normally out of range of human awareness.

We exercise this capacity in states ranging from dreams and deep sleep to meditation experiences. Even everyday consciousness can create new neural pathways. This plasticity of brain function is enhanced when a flexibility of psychology comes together with pure consciousness in a highly coherent and effective way.[4]

Human beings are innately designed to live in a frequency state of love. The coherent emotion of love creates a multisensory benevolent awareness that inspires a sense of service to humanity. The interface between the intelligent resonance of the heart and the densely packed information of the brain/mind field has the capacity to activate codes dormant in the DNA. Love produces a sacred circuit that creates resonance between the heart and brain. In this state of love, the seven-layered heart muscle is the focal point of all feeling, acting as a liquid crystal resonator. The vibratory connection between the heart and brain provides neural pathways that create an intelligent resonance within each cell of the body. The extent to which this vibratory connection is present determines which genetic codes within the DNA become active and which remain inactive.[5]

The variability of our thoughts, feelings, and emotions is encoded in the DNA. The higher-frequency field of love is a shorter, faster wave with a greater number of complete waves expressed per unit of DNA. Our personal reality is spun out of our thoughts, feelings, and emotions; these multi-generated frequencies then feed into the geomagnetic grid of the Earth.

Stabilization of higher consciousness produces an experience in which language becomes a more direct, nonlinear expression of deep conceptual structures. The areas of the brain responsible for language can then become more representative of the integration of thought and feeling. This shift in intelligence enables one to develop a direct inner link through which empathic and cognitive communication with Earth as a living being becomes possible.

The emergence of galactic status for humanity is established through the experience of love. Love as an established state on the personal and transpersonal levels of awareness gives rise to the behavioral expression of reverence towards all life. A healthy and evolutionary symbiotic relationship between humanity and the Earth is established through the expansion of love. As love courses through the veins of people and the Earth, the integrity structures that support life are reconstituted.

SACRED GEOMETRY: A ROADMAP INTO THE PSYCHE

Sacred geometry is the language of creation. It is the means through which intelligence moves from the unmanifest subtle dimensions to manifest form. Sacred geometry's signatures can be seen in plants, gems, stars, and all of Mother Earth's designs.

The human being is birthed out of this same blueprint of fundamental manifestations of nature. Knowing this, we can use the gift of sacred geometry intelligently and intentionally, applying it to our healing and our awakening to higher levels of consciousness. **When we understand or have even a "feeling" knowing that we are sacred geometry, we can embrace the power of the geometric structures that support, nourish, and uphold our divine design.**

One of the most basic geometric shapes is the Golden Mean Spiral, a mathematical ratio referred to as the divine proportion, or Pi Ratio. The Golden Mean ratio 1.618 is the most efficient of all ratios; when energy is phase-locked with this ratio, it cascades between frequencies without losing energy or memory of itself.

The Golden Mean Spiral ratio of the heart and other structures of nature is a superconductive information highway between the personal and transpersonal, the physical and subtle dimensions. It unfolds in a numerical sequence called the Fibonacci series. The Italian mathematician Fibonacci discovered that each number is the sum of the preceding pair of numbers, such that $1 + 1 = 2$; $1 + 2 = 3$; $2 + 3 = 5$; $3 + 5 = 8$; $5 + 8 = 13$, and so on. This numerical sequence gives mathematical correlation to the movement from biodynamic energy to materialization. Pervading the world of nature, the Golden Mean is encoded in the anatomical structure of organic life forms, including humans, seashells, plants, and other naturally occurring phenomena such as galaxies and star clusters.

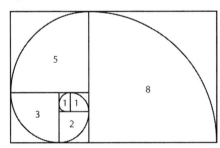

Golden Mean Spiral

When the Golden Mean Spiral unwinds as a short-to-long waveform in its spinout, it creates the fractal image of the heart. A fractal is a geometric shape that can be subdivided in parts, each of which is a reduced-size copy of the whole.[6]

The deep internal focus of the heart weaves all waveforms into one. The subtle layers of the heart reveal its shape and form; its sacred geometry opens into the entire manifest creation. The heart is the human definition of the space/time fabric; it is a portal into infinity and back.

The Golden Mean ratio is embedded in all of the primary geometric forms, known as the Platonic solids. The language of the heart is spelled out of the most basic of these geometric structures, the tetrahedron. It is the symmetry basis for all Platonic solids, the five primary geometric structures that allow intelligence to organize itself into physical manifestation.

As we have come to understand the correlations of the heart to geometry, it has been calculated that the seven spins of the tetrahedron correlate to the seven layers of the heart muscle, which are exactly tilted to the seven axes of the tetrahedron.[7] These spins create vortices. Each vortex appears as a self-replicating loop that moves through the heart. The sacred geometric codes appear as flame letters (seed letters of the Hebrew alphabet), which correspond to the living intelligence expressed in sound vibrations that give rise to the meaning of words.

Electrically encoded intelligence contained in the heart permits higher brain functions to open the gateway between personal and transpersonal dimensions.[8] Coherent brainwaves sonically resonate with the heart. Studies reveal that when the heart's electricity becomes coherent, a person is highly focused on the experience of love. As one experiences love, the energetic spin of the heart (measured by EKG) displays the same ratio structure as the Golden Mean Spiral: 1.618. As previously noted, this perfect mathematical fractal is the most energy-efficient conductor of information between frequencies or dimensions; it maintains memory of itself.[9]

A heart-centered physiology releases abundant amounts of psychoactive chemicals in the brain.[10] When the heart expands, the frequency bandwidth of harmonic information, the Golden Mean ratio of 1.618, is evident as measured by EKG; the heart uses its fractal spin pattern to send electrical energy and information to the DNA.[11] **The vibratory level of love creates**

a background for pure knowledge to paint the picture of life in the mind of the cells.

When the mind/body/breath is unified in the ecstatic love frequencies, the physical and spiritual hearts are supported by this immortalizing geometric pattern that infinitely self-replicates. The subtle layers of the heart reveal the shape, form, and structure of the fundamental mechanics of space/time.

As we come to understand and experience the heart from the level of its own language of space/time geometry, we are in a position to see how the body mirrors these innate primordial forms. An example in biology is that during embryonic cellular division, the cells reorganize geometrically, with the first structure of organization being the tetrahedron. In nature, the tetrahedron converts liquid into orderly crystal. It defines the space for the biological unfoldment of life through time.[12]

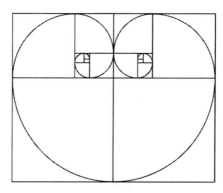

Fractal of the Heart

The human is birthed out of the universal principles of nature. To envision the possible human, it is necessary to make the association between our physical form, everyday reality, and the intricacies of the mystical blueprints that form the basis of creation.

The body has a mind of its own—a "delicate web of intelligence," says Dr. Deepak Chopra. Since the body's intelligence is non-localized, existing simultaneously in multiple domains of space/time, its structures are specialized fields of quantum intelligence radiating from a single source: pure unified awareness. The very fine levels of matter revealed through quantum theory help us to understand how the body reflects such a complex specificity yet retains the character of wholeness that allows the individual identity to have a personal point of reference in creation.

To be true to our natures, we must use healing approaches and therapies that follow the basic human architectural principles found throughout nature that create, maintain, and sustain life. These are the topics found in the following chapters, merging the mystical and the practical.

2

THE MYTHIC LANDSCAPE OF HEALING
A Multicultural Perspective

All religions, all this singing. One song.
—Rumi

Knowledge of the holographic human is not new; psycho-spiritual systems, traditions, and practices for transformational, soul-level healing are found among indigenous peoples throughout the world. These traditions show how the natural world synchronously reflects movements of the human mind, body, and spirit. The indigenous healing traditions developed forms of medicine that recognize spirit as the predominant influence behind well-being and that view the physical body as a template for the transformation of soul required for the solidification of the dense aspects of material creation. Seers who are able to view the body from a subtle perspective see it as a sanctuary for the spirit.

This contrasts with the modern Western view in which the physical body is seen merely as a mechanical platform for the mind. People in indigenous cultures trust their medicine people as we would now trust the most illumined members of our clergy—that is, with our soul, not just with the pathological anomalies of the body.

The interest in holistic health that has developed in the West over the past twenty-five years has produced a resurgence of modalities and traditional understandings that borrow much of their richness from long-established indigenous cultures. Indigenous peoples developed medicine that reflected their understanding of ancestral and soul influences in the building of a healthful, workable communal landscape.

Traditional medicine people viewed—and still view today—plants, gems, minerals, elements, animal totems, celestial bodies and star systems, etc., *as allies*, meaning ways of getting under the skin of disease itself and understanding the human condition from the level of the soul. This differs from the allopathic approach of simply alleviating symptoms. The effect of incorporating these healing systems into mainstream Western life is to return us to a fundamental level of our own nature and awakened understanding of the purpose and meaning of existence.

The landscape of traditional healing involves a complex blueprint of the nature of psyche and body, such as the chakra system, the archetypes of the astrological zodiac, acupuncture points and meridians, and the *doshas* and five elements in Ayurved. The language that has evolved to describe such principles varies, but it is fundamentally geared towards arriving at a tele-pathic link that moves in the direction of seership, rather than simply an intellectual grasp of detail, analysis, and recapitulation of disease and symp-tomology. This knowledge maintains a depth of originality, spontaneity, and organization of a higher order.

This chapter looks at six prominent healing traditions imprinting our Western culture today: the Ayurved system that originated in India, Native American spirit medicine, West African spirit medicine, Amazonian Shamanic medicine, Aboriginal spirit medicine, and Western metaphysical traditions (including flower-essence therapy). The chapter will also briefly discuss gem therapy and its use in many ancient societies.

AYURVED: GUIDE TO THE TEMPLE OF THE SOUL

Ayurved is a five-thousand-year-old system originating in India that goes deep into the fabric of consciousness. Its purpose is to integrate the human psyche with the elements of nature. The Ayurvedic system emphasizes balance, spiritual evolution, and enlightenment. It views the perfection and maintenance of the body as the temple of the soul.

In ancient times, seers of truth known as *rishis* directly perceived the laws of creation; the Ayurvedic system evolved out of this cognition of the inter-relationship between humanity and the cosmos. The purpose of Ayurved is to promote self-realization; its practices are rooted in the concepts of purification and regeneration as interwoven cyclic processes of the body/mind/soul.

The ancient rishis developed powers of memorization and higher uses of the mind, including cognition and intuition. Modern Ayurvedic practitioners continue the tradition of "seeing" the physiology through pulse diagnosis and a thorough knowledge of the chakra system. Plants, gems, minerals, light therapy, color therapy, and sound therapy are chosen for the patient through objective and innate knowledge of how they will function within the framework of the patient's mind/body complex.

The Ayurved system is based on the understanding of the five elements that give rise to the human physiology. Ancient rishis identified the five elements as the foundation for balancing the body/mind/soul as one of the first principles of health. Understanding the function of the five elements explains how material existence was formed and how it continues to link all sentient life together at its core.

The first of these elements, earth, refers to the ground state of matter. Earth brings physical abundance and moves the individual beyond the rudimentary comfort of mere survival. Earth links the individual with the precepts of elemental existence based on the sacred architecture of proportion, form, and creative power.

Water, the liquid state of matter, is the most impressionable element that constitutes the human body. It has a magnetic power of attraction and allows for the mind/body/psyche to receive information and store it in the form of crystalline patterns. Water is readily imprinted with the universal life force that shapes the mind/body/psyche. For this reason, it can also create a condition of inherent fixity, or stagnation, that locks in limited conditioning and the repetitive habits of ancestral programming.

Fire, through the powerful heat of transformation, consumes matter and vaporizes liquid. The result is a spontaneous upsurge of spirit that activates the imagination and gives light to life. Fire reduces material form to its essence. New expressions of life emerge out of the ashes of creation.

Air, the gaseous state of matter, is the most mutable and formless of the elements. In a sense, it is the pivotal element between the invisible plane of matter and the felt movements of time. Air is the conductive element. It provides the medium of communication within a specific space/time context.

Ether is the field of space from which everything is manifested and to which it is returned. The ether element is the domain of reality in which cosmic data for creation mechanics is stored. This ether field is a medium out of which the Godhead speaks the language of direct knowledge through dimensions.

Ether/space is the birth hatch for the archetypes of the psyche. When one is immersed in the vastness of the ether/space element, one lives in the realm of divine revelation, not bound by the limitations of psychological time or the artificial boundaries of manmade space.

The system of Ayurved is used to describe the levels of organization in the body, mind, and spirit.[1] The five elements form the three doshas within each person: *vata, pitta*, and *kapha*. Vata governs the nervous system and all body movements. Pitta governs the balance of the body's kinesthetic and potential energies; processes governed by Pitta include digestion, activity, and the metabolism of substances, emotions, and thoughts. Kapha, the principle of potential energy, governs the body's inherent strength; it supports lubrication and provides the stability needed for the mind to grasp a single thought in time.

The balance of these principal energies allows the evolutionary currents of health and consciousness to unfold in accordance with one's highest spiritual potential. This is the central goal of the Ayurvedic system.

In Ayurved, plants, herbs, and food play a significant therapeutic role. Each is classified according to the five-element theory. Each is also classified according to its influence on the doshas, the organs, the meridians, and the taste it elicits (which speaks directly to the body/brain).

The use of plants in particular has been brought out by one modern practitioner of Ayurved, Dr. Vesant Lad. Dr. Lad has made an important contribution to Ayurved in the West by bringing out the role of plants as a direct reflection of consciousness. Lad views the human nervous system as a tree whose plant essence is human. The human nervous system is a universal network that mirrors the organization of the plant kingdom. **Through** plants, the human enters into communion with the energy of the sun, the power of light to give life and consciousness. Within the plant is the potential of the human being; within the human being is the underlying energy structure of the plant.

Plants impart a level of unconditional love inherent within Nature. In Sanskrit, the word for plant is *osadhi*, which means "mind" (*dhi*) in which there is burning transformation (*osa*). According to Lad, "The human being is the plant of consciousness."[2] He states that healing is always a matter of unification.

Consciousness in plants is at a primal level of unity and therefore psychic and telepathic. Plants exhibit a pure level of feeling whose purpose is to imbue the environment with life-transmitting messages of power, beauty, and organization.

Another modern-day rishi whose teaching has received worldwide recognition is Maharishi Mahesh Yogi. His life work involved original cognitional insight into the Vedic Sciences. Maharishi sought to comprehend the unimaginable in the human being.[3] His illumination of the Ayurvedic system correlates the structure and function of physiology with the structure and function of the Vedas, which are ancient Indian spiritual texts. His teachings counter the academic view of the Vedic texts as mere mythological stories that were recited during Vedic rituals and ceremonies. Rather, he elucidates the Vedas as an underlying blueprint for all of creation, both manifest and unmanifest.

According to Maharishi Ayurved, human physiology has at its basis *Nitya* (eternal) and *Apaurusheya* (uncreated). Maharishi stated that it is from this self-referential level of intelligence that the physiology can perfect itself at the ground level from its transcendental source.[4] Alignment with the laws of nature increases longevity as well as the potential for the development of an illumined, immortal consciousness. This is the gift of Maharishi's contribution in returning the understanding of Ayurved to its original truth.

NATIVE AMERICAN SPIRIT MEDICINE

It is estimated that prior to the arrival of the white man, there were up to two thousand separate Indian cultures in the Northern Hemisphere.[5] However, the European settlers' belief in the superiority of the European way of life created a destructive and judgmental force that led to a profound misunderstanding of the mores, spiritual perspectives, and practical knowledge of Native American cultures. This led to a profound gap in the rendering of historical information about the Americas, which stands to this day.

Although each tribe was unique in its spiritual perspective, many areas of shared understanding tied the nations of native peoples together. Most Native American cultures continue to be based largely on the tradition of ancestors, who are seen as spiritual gatekeepers. The ancestors are experienced as sentient beings that guide, protect, teach, and love from their position in the spiritual world. The ancestors are braided into the overall human/divine interconnection and serve as vehicles of healing.[6]

Native American tribes view religious experience as a state of being that surrounds humanity at all times and in all circumstances. Creation is viewed as a process of eternal happening, and the assessment of health takes into account all facets of life: physical, mental, and spiritual.

For example, in the Hopi tradition, it is believed that unless one can project oneself into the spirit world, one cannot achieve true healing and spiritual experience.[7] In the Navajo tradition, one goes to a shaman/medicine person to reestablish one's relationship to Nature. The Navajo sees life as a three-way partnership between plant, animal, and human.

The Pueblo Indians see the universe as a spiritual domain that elicits active reciprocation with all of creation. The model of sacred space/time for the world is replicated through the teepee, hogan, or kiva. This creates images that are deeply holographic in nature, with each structure representing macrocosmic principles that are guided by ancient, pictographic information. These dwellings are the central access points between Heaven and Earth that pierce the multiplicity of the worlds.[8] The Pueblo Indians experience life as an interactive process at every level.[9]

The symbols of the Navajo tradition hold the power to cure physical illness and to change the shape of things in the physical world. Both Navajo and Hopi view symbolism as the bridge between the manifest and unmanifest aspects of creation. [10]

The capacity to see the underlying supernatural components of disease or emotional imbalance is fundamental to all Native American traditions. It is assumed that what is invisible—namely, the core structures of the psyche and its relationship to the creative force—must be addressed for health to be fully realized.

The offering of one's self—as in the Sundance ceremony of the Lakota, Oglala, and Ute tribes—is based on one's connection to a supernatural power. In this ceremony, the body becomes a living ritual offering for divine awakening. Self-sacrifice is not seen as a form of martyrdom, but as a powerful, internal decomposition of all that one knows to be self, in light of a core realization of a larger level of self that surpasses the powers of mind or reason.

In Native American traditions, supernatural beings are symbolized in animal form. A deep knowledge of how animals communicate and their capacity to provide spiritual, mental, and emotional information to human beings is inherent in Native American practice and understanding. Once the awareness of an animal totem is awakened through spiritual initiation, it functions similarly to the mantra in Eastern spiritual practices. The animal totem takes on a life of its own in the core essence of being, enlivening traits of character and harmonious resonance that unite one profoundly with the earth, the sky, and the many worlds of spiritual life.

Native Americans, like many indigenous cultures, view the causes of disease as sorcery, taboo violation, disease object intrusion, spirit intrusion, soul loss, and unfulfilled dreams or desires. This also extends to spirits of animals that have been slighted or abused, disrespect towards fire or rivers, or human ghosts who have lost their way.[11] A medicine person's goal is to determine the spiritual cause of disease and to administer the appropriate treatment based on the supernatural understanding of plants and animals as magical healers.

The medicine man/woman, or shaman, is essential to Native American healing. He or she is viewed as a healer, sorcerer, seer, educator, and priest.[12] Through birth, initiation, or gifts of power often gained through warrior magic, Indian medicine people through the ages have been gifted with clairsentient abilities, prophecy, and the knowledge to heal. The medicine person's talents include being able to identify the spirit properties of plants and how the spirit of the plant casts out demons or illness in the system. The medicine person performs healings according to tribal lore at times of birth and death.[13]

In modern psychological thought, healing through ceremony is viewed as a matter of shared belief, rather than as magical or supernatural intervention. The key to understanding the medicine of Native Americans in light of twenty-first century research is to recognize the capacity of beings that can authentically enter the holographic universe, investigate states of being, and understand the mysteries of our inner conditions.

Over many generations, European settlers learned about the indigenous plants the Native Americans used. This knowledge became the basis for American folk medicine: a blend of the herbal lore of Europe, the Americas, and some parts of Africa. Settlers who were taught indigenous medicine were called "Indian doctors."

Since 1820, more than two hundred indigenous plants that were used by one or more Native American tribes have been officially entered into the pharmacopoeia of the United States.[14] It should be noted that plants form the basis for synthetic drugs, and more recently, for neutraceuticals.

WEST AFRICAN SPIRIT MEDICINE

In West African traditions, the world is divided into two realms: visible and invisible. Human beings exist in both realms, but our real being is interior and invisible.[15] Human beings are in fact composed of four parts: body, vital principle (the breath that animates), dya (the shadow, or the invisible double that learns directly from the invisible realm), and the interior (the center of intelligence and perception).[16]

In this tradition, the healer's ability to heal depends on a profound understanding of the role of sacred plants and a mastery of consciousness practices that are used to alter states of being in others. The knowledge to heal is acquired through herbs, fetishes, and magical or sacred words.

The Ibo and Yoruba of Nigeria see physical and mental illness as a result of the work of spirits or supernatural influences. Healers are often highly skilled musicians who can bridge the planes of existence, bringing a person into harmonious relationship with the Self and the world. Magical doorways are introduced for the practice of religious rituals that involve adept practice of trance. During these interdimensional voyages, utterances that are charged with a supernatural potency are cognized and voiced.

Plants are ingested to activate the primordial levels of cellular memory that invoke knowledge of subtle levels of image, sound, and breath. In the ceremony called *nia*, elders give trance-inducing herbs to assist those who wish to enter a state in which they become messengers for the ancestors and the invisible realms.[17] Herbal remedies—along with the sacred word, music, and dance—are used to heal and restore harmony on all levels.[18] The spiritual adept who has made a link between the conscious mind and the supra-mental body is able to dip into the primordial regions of the psyche and retrieve information from levels heretofore unspeakable.

The West African tradition of the Minianka recognizes the circle of ancestors first. Humans are in contact with other beings and forces in the invisible realms that include the ancestor circle, which guides and gives protection and knowledge.[19] The Minianka perceive a spirit in everything and acknowledge it for its role in creation.

The Dagara are holographic in their orientation, viewing healing as a schism mending in the fabric of consciousness, seamlessly weaving together past, present, and future into the now. Rites of initiation are designed to find the individual's center as he or she navigates deeper levels of existence. Healing energy is focused on matters that concern the growth, refinement, and education of the soul. The soul is expressed as an interpenetrating energetic structure that defines a living being as a fully formed and mature circle. Dagara knowledge is liquid, alive, flexible, spontaneous, and breathing, as well as time bending.[20]

Like the Minianka, the Dagara recognize the centrality of the ancestors. As Malidoma Somé, a native Dagara, writes, "Ancestors are the real school of the living."[21] The Dagara also give primacy to spirit. Each person is regarded as an incarnation of spirit that has taken on a body.

The Dagara live in a completely open-ended relationship with spirit that is more than human in its most intimate sense. Having mastered the capacity to exist in an interdimensional state, they are able to move beyond simply the orchestration of spiritual journeys. They have come to a state of adepthood in which they are permanently immersed in the spiritual from the perspective of the incarnate.

Living in this world, they view solid matter as a nonlinear and transpositional alchemical process. They function as a fully embodied spirit incarnate. From this state, they are able to involve themselves in initiation quests that are living illustrations of quantum mechanical processes.

The purpose of these quests or rituals is to heal and create harmony between the human world and the worlds of the gods, the ancestors, and nature. The rituals take initiates through a long series of highly dangerous missions, which from the outside might appear torturous or inexplicable in their intensity. Such tests awaken the powers of the soul. Sacred spiritual knowledge can then be brought back for the benefit of humanity as a whole.

According to the Dagara, the life mission of the incarnate soul is to find out who he or she truly is—a quest that is orchestrated by the healer or shaman, who commits to a lifelong examination of the physical and spiritual energy fields of groups and/or individuals. The Dagara see existence as an opportunity for service on a scale wider than the Dagara themselves. The individual initiate is given the opportunity to fully mature and develop through the imprinting of ancestral landscapes that are downloaded directly into the DNA.

Such processes are rare in the world at the present time, and the knowledge that feeds them is rapidly fading. The purpose of such people as Malidoma Somé is to be a living embodiment of the synthesis of Western technological society and the profound knowledge of West African cultures. It is a challenging and heartfelt mission that the soul chooses to undertake.

AMAZONIAN SHAMANIC MEDICINE

Shamanism connects the human psyche with the archetypal forces of Nature. The shaman elicits an altered reality by creating a backdrop of sound, color, taste, or smell that drops the participant out of the realm of everyday sense experience and lands him or her in a realm in which the intelligence of Nature can speak directly to the holographic psyche. The shaman can accomplish this task through the use of plant medicine, drumming, sacred fire, ecstatic dance, breath work, or other pathways to expanded awareness.

The use of plant medicine in shamanic practice is one of the principal vehicles for eliciting entry into other realms in order to gain knowledge of one's personal and cosmic reality. Plants function as teachers or messengers for the individual who has taken communion and ingested the plants' intelligence. They teach the human psyche how to navigate through personal and biological history.

Plant-based teachers facilitate a journey into transdimensional reality that is sourced out of the Self. This mechanism of teaching is initially through visionary, kinesthetic, and sonic linguistics that inform the collective repository of consciousness. Information gained through pure visionary, kinesthetic, and sonic awareness has the capacity to catalyze quantum shifts in the field of human consciousness and science. This process elicits a unique sensitivity to the mechanics of the unified field, the backdrop of dimensional expression.

The Indians and mestizos (people of both Indian and white blood) of the Upper Amazon practice an indigenous form of shamanic healing. They utilize an herbal psychotropic mixture commonly known as *yage* or *ayahuasca*.[22] Shamans recognize ayahuasca as a plant teacher that infuses them with healing skills and powers.[23]

Ayahuasca is an alchemical expression of the feminine principle. In this context, the plant is known as "The Grandmother" that embodies the wisdom of creation medicine. It utilizes two or more indigenous plants, the principal green materials being the *banisteriopsis coptis* and the *psychotri* leaves. The Vine of the Soul, as ayahuasca is commonly called, catalyzes a subtle alchemical holographic imaging system. The Vine imprints the elemental matrix and creative maternal forces into the blueprint of the journeyer's consciousness.

In this tradition, the use of plants to contact the spirit is the primary path to knowledge. Ayahuasceros know that the inner world is real and the external world is illusory. This is similar to the Hindu concept of *maya*. Visions are viewed as direct response pathways to the archetypal reality of our being, rather than simply as metaphorical psychological constructs.

Ayahuasca liberates one to live life in multidimensional realities, freed from everyday conditioning. These are plants of the gods whose powers originate from supernatural forces.[24]

Unlike other psychotropic preparations, ayahuasca is principally an awakener of the physiology that naturally restores order to the primordial functioning of organs and systems. Organs are like retaining walls for the stored psycho-emotional collection of memories and beliefs.

Ayahuasca elevates the capacity of the brain to uptake extrasensory information. One perceives a heightened integration of spirit and intelligence that defies the rigid boundaries of cultural norms. This acts as an antidote to the realm of the ordinary mind, which is imbued with egoistic conflict and stripped of a connection to the core Self. In the more holographic context set forward in shamanic practice, such disassociated mind patterns and resulting decisions can be re-evaluated and made anew.

In preparation for work with the plant spirits of ayahuasca, a dietary structure that purifies the body is suggested. This diet imbues one with the clarity to receive and translate spiritual visions. The diet also enhances the ability to discern the spiritual significance of songs of power traditionally associated with plant medicine given by the plant to the Ayahuascero. One seeks contact with the intelligence of spirit behind each medicinal plant. One awakens to the inner knowledge necessary for divining, diagnosing, and healing.

Ayahuasceros, like medicine people of other Indian cultures, believe illness is produced by the intrusion of pathogenic objects, soul loss, contamination, or breaching of a taboo. The shaman is able to produce and heal with a magical phlegm called *mariri*.

Shamans travel consciously in the spirit realm, accessing information about themselves, others, and the world. They recognize the infinite panorama of color gradation that creates the beauty and complexity of the visionary world, and they are able to perceive how plants express themselves in this liquid language of light that is filled with geometric mathematical statements about the structure and function of existence.

Ayahuasceros report that during their travels in the spirit realm, they make contact with advanced extraterrestrial civilizations and interdimensional beings. They report that complete cities, as well as temples replete with advanced spiritual practitioners and celestial libraries, are located on the inner planes. The celestial beings that dwell in these interdimensional habitats feed on the aroma of flowers and use a balsam that allows them to live for thousands of years. The shaman travels to these magical locations to receive knowledge and instruction from ambassadors of the different higher-vibrational schools of spiritual/physical healing.[25]

Shapeshifting, interdimensional travel, and flying are the skills and powers that the shaman learns directly from the plant/spirit teachers. The shamanic healer develops the creative capacity to cognize tools of light and energy that assist or give access to magical properties. These tools include the cognition of bright surgical lights, magical arrows, and angels.[26] The shamans also gain the assistance of spiritually adept physicians from other dimensions who have resonance and access to our temporal reality. This information may be expressed archetypically in the form of mermaids, fairies, or dolphins, as well as in the form of beings not known in this dimension of existence.

Amazonian shamanic medicine, like all indigenous methodologies of healing, is fundamentally holographic. It lifts both practitioner and recipient from the illusory world of duality and separation into a more truthful world of harmony and unification. The brain stretches its innate capacities; it moves from being simply a receptor for what is commonly accepted or known to that which is mystically deep, unfathomable, and surprisingly attainable.

The purpose of shamanism is to help humankind. Ultimately, one journeys on behalf of humanity to spiritually reconnect with Mother Earth. On the shamanic path, one experiences Nature as one's Self. Through such journeys one can gain valuable teachings from plant allies and celestial beings, as well as dimensions normally beyond our awareness. Transcendental illumination brings clarification and healing to the journeyer and, in advanced stages, is capable through a single atom of piercing the veils of humanity's deep sleep.

ABORIGINAL SPIRIT MEDICINE

Aborigines live in what is known as Dreamtime, a timeless state of being that allows one to live in the holographic universe. Dreamtime is that stream of life and power that is not hampered by the limitations of space and time.[27]

Much discipline and training goes into mastery of the human mind and the influence of the mind on the body. This is done through the death-and-rising ritual. The goal of the medicine man in working with the patient is to bring back the wandering soul. If he cannot extract the cause and bring the soul back, the suggestion of death is imparted telepathically and the patient joins the ancestors in the Other World.

In aboriginal life, the medicine person acquires powers through the supernatural beings in the Dreamtime—the rainbow serpent, the sky gods, and the ancestors (spirits of the dead). It is reported that medicine men in aboriginal tradition go through extensive initiation rites of literally dying and returning from the Other World. It is said that often their bodies can be dismembered and reconstructed. Magical crystals can be placed in their bodies during this process.

The result of these initiations is that the medicine men are capable of flying, traveling at great speeds, acquiring precognitive information to cure, making rain, and even dematerializing and rematerializing in other locations.[28]

WESTERN METAPHYSICAL TRADITIONS

In the 1500s, Paracelcus (born Bombastus von Hohenheim), a native of Switzerland, emerged as a metaphysican and alchemical philosopher of medicine whose practice was largely based on the occult sciences. His approach to healing laid the foundation for Western herbalism, homeopathy, and flower essence therapy.[29]

Paracelcus's philosophy unified the spiritual with the material, the parts with the whole, and the divine with the natural. His ideas included the application of life-force principles, the wisdom of nature, and the spiritual domains of human existence.[30] Threads of mystical, occult, and shamanic themes appeared in his writings. He said, "I write like a pagan, yet I am a Christian."[31]

Paracelcus identified the life-force principle as a directing intelligence that maintains and repairs a living organism. He called this vital force "arch-principle," an all-pervading force that governs life by a self-regulating and self-healing intelligence. It was his influence that was passed on through the homeopathic principles of Hahnemann, Thomsonian herbalism,[32] and the Western clinical herbalism practiced today.

Paracelcus's "doctrine of correspondence" states that life is an organizing principle that receives its information from the light of nature. The natural world intimately corresponds to the archetypal world, giving it form and meaning.[33] His philosophy was that the essence of substances was directly received through divine power. The divine power must first pass through the realm of the stars, the *astrum*, during which the stars become polarized to reflect either positive or negative influences. This does not imply a value judgment, but simply describes the dualistic nature of manifest creation.

Another contribution for which Paracelcus is noted is his "doctrine of signatures." He observed that shape, color, taste, smell, and environment could be used in healing. Every plant embodied its own set of knowledge, enacted in medicinal application and symbolized by the part of the body afflicted or its inherent cause.[34] For example, the flower essence bleeding heart is pink, heart shaped, and downward gesturing; its subtle medicinal application is to ameliorate emotional issues that bind the heart.

Paracelsus once more presaged the holographic sensibility of life as a complex, interwoven sum of all its seemingly disparate parts. The core essence, the *Arcana*, is a configuration or identity pattern that forms the matrix for all natural substances. This can only be seen through the light of nature or the spiritual eye. This is a founding principle in flower essence therapy.

A century after Paracelsus, during the 1600s, Nicholas Culpepper practiced herbal medicine in England. He mostly tended to the common folk and primarily used indigenous plants. In 1649, Culpepper published the first herbal reference manual with the common names of plants. He was most known for his astrological theories that correlated plants and planetary energies. He emphasized how diseases and plants could be astrologically classified, and his use of plants was based on the positions of the heavenly bodies.[35]

Johann Wolfgang von Goethe (1749–1832), Germany's foremost man of letters, was also a scientist who illumined the inner reality of the natural world. His true subtlety in consciousness, his special talent to describe worlds heretofore beyond most people's sight or touch, laid the groundwork for our contemporary understanding of vibrational medicine. The present-day science of allopathic diagnosis that includes the use of CAT scans and MRIs, as well as the subtler mechanics of Kirlian photography and thermographic imaging, has its underpinnings in Goethe's understanding of the geometrical forms that underlie material creation.

According to Goethe, plants are organized on the Earth in such a manner as to express organic relationship to the sun and the celestial universe. Goethe also describes the "staff of Mercury," the caduceus, as symbolized in plant growth. The central axis of the vegetative part of the plant is hollow and denotes the "infinitude within."

The line of force through the central axis draws forth the plant form. Along its axes are the nodes of power that signify potential development. The symbol of the caduceus represents such a natural form, mirroring the force of energy found in green leaves as they spiral in a rhythmic sequence up the stem of the plant.[36]

Goethe's fine levels of discriminative observation reveal the cosmic energies of the phenomenal world. He sought to investigate the true nature of plant life, the one expressing itself through the many. He saw the higher life of plants as a rhythm of expansion and contraction between darkness and light.[37]

The morphology of plants is based on projective geometry and the interplay of polarities.[38] The morphology of plant growth as defined by Goethe parallels the Vedic system of the chakras and the rise of kundalini, the evolutionary life-force current found in the subtle human nervous system. Kundalini rises up the central axis of the human spinal column, expanding and contracting between the polarities to form the vortices of multidimensional life.

Rudolf Steiner (1861–1925), a student of Goethe, recognized the world as a system of inner relationships whose messages and content reveal the "Laws of Nature." Steiner provides detailed commentary on Goethe's work, *The Metamorphosis of Plants*, which deeply examines the inner forces that give rise to the metamorphosis of organic form. Steiner stresses the need to redefine in scientific terms the realm of nature and the forces that shape and sustain living forms.

Steiner's mode of research is based on direct higher sense perception, modern mathematical analysis, and projective geometry. His work reveals that the cosmic geometry of the universe exists as a proportionate mirror to the rigid boundaries of finite space. The processes that build and create living tissue find a clear basis in modern mathematics.[39]

Steiner sees the staff of Mercury as representative of the continuous process of expansion/contraction between the polarities of positive/negative space.[40] He holds the view that the universe sends its forces through space, drawing light out of the unmanifest. Steiner brings out how forces from the realm of cosmic space work on the earth plane, manifesting the world of plants. The light from beyond earth is upheld through the plant world.

Steiner also identifies the sequential organization that underlies natural forms. These spirals, founded on the mathematical sequences of the Golden Mean, denote the infinite life patterns of natural organization that, by definition, are concentric and continuous. As examples in Nature, he refers to florets in the composite species such as sunflowers. He also identifies the Golden Mean spirals found in pinecones and seashells, comparing them with the musculature of the human heart.[41]

Steiner observes that the spiral itself is the doctrine of signature that distinguishes organic and inorganic life. The interplay of planes, lines, and points depicts what he refers to as archetypal space, denoting infinite possibilities in the reality of Nature. Steiner refers to these concepts as "negative or counter space," "ethereal space," and "sun-space." He sees the seed and cotyledon as ethereally vast, sustaining all life forms from a central point of organic reference.[42] From macrocosm to microcosm, the seed forms the model of the body as a mirror reflection of the cosmos.

Steiner forms a correlation between the inward experiences of the soul and the external formative forces and principles that shape and define Nature. He sees the process of healing as a mechanism that employs the external forces of nature to strengthen the function and facilitate the evolution of the mind/body system. He sees plants as external forces of Nature that have the capacity to reunite with the human organism. Plants have the capacity to restore the formative forces in the human body that Steiner depicts as evolutionary, healing, and ascending.[43]

Plants mirror the opposite, complementary structure to the human organism. For example, plant roots unfold earthward, and the blossoms—which contain the reproductive organs, the fruit, and the seed—all spring upward. The evolutionary pattern of Human is seen as directly opposite to this path, with the roots being identified in the head and the reproductive system and organs reaching down toward the earth.

Soul forces extend both vertically and horizontally and are operative on the cellular levels. The whole earth is viewed as a single entity, and the vegetable world is in direct correspondence to this expansion. One cannot regard a single plant as an independent organism. Thus, the earth has a basic constitutional unity. **The human being is individualized as a being of soul and spirit whose inner life is in union with the universal process.**[44]

PIONEERS IN THE FIELD OF FLOWER ESSENCE THERAPY

At the beginning of the twentieth century, Dr. Edward Bach developed a unique system of soul therapy involving the application of plant essences. The primary method of preparation was a "solar infusion," prepared by placing blossoms in pure water collected at the peak of their spiritual efficacy. The original thirty-eight Bach flower remedies were developed to address personality imbalances, emotional conflict, and mental thought-forms that formed the underlying patterns of the disease state.

Bach flower essence therapy centers on issues of the personality that cause conflict in the heart and soul of the individual. Flower essences are chosen to alleviate states of mind or emotion, such as worry, loneliness, and fear.[45] Greater harmony between soul and personality leads to the actualization of health, peace, and happiness.

The Bach model of flower essence therapy views life as a series of life lessons or challenges in which obstacles are created for the purpose of evolution. The soul is seen as the Divine guiding force of life.[46] Bach researched flower essences through direct experience within his own consciousness. Through in-depth self-inquiry he was able to discern how these plant essences influenced mind, body, and emotion. He established the importance of the mind/body relationship within the context of Western medical culture.

Bach's work has been validated scientifically. Patricia Kaminski and Richard Katz conducted extensive research to advance flower essence therapy to be able to address contemporary issues of human development and soul-level actualization, including modern-day sociological, cultural, and other collective issues.

In the late 1970s Kaminski and Katz expanded the thirty-eight original essences to include research and documentation of more than three hundred additional essences (ongoing to this day). Kaminski and Katz emphasize that flower essences facilitate a dialogue between the archetypes of Nature and the human soul. They created a system of flower essence therapy based on the premise that issues of the collective consciousness could be seen within the context of the life of an individual soul. For over a quarter of a century, this dynamic team has carefully documented fundamental changes in the underlying value structure of human development and the role that flower essences can play in it. They define a flower essence as a holographic imprint of the essential qualities of the plant, each drop of water containing the whole matrix of the plant's archetype.[47] Through the process of solar infusion, the blueprint of the electromagnetic structure of the plant is imprinted into the receptive water element.[48]

This is a different process than the preparation of a homeopathic formula. Clear intention is seen as an important prerequisite to this process, as well as choosing the optimal time to collect and process the flowers to be used to create remedies. Mother essences, as they are called, form the most powerful and clear embodiment of the electromagnetic signature pattern of the plant form. The liquid floral essence is the receptacle for the bio-magnetic energy discharged by the floral bloom at the time of its most vital life force. The liquid consciousness of the flower essence reconstitutes the bio-magnetic auric fields and bio-geometric pathways inherent in the human mind/body complex.

Flower essences create new neurological pathways that affect the neurochemistry of the brain, providing new information to the DNA. This process has been confirmed through psychoneuroimmunology, a branch of science that studies the physical effects of beliefs, attitudes, and feelings on the biochemistry of the body.[49] Neurophysiological states become optimized in direct response to the power and source of thought as an electrical impulse generated from a transcendental level. Greater levels of pure consciousness are actualized in the nervous system at the ground level of being. Flower essences generate pure consciousness by returning awareness to the unity value of the heart. Through the introduction of natural rhythmic patterns stabilized through the use of flower essences, the integrity of the unified field of awareness can be more easily maintained.

Kaminski has also developed a system for applying flower essence therapy to what she has termed the "meta-levels" of life. She views the process of human evolution as an ever-changing dialogue between the needs of the personality and the destiny of the soul as one traverses psychological, sociological, and transpersonal realms.

The eight primary "meta-levels" of soul development include the following:

1. Extending the emotional repertoire
2. Building a home in the body
3. Cultivating consciousness, learning, growing, and changing
4. Finding life purpose, social service, and community life
5. Building the chalice of the soul, sensitivity, artistry, and personal relationship
6. Shadow and soul: recognizing and transforming karma; meeting death
7. Cultivating the spiritual self; transpersonal awareness
8. Nurturing our connection to Nature; knowing the earth as a living being[50]

Thoughts, feelings, and experiences of the human psyche are reflections of cosmic laws inherent in growth patterns, shapes, colors, fragrances, and vital energies of Nature as expressed in the flowering plant.[51]

A valuable adjunct to the research done by Kaminski and Katz is the work of Kevin Ryerson, a professional psychic researcher who developed a cosmology for flower essences in the 1970s. Through his psychic cognition processes, he revealed that flower essences activate ancient doorways to levels of consciousness held within the structure of creation.

Archeytypal energies are holographic and universal in nature. They are lively within the energetic blueprint of the plant form and transmit an inherent signature of purpose and presence. The vibrational patterns of flower essence petals are a hologrammatic diagram for the electrical impulses that structure the mechanics of cellular function.

Further work has been done by Machaelle Small Wright, who portrays the devic sensibility of the plant "kin-dom" as expressed in sacred spirit medicine. The pioneering beauty of her Perelandra gardening project showcases the dynamics of manifestation in the natural world. Plants develop according to the mathematics of dimensional expression as displayed on this plane. The world of plants, animals, and other living organisms relies on the sympathetic resonance of form and structure.

Wright has worked directly with the devic orders of intelligence to create exquisite Findhorn-like gardens that transmit specific energetic blueprints. She has shown the profound influence that plants play in holding the template for the human condition. The human nervous system is an intricate conduit for the intelligence of plants as expressed in our everyday actions and feelings.[52]

Wright further explains that plant essences can support the circuitry of the subtle and gross levels of the human nervous system. They can rejuvenate and rebalance fine levels of electrical conductivity. They send impulses through the physiology to support the order, function, and communication of the glandular system.

Wright has worked extensively with the human immune system, developing essences that work to strengthen and refine human responses to potentially invasive influences. She developed a specialized system of rose essences that align the subtle bodies during periods of intense trauma or spiritual transformation. She believes that contained within Nature is a pattern of healing that responds to every disorder of humankind.[53]

ORIGINS OF THE USE OF GEMSTONES FOR HEALING

Gemstone therapy dates back thousands of years. The ancient civilizations of the Egyptians, Greeks, Hebrews, Aztecs, Chinese, and Incas all practiced gem therapy. Kings, queens, and pharaohs wore gems on their crowns because of the occult powers the gems were known to possess. The gems were seen as conduits for the subtle forces of nature, offering the wearer the possibility of superhuman abilities and even eternal life. The gems were seen as protective shields that would ward off disease, hardship, famine, and natural disasters. Even today, in monarchies around the world, the tradition of wearing ceremonial crowns and gems confirms a power of authority beyond our terrestrial boundaries.

The Ayurvedic tradition of India developed an elaborate science utilizing the healing application of gems and their relationship to the planets and nine cosmic rays—which include the primary colors red, orange, yellow, green, blue, indigo, and violet, plus the invisible ultraviolet and infrared. These cosmic rays are said to be the essence of the nine planets.

The Vedic texts of Jyotish (astrology) and the Guruda Purana provide instruction about the use of gems for healing of the physical, mental/emotional, and spiritual bodies. Gems are utilized for ameliorating astrological afflictions and imbalances in the planetary birth chart. They are also used for accentuating auspicious powers.[54] Gems are in bio-resonant attunement with cosmic energies and the celestial planets. Recommendations are made for the amelioration of astrological afflictions and imbalances in one's natal or progressed chart or to accent a beneficent planetary configuration.

The Chinese advocated gem usage in order to balance the yin/yang aspects of the human energy field and build *chi*, subtle life force energy. Gems were seen as reflections of the cosmic order, which when applied to the subtle emanations of the aura could lift the spirit and relieve burdens of the psyche. Chi was seen as a protective and radiating blanket that permeated the physical and subtle bodies. An individual's unique position in society was calibrated to his or her chi, as well as to innate proclivities.

In most cultures, gems were also introduced either as attire or as layouts placed on the individual's body on specific acupuncture points, *nadi* points, or *marma* points for one's emotional, physical, and spiritual benefit. These spiritual accoutrements were seen to enhance the flow of the chi that had been damaged due to trauma, psychological disturbance, or negative environmental influences. The Chinese believed that jade was the most precious of all stones and contained the "five great virtues": charity, courage, modesty, justice, and wisdom. It was also thought to have powerful curative values in the treatment of illness.[55]

In Western spiritual tradition, Biblical stories tell of many instances in which the Hebrews used gems to create talismans that focalized the power of spiritual energies in this dimension for specific purposes. The blue sapphire was thought to be the stone of which the tablets Moses brought down from Mount Sinai were made. The blue stone was believed to open awareness to the celestial planes and provide clarity of cognition. Noah used a wine-red garnet that had the power to reveal what was hidden, illuminating higher awareness.

In early Judaic tradition, the breastplate of the High Priest was known to contain many precious gems. The Old Testament describes a "breastplate of judgment" or the "breastplate of Aaron." The breastplate contained twelve gems representing the twelve tribes of Israel. The gemstones were each engraved with the name of one of the tribes. It was believed that touching any of the stones would call forth psychic and spiritual influences. The breastplate served as a communications source, a hidden language or code that enhanced these properties or powers. The channels, or psychic forces, inherent within the breastplate allowed the High Priest to serve as a prophet and a sage through dream and vision.[56]

The Egyptians used stones for the enhancement of spiritual power, the making of talismans or amulets, and personal adornment. They wore gems on all parts of the body and clothing, and they also carved gems into scarabs, falcons, and other creatures that served for protection and good fortune. Sages and mystics understood the esoteric knowledge and powers of the stones and kept them sacred in folklore, legends, and world traditions.[57]

The word *gem* means "that which is seen as perfect." Gems are formed through intense heat and tectonic pressure from within the earth. They are created over thousands, and in some cases, millions of years. Gemstones have the ability to absorb, reflect, and radiate varying frequencies of stellar light, becoming conduits for the subtle forces of Nature. They are crystalline forms of energy that are highly sensitive and capable of broadcasting their frequencies over great distances. When a person wears a gem or imbibes a gem elixir, the electromagnetic force field of the gemstone imprints the electromagnetic energy of the human body.[58]

Gems are the most concrete of the celestial forms that embody the universal cosmic rays. Each cosmic ray of chromatically coded light travels to Earth as a vibrating light frequency. The light-coded information organizes itself into crystalline patterns. Each cosmic ray stores information in a compressed fractal sequence. When the cosmic information ray reaches the Earth's subtle atmospheric zones, the information unravels itself according to its divine design.

Gems are crystalline matrices, the ancient record-keepers of Earth's history and its relationship to intergalactic life. In this respect, they fulfill a different function than do plants. Within each cycle of existence, plants embody the codes and blueprints of the evolving plan inherent in Nature. Plants travel through cyclical periods of evolution in which they die and are reseeded, to be born again at a different sequence in the seasonal spiral of time. Gems, on the other hand, are an ancient, stable, and in many cases, more historical record of the laws of Nature of a given locale. Gems record the historical space/time codes of civilizations across eons.

3

PLANTS IN THE LIGHT OF HEALING

Aligning Mind/Body/Soul

Earth laughs in flowers.
—Ralph Waldo Emerson

Earth has no sorrow that earth cannot heal.
—John Muir

We live in a world of plants. Plants are pure light intelligence; they live in the field of love and unification of all living energy systems. As such, they are one of the primary tools to support the mastery of our potential within the universal blueprints of the chakras and the zodiac. They are also key to supporting the body being the temple of the soul.

All plants are visionary teachers and healers whose role is to act as an inner guide, speaking directly to the soul in the language of light, sound, kinesthetic experience, smell, and taste. Plants interface directly with the human nervous system. As light messengers, they send chemical codes of intelligence via receptor sights to the organs and systems of the mind/body, relaying information that inspires, regenerates, and propels the inner being toward the all-possible human. They serve to remind us that the three-dimensional world in which we appear to live is not our whole reality.

Plants open the pathways of our minds to new vistas of insight. They activate awareness to pan the landscape of our inner psyche, revealing the fabric of consciousness. They identify the gap between energy and matter, reweaving the tapestry of consciousness.

Gradually and with precise mathematical methodologies of creation, plants call forth the inner witness that directs our awakening process. **The privilege and responsibility of a person who seeks the healing messages from the natural world is to create a doorway for the union of plant and human consciousness.**

Knowledge of plants offers multidimensional gateways into the human developmental process, which historically centered around priests, priestesses, healers, shamans, and doctors. The present time calls to all humans to access and apply the knowledge and consciousness of plants for the birth of a new civilization on the planet. Civilizations have come and gone, leaving us with sacred knowledge that maps and supports the advancement of our human species and collective consciousness. Each individual is in a unique and powerful position to embody the understanding of the human/plant/ planetary interface.

To move into a future in which we recognize that plants are our allies and co-creators, we must begin to imagine, realize, and define the human species beyond the confines of the physical, emotional, and psychological realms. Plants speak to us in the language of the soul, which empowers and awakens us to deeper realities of our inner life as well as our physical reality. When we open to the healing realms of the soul, we examine and integrate states that are pre-linguistic, symbolic, and archetypal within the psyche.

In this chapter, we'll journey into the mystical nature of plants, how they heal and speak to the human mind/body/soul. We will also highlight practical plant preparations for maintaining health and wellness in life.

PLANTS AS LIGHT-CODED MESSENGERS

As symbolic representations of consciousness, plants are established in the unified field of nature. Their light-coded information is often communicated through visual revelation. Plants are also mathematical replicas of perfection, illustrating the precise unfoldment of creation known as the Golden Mean spiral. Examples of this celestial structure of nature are seen in the center of the sunflower, the Shasta daisy, the pinecone, and the ratios within the human body.[1]

The ratios of the Golden Mean spiral (introduced in Chapter 1) are identified through Fibonacci intervals, a sequence such that the preceding two numbers always add up to the third (i.e., 1, 1, 2, 3, 5, 8, 13, 21, 34, etc.)[2] This sequence creates a portal through the heart into the subtle dimensions of the soul.

Plants meet us where we are. They awaken the soul force, navigating through the psyche, identifying fuel for the fires of transformation. The soul is an intermediary between inner and outer reality, between body and spirit. The soul is fluid in nature.[3] Soul-level work and transmutation can be viewed as symbolic alchemy.

Human evolution is presently involved in the process of training the body to act as a light reservoir for spiritual consciousness. Plants play an integral role in this process by transmitting configurations of light into the nervous system. These light-coded messages engineer the repair and construction of our subtle, or celestial, dimensional structures. These light-body structures are an integrated aspect of the sacred geometrical principles that inherently animate all levels of the holographic mind/body.

When we look at the relationship between plant and human consciousness, we must include our relationship to the whole of Gaia. Plants are mediators, or linguistic translators, for Gaia's evolving intelligence matrix. Human, plant, and planet are fractal interpretations of life unfolding from the grossest outer levels to the finest inner levels of organization and integration.

Plants heal on the level of the heart. The spiritual interface between plants and the heart is the center of reorganization for the evolution of our species. Plants maintain a state of unity with all creation. Since plants are boundless in their state of being, they maintain a coherent frequency of wholeness that resides within the unified field of love. Through their basic nature, they are endowed with the chemical and spiritual power to interface with the human body/mind/soul.

Plants serve as messengers of the evolving Earth. They convey the essential information to our hearts and to the repository of genetic material. There is an exchange of biological resonance between Earth, plants, and human beings. This sonic entrainment is embedded like a fractal within each plant and human entity, as well as within the planet as a whole. The human heart and the heart of Nature synchronize through the use of plants, collectively moving all sentient life toward a quantum expansion of love. Love is the only frequency that can cross dimensions.

The energetic frequency of love is grounded in the biochemistry of the brain. The capacity to identify, activate, and stabilize multidimensional states is both a spiritual and a physiological process. It involves a chemical called DMT (dimethyltryptamine), which is naturally found and produced in the human brain and which elicits an experience of heightened states of awareness. DMT transmutes the chemical language of plants into the visual language of the soul. It lifts emotional and psychological boundaries, enabling consciousness to map the history of the species as a continuum of singularity fusing past, present, and future.

Plants are biochemical agents whose ultimate impact is on the genetic constitution of the species.[4] The internal blueprint of the plant in its crystalline matrix merges with the collective unconscious and forms a backdrop for alchemical transmutation in the human psyche. All plants have the capacity to register their intelligence deep in the substructure of the human heart and mind.

Plants are unique and incomparable messengers of universal intelligence. They should be approached from a place of reverence and given sacred stature on the altar of the soul. A plant need not be purposefully "psychedelic" to deliver a higher order of information. Receptor sites in the consciousness of the individual, suitably prepared through intention, prayer, and invocation, make the utilization of plants for healing spiritually potent.

Plants entrain the heart and mind of the individual to be in phase with the evolving consciousness of a higher order of earth-based reality. The universe provides many allies that aid the journey to the awakened Self. Sacred remedies—prepared as herbal tinctures, homeopathic formulas, essential oils, gem elixirs, and flower essences—have historically been primary vehicles of alchemical transmutation.

Spirit-based bio-resonant remedies transmit organic fluctuations and changes in the heart, mind, and soul of Nature. These preparations create a framework that takes the individual beyond the mental constructs of the thinking mind to a depth of personal self-revelation that has the capacity to break the boundaries of collective consensus.

It is important to recognize that plant therapy plays a key role in addressing the contemporary transformational issues that the human soul bears, individually and collectively. Unification of the body/mind/soul complex can occur through integrative and transpersonal systems, such as traditional shamanic healing practiced in many cultures around the world and the use of flower-essence therapies, essential oils, and other botanical preparations. These ancient and modern approaches assist in the development and mapping of the emergence of new levels of consciousness in humans (see Chapter 2).

This book is an attempt to identify the universal and unifying values shared by ancient and contemporary traditions and systems of natural healing. The organization of botanical formulas in this chapter is rooted in the understanding of the energetic anatomy and principles of the human subtle bodies.

MULTIDIMENSIONAL BOTANICAL THERAPY: HOW PLANTS HEAL

Botanical therapy is a full-spectrum approach to healing that leads us into the deepest realms of human awareness. Plants are the purveyors of bio-light on Earth. Living entities, they are first receivers of impulses of cosmic intelligence, then translators of this information to human consciousness via sound and light. Their capabilities stretch from Earth throughout the cosmos, storing and relaying specific information about all of the vegetation and existing species on the planet.[5] Receptor sites throughout the human physiology are fed creative intelligence directly from plants.[6] These receptors respond to complementary chemical substances found in plants.

The information received by the body/mind/soul complex carves sacred evolutionary pathways into the heart and soul of human beings. For example, when one ingests a flower essence of Holly, the bio-energetic signature activates a resonance field within the psyche that produces the realization that one is not separate or alone in the world but is, in fact, lovingly connected to others.

Plants assist the ego to act as a semipermeable membrane; the ego learns to function in a nonsolid, fluid state in which it allows information and guidance from the Higher Self and other realms to enter its field of conscious awareness.

The infrastructure of plants is crystalline in nature. Layers of geometric crystalline structure are symmetrically inlaid, creating fractals, which are infinite mathematical configurations emerging one from another. As each pattern reveals itself, these packed forms of energies unfold information, describing the mechanics within creation. The crystalline structure of the plant releases information by establishing a lattice of ethereal information between the plant and human nervous systems. This supports ongoing evolving processes of ordering that advance the organization and integration of the body/mind/soul complex.

As our human nervous system becomes more fully interactive with the crystalline structure of plants, we are initiated into realms that command us to actualize the creative intelligence of the God-force. Through a technique known as Kirlian photography, which was developed in the former Soviet Union to document the functioning of the human energy field, we are able to see the crystalline matrices that a specific plant form embodies.

Plants are living archetypes. When we ingest them through any one of the senses, we activate a unifying bio-resonant field. They then catalyze consciousness through a process of shared imaging.

Plants reveal ancient information held in the multiple forms of Gaia. Through his work with breath and plant medicine, Stanislaus Grof (a pioneer in the field of transpersonal psychology and consciousness research) experienced that archetypal realities become available via the expansion of our sensory modalities (i.e., clairvoyance and clairaudience).[7] By traversing the biological, psychological, mythological, and spiritual dimensions of one's psyche, one can experience an imprinting that awakens realization of one's place in the architecture of creation.

A mapping of a new typography of the psyche will include soul mapping of color and geometry as gates into the unconscious. Plants transmit cosmic color rays that speak to the body/mind/soul; their forms embody packets of geometric intelligence. Therefore, using plants to access different frequencies of information, an individual's nervous system is capable of quantum-shifting entire realities and belief systems within the psyche.

Since plants as a living system of intelligence are an inclusive continuum of past, present, and future, the daily use of plant essences liberates space/time boundaries that have been previously set. The domain of time becomes fluid, and points of reference for healing become nonlocal.

The intelligent field of human/plant life unfolds the healing process by downloading the light values through the heart and nervous system. In the mind/body field, events, emotions, and conditions of mind become fixed through past circumstances, but plants set up a resonant field that penetrates the past conditions and begins to dissolve them, thus retrieving kinetic energy that has been lost.

At this point, as the frozen energy dissolves and integrates into the present, awareness may hold insights and realizations about one's life. Retrieving aspects of the soul and energy locked in the past can reconstitute the present and future of one's life.

For example, in one case, I was working with a young man of about thirty who was a professional writer. He was having difficulty accessing his creativity, and I recommended a formulation of flower essences. For several days, he reported memories and flashbacks from his childhood previously out of his normal range of memory. In this process of retrieving lost memory, he experienced surges of energy and inspiration that allowed him to complete an entire screenplay within two or three weeks while taking his personal flower essence formula. The ingestion of the plant formula released the frozen energy and freed the locked memories. In this instance, the client reported an increased sense of being in the present, enabling him to overcome past experiences that had blocked his creativity. The resurgence of creative experience was measurable, not only by virtue of the creative product he manifested, but also by an increased feeling of well-being and gratitude; the client experienced a freedom through psycho-emotional release that translated into a more coherent and inspired creative expression.

MIND/BODY BOTANICAL THERAPIES: CORNERSTONE OF HEALTH

My intention is to catalyze you, the reader of this book, into a direct experiential relationship with the natural world of plant intelligence and its power to make whole. The information presented is aimed at restoring our knowledge of who we are and why we are here. The formulas described in this chapter and throughout the book facilitate a greater experience of the spiritual values of the plants; this creates a broader field of influence that facilitates personal awareness and identity in shifting toward a transpersonal state.

The application of botanicals transmutes one's personal, history-bound reality into a transpersonal state free from referencing to the past. This occurs on the level of the chakra system and the mythological, or astrological, archetypes of the psyche. All of these hold primordial keys to unlocking this vast nature of our individual potential and cosmic life.

Botanical therapies facilitate an organic healing process and self-discovery into the nature of personal reality. Botanical formulas and applications call forth the knowledge of the physical, energetic, and spiritual interrelationship of plants. The most popular preparations include fresh fluid botanical extracts, herbal-based topical oils, flower essences, and essential oils.

These plant preparations are created with the intention to heal both the physical and subtle energetic bodies. Each method of preparation described below is specialized in its ability to access the human sheaths of the subtle bodies. Each unique botanical preparation method provides vital information to the living system of the human being to invoke greater health, awareness, and wellness.

As we work with plants, we rapidly understand that our own consciousness is enlivened by divine grace and intelligence. A true healing system is grounded in the source from which the creative forces of light and sound originate. Such is the world of nature and the kingdom of plants.

The preparation of plants for healing purposes is a spiritual discipline. Each of the specialized preparations—which include herbal extracts, herbal-based topical oils, flower essences, and essential oils—accesses a specific realm of healing that enhances communication within the body/mind/soul complex.

Herbal extracts embody the chemical messengers that speak directly to our physiology, restoring the natural levels of organization necessary for healing.

Essential oils embody the most vital part of the plant in high levels of concentration. The aromatic essential oils communicate information directly to the brain and nervous system. They awaken the cellular memory of wholeness, refining the feeling and uplifting the spirit.

Herbal-based topical oils are applied to the skin, conducting plant intelligence throughout the cellular level.

Flower essences, which are a solar infusion of vibrant blossoms, directly communicate the spirit of the plant to our consciousness through a crystal-line matrix. This activates an integrating process that speaks to the emotional and psycho-spiritual parts of the psyche.

Herbal Extracts: Regeneration and Nourishment for the Body

An organic grain alcohol, mixed with pure spring water, is one of the most effective mediums for extracting a wide range of plant constituents. After the extraction process, the grain alcohol can be rotary evaporated out of the extract, after which vegetable glycerin can be added to keep constitu-ents suspended in liquid without an alcohol base. Ideally, herbs should be organic, wild crafted, and verified free of any contaminants. They should be saturated for a period of two to four weeks.

To capture nature's vital healing powers, many conscious standards have to be met in the art and science of making plant medicine. Using herbs that are either ecologically wild-crafted (so as not to disturb or deplete the natural environment) and/or certified organically grown is of primary importance. To be certified organically grown, herbs must be cultivated without the use of herbicides, pesticides, chemical fertilizers, or genetically engineered seeds.

The herbal extract embodies the life force activity present in the taste, color, texture, and aroma of the plants. The extract restores life-giving patterns of intelligence; the plant's chemical messengers feed directly to receptor sites throughout the human physiology, providing specific infor-mation related to restructuring and healing on the level of cellular memory.[8]

Essential Oils: Celestial Fragrances to Lift the Spirit

Essential oils carry the vital force of the plant in its most condensed and primary form. The essential oil preparation carries the pure aromatic potency of the plant; its smell is the primary therapeutic pathway for the oil to activate the healing process. These oils may also be blended with other plant extracts and applied to the skin, where they are absorbed and carried into the blood and lymphatic systems, purifying and restoring vitality to the systems.

The purpose of the essential oil is to transmit vital energy from the medium of the oil to the medium of the cell. The oils uplift the spirit, awakening the individual's will to heal. The fragrance of the oil activates personal and transpersonal aspects of memory. Information gained in this manner is fed through the olfactory to the limbic system of the brain (the processing center for emotions) as well as the central nervous system, stimulating the genesis of spiritual awakening.

Hundreds of pounds of fresh herbs and/or blossoms are gathered to create as little as one pound of oil. In steam distillation, the preferred form of extraction, the aromatic volatile oil is separated from the water and material content of the plant. The steam is capable of extracting small droplets of fragrant oil from the plant, carrying them upward. The oil then passes through a cooling tube and enters a receptacle filled with water, allowing the oil to float to the top. The oil is then collected and placed in glass jars tinted to prevent exposure to heat and light.

The steam-distilled essential oil is completely pure, in contrast to those generated through synthetic or chemical extraction. Like the flower essence, the essential oil embodies the intelligence of the plant spirit. As noted above, the first access point for entry into the human energy field is the sense of smell and its ability to deliver information to the brain and nervous system.[9] In some cases, pure essential oils are blended with herbal extracts for internal therapeutic uses.

Herbal-Based Topical Oils: Anointing and Nourishing the Body

Herbal-based topical oils are extracts of vibrant plant blossoms set in a base of one or more oils, such as cold-pressed olive, almond, and castor oils. They are generally set in the sun for a minimum of two weeks, creating a solar infusion of the healing properties of the plant into the oil base.

The purpose of the oil base is to provide an influence that is both nutritive and penetrating. Through contact with the skin, the healing power of the plant's intelligence can be offered at every level of being, from the tissues to the finest levels of consciousness. Inhibitory patterns that have been stored in the tissues and musculature of the body/mind are easily released through the use of these oils. The result is that the individual is assisted in developing more evolutionary patterns of awareness and behavior.

The skin encapsulates the physical body and functions as a vehicle for its definition. The skin is the largest organ of the human body, constantly communicating the physical and subtle information it gathers from its environment. Herbal oils feed the physical and etheric bodies; the etheric body is the consciousness matrix for the sequential unfoldment of the physical form. Herbal oils help to reestablish and strengthen the etheric/physical bodies, penetrating deeply into the somatic level.[10]

Flower Essences: Wordless Prayers from the Mystics of the Earth

Flower essences are liquid solar infusions that carry the subtle energetic patterns of specific flowers. Flower essences are vibrational in nature. They are generally ingested orally, initiating an interactive process between the plant and human energy fields. Flower essences create a resonance within the individual field of human consciousness, thus awakening specific qualities inherent in the soul.

The vibrational frequency introduced through the medium of flower essences reaches the deepest core of our being; it enlivens consciousness and integrates psycho-emotional perception. Flower essences direct consciousness to the attributes, virtues, and potential of the soul that seek to be actualized and expressed in one's life.

The flower essence unifies the vertical and horizontal growth axes in life. The bloom unifies these two values, creating a vortex of light in the heart chakra. The bloom represents the infinite value of the eternal expression of beauty and grace. The moment in which a flower comes into its full expression is the moment in which it embodies the totality of the essence of its being. At that point, it is in full communication with the divine cosmic influences and light.

When the flower reaches full bloom, it has attained the pinnacle of its journey toward the light and upholds the values of its creative intelligence. This is the zenith at which the plant's growth process becomes suspended in timelessness. This is an interdimensional window in which the essence of the plant is lively both in its manifest and unmanifest values. It is at this gap in space and time, the eternal peak expression of reality, that a flower essence is prepared.

The life-force essence of the flower is a vibrational quality that contains the blueprint of form, space, and time, yet is not bound by it. It is on this basis that a flower essence preparation is a time traveler/healer. Without the ability to move forward or backward in time, we are caught in an unchangeable, fixed version of what we perceive to be reality.

Time is unbounded, without object, and stretches infinitely across the range of intelligent experience. As Janet Sussman says in her book *Timeshift*, "The circular, ever-bending subswing of time allows us to lift free from caged possibility."[11] Such is the gift and the subtle power of flower essences.

Simply put, a flower essence is a wordless prayer, an energetic formula that communicates the God-plan to our very heart, mind, and soul. The flower symbolizes and resonates with qualities of consciousness shared by both humanity and nature. An essence acts like a sutra, a yogic formula that awakens specific channels in the field of universal consciousness.

Flowers are symbolic representations, living archetypes of consciousness found in the field of nature. Flower essences expand the boundaries of our limitations, psychologically and emotionally. Let's look more deeply at the capacity of flower essences to awaken the holographic psyche.

Flower Essences: Technicians of Holographic Healing

Flower essences live in the timeless continuum of life and thus have access to the range of past, present, and future. Flower essences are time travelers that heal through their limitless ability to move through what we understand as conceptual time.

As we ingest a flower essence, the body receives information through the nervous system as coherent electrical impulses, the vibrational or electromagnetic information inherent as that essence.

The heart matrix carries the waveform generated by the use of a flower essence through the physical and subtle bodies. As this healing process unfolds, an enhanced fluidity in the etheric body moves consciousness, allowing for the psyche to have greater range of motion and fluidity. A sense of time-bound reality is released, and information from other coordinate points can be accessed. It can be understood that essences dissolve the timelines locked in the past and retrieve portions of the soul that have been psycho-emotionally frozen, fixed, or lost, due to some trauma or condition in the emotional or mental subtle bodies.

The soul makes available information from other dimensions or times where related events have been experienced. The information retrieved by the body/mind/soul is in a resonant phase loop with present evolutionary codes unfolding from the soul. Healing or reconstruction of the physical dimension and body/mind/soul can take place through this process.

Flower essences enter the information network of the soul through the nervous system. Flower essences are electromagnetic in nature, communicating their impulse matrix to the human nervous system. The life-force energy and vibrational patterning of the essence—which is visual, kinesthetic, and sonic in nature—enters the human auric field through the etheric body, the chakra system, and the body/mind complex.

The pineal gland, due to its special crystalline structure, receives information from the soul and subtle bodies, translating this knowledge to the entire physical and subtle nervous systems. Flower essences adjust the flow of consciousness, allowing karma to dissolve. They elevate the healing capacity of the individual, breaking it away from inherent limitations and creating stable changes in the body/mind/soul. Flower essences illumine the junction point where consciousness transforms into matter. They reconfigure emotional, mental, and karmic conditions to allow them to integrate at the level of Self.

As flower essences create new electrical pathways through the spinal column, the circuitry is reconnected, and dysfunction of any kind—physical, emotional, mental, or behavioral—begins to reverse itself.[12] The revelatory application of flower essences leads to an interface with individual human consciousness.

Flower essences catalyze the transmission of holographic information to the soul. New developments in flower-essence therapy will investigate the psychic/spiritual links in the epigenetic field of study.

Prenatal ancestral patterns have transbiological roots essential for healing and transformation.[13] Flower essences identify familial imprinting in the ancestral psyche and reveal how genetics are expressed as the individual's persona. As ancestral imprints are illumined by the light of consciousness, there is a simultaneous dissolution and resolution of karmic blueprints. This can also be understood in progressive science as an epigenetic transformational clearing-and-healing process.

The ingestion of a plant essence brings the human soul into direct contact and communication with the plant spirit.[14] **The soul is the ground state for interactive processes between species and worlds.** It is a collective field of consciousness whose presence unfolds the time loops that create past, present, and future. As the soul arcs between dimensions, superconductive conduits of light-encoded information from the essences are configured into symbols that communicate directly with the soul.

Like all life, plants are organized mathematically. The mathematical arrays of the soul are enhanced through the use of plants. These mathematical codes are fractal in nature and appear as visual archetypes that arise out of the unmanifest. Inherent in these codes are the blueprints of creation. Plants reinforce and reference the body/mind back to one's state of divine, healthy origination. This process is very conceptual in nature and elusive in its abstractness.

Plants and flower essences enliven the original memories embedded in the intelligence of Nature. The harmonic frequencies of the flower essences are fed to the human light body in a step-down series that provides the mathematical codes from which the knowledge of DNA is drawn. Plants are portrayed in archetypal forms. For example, Mariposa Lily is an expression of the Divine Mother principle, while Sunflower is an expression of the Divine Father principle.

The light-encoded information carried within these archetypes is transmitted telepathically, electromagnetically, and biochemically to human consciousness through the neuro-net of the nervous system. Thus, human souls and the intelligence of Nature develop an empathic synchrony that resonates directly in the structure of the human nervous system. This process underlies the fundamental continuum whereby humans can communicate directly with the natural world.

Advancement of our species is not commonly sought by the mainstream population. This evolutionary gesture is a trans-temporal phenomenon that can be described as the "future-now." When the soul is actively in these trans-temporal shifts, a type of pre-linguistic intelligence comes to the foreground of consciousness. The late Terrence McKenna, a consciousness researcher and visionary philosopher, posed the question of whether language is simply a shadow of the hyper-dimensional mind or whether it plays a more significant factor in the future development of higher levels of cognition.[15] I believe that the role of plants in all their healing and intelligent communication capacities brings us to the doorstep of our future selves.

Plants are bio-resonant communicators that feed light intelligence to the human nervous system. Plants are encoded sound frequencies that can be heard at the level of their subtlest value, leading the personality back to its essential origin. Through trans-linguistic experiences, the sonic frequencies of the plant expand consciousness to redefine the realms of meaning and significance. The unveiling of these sonic tones or frequencies creates inner feedback loops that guide awareness to its most primary or causal level of expression.

As we have seen, throughout the ages, indigenous cultures have used medicinal plants as part of their healing rituals and spiritual practices. The spiritual attributes of the plants have acted as enlightened teachers, reaching into the soul of the recipient and unlocking the knowledge of holistic life. Each plant has been viewed as a conductor of higher emotional/mental frequencies that have brought individuals and civilizations into contact with the infinite nature of the universe.

In modern times, healing has reverted to a more mundane and superficial level, relying on medicine more as a stopgap measure to ease pain and suffering than as a means of tracing the roots of that suffering to the core of the human condition and our relationship with the divine. In present times, healers, therapists, and physicians are poised on the edge of realization that transformational healing can awaken an individual into his or her true nature.

THE UNIFYING HEALING POWERS OF HERBS, FLOWER ESSENCES, AND ESSENTIAL OILS

The unifying powers of fresh herbal extracts, essential oils, and flower essences create a full-spectrum approach for the promotion of deep core resonant healing in the whole mind/body complex. The blending of herbal extracts with flower essences is founded in the understanding that the flower essences have the innate capability of enhancing and expanding the healing properties of herbs. In this way, the whole value of the plant can be accessed and utilized, restoring the synthesis of its chemical and nonchemical components, its physical and nonphysical spiritual properties.

The blending of flower essences with herbs is an important step in the energetic utilization of intelligence within the individual, as it establishes a clear and vital light body. The physical component of the herbal preparation creates a cushion, or foundation, for the flower essences to be more fully activated in consciousness. The herbal component clears and vitalizes the cellular level, while the essence fills the cells with properties of light. The life force energy of the essence enters the human being through the physical, the etheric body, and the chakra system.[16]

There is an inherent connection between imbalances that occur on the physical level and the mental and spiritual aspects of an individual's psyche. For example, an individual expressing weakness in the liver area might also experience feelings of anger, resentment, or hostility. Intervention from a healing perspective traditionally addresses this reality through the physical vehicle with an herbal formulation or at a psycho-emotional level with the use of a flower essence. **The synergistic blending of herbs and flower essences into a single formula maximizes the therapeutic value of each of these preparations and broadens the spectrum of influence from the physical into the subtle realms of healing.**

In creating a full spectrum herbal/flower essence formula, the plant can be prepared as a fluid extract, an essence, or an essential oil. For example, Echinacea as a fresh plant extract is an immune-potentiating herb. Echinacea prepared as a flower essence assists in establishing integration of the core self, which plays a principal role in the integrity of the immune system.[17] The essential oil of Echinacea supports both physical and etheric aspects of health. Thus, the therapeutic theme of the herb and the essence is innately expressed as a whole. Finer and finer levels of intelligence unfold themselves through the different extractions of the plant.

The other principal approach is to choose a flower essence that is complementary to the herb. For example, Hawthorn prepared as an herbal extract acts to strengthen the connective tissue and enhance cardiovascular capacity and circulation.[18] It may be complemented by an essence such as Holly, which expands the value of the heart chakra, increasing and circulating one's feelings of unconditional love. The flower essence then acts to enhance the healing potential of the herb from a subtler energetic level. A Hawthorn essence could also be used in conjunction with the Hawthorn herbal extract, as discussed above.

Another type of formula design incorporates herbal-based oils, flower essences, and essential oils. In this case, the aromatic essential oils are added for the purpose of directing the vital force of the plant's intelligence deep into the brain and nervous system, through receptor sites on the skin and the sense of smell. The essential oils are added in a complementary way to access and bring out the therapeutic theme for which the whole formula is intended.

For example, one may have a preparation of Arnica as an herbal oil that, when applied topically, assists in repairing trauma, shock, tears, or strains to the physical structure. Arnica flower essence facilitates the repair of the shock, trauma, or tears in the etheric body, thus speeding the healing process.[19] An essential oil of Chamomile creates a soothing and quieting influence on the nervous system, releasing stress. These herbal preparations, applied through the skin, nourish and feed the entire mind/body system from a cellular level.

Oral ingestion of herbal/flower essence formulations involves many different protocols. When profound imbalances in the physiology are manifest, a therapeutic dose should be taken as prescribed by your health care professional. For example, in some cases this could be thirty or forty drops taken two to five times a day in water. This frequency would most directly address the physiology. When the pattern of imbalance is more on the subtle psycho-spiritual and emotional level, application could be three to five drops taken four or more times in a small amount of water. In every situation, it's best to seek the advice of your health care provider.

FIVE HERBAL/FLOWER ESSENCE BLENDS FOR BUILDING THE BODY AS THE TEMPLE OF THE SOUL

The following five botanical formulas (developed by the author) are keys to cleansing, strengthening, and creating a healthy physical body and vital energetic pathways—enhancing the body as the temple of the soul. As the body grows in light, health, and vitality, it can enable the power of the soul to manifest its highest destiny in one's life. Each formula holds a vital key to creating a clear, balanced, and strong system, capable of housing the ever-expanding presence of one's divinity.

The information presented here is based on historical use of the botanicals and flower essences mentioned. It is for educational purposes only; it is not intended to treat, diagnose, prescribe, or mitigate any illness or disease. Always seek the advice of your physician.

1. Hawthorn/Holly Blend: A Vitalizing Cardiovascular Tonic for the Heart Chakra

Primary Colors: Red and White (red fruit and white flower)

BOTANICALS USED IN HAWTHORN/HOLLY BLEND

HAWTHORN (*CRATAEGUS OXYCANTHA*)

Part Used: Ripe fruit, leaf, and flower

Constituents: Flavonoids, glycosides, saponins, ascorbic acid, and tannin[20]

Hawthorn is a general tonic for the cardiovascular system. It has a restorative and strengthening effect on the heart. It improves circulation and oxygenation of the blood. It regulates heart action, depending on the need of the body to restore homeostasis. Hawthorn enhances recovery of both energy and metabolism; it can lower levels of lactate, indicating cardio-protective effects.

Recent biochemical analysis indicates Hawthorn's medicinal properties are due to bioflavonoids called flavans. Hawthorn exhibits supportive influence on the connective tissue in the lining of the arteries and heart, as well as the lining of the synovial joints. Hawthorn's procyanidins cross-link the connective tissue's collagen and elastin, optimizing the tissue's elasticity and resilience to stress and aging. The flavans optimize the heart's calcium metabolism. Hawthorn also dilates the coronary artery, enhancing supply of blood to the heart muscle.[21]

Modern research indicates that extracts of Hawthorn exhibit the major flavonoids such as vitexin, rhamnoside, rutin, and hyperoside in the flowers, with the addition of vitexin in the leaves. Flavonoids are bioactive plant pigments that have shown antianaphylactic, antiallergic, anti-inflammatory and antithrombotic activity, as well as cardiotonic, hypotensive, and anti-arrhythmic effects.[22]

In over 100 years of clinical use, Hawthorn preparations have shown to be highly safe, exhibiting no known cases of toxicity even in high doses.

WILD OAT (*AVENA SATIVA*)

Part Used: Oats

Constituents: Proteins, C-glycosyl flavones, avenins avenacosides, fixed oil, vitamin E, starch

Wild Oat exerts a calming influence directly upon the brain, increasing nerve force and improving nutrition to the entire system. Wild Oat is used to aid in relief of cardiac exhaustion, general muscular weakness, nerve tremors, and anxiety. Wild Oat neutralizes gastric acidity and is used for lack of circulation to the extremities.[23]

The German Commission E monograph notes the use of Wild Oat for helping relieve acute and chronic anxiety, stress and excitatory states, and weakness of the connective tissue; it also serves as a tonic and restorative. Preparations are used to support the cardiovascular, nervous, and respiratory systems, as well as for pulled muscles and cramps. The oats from the green tops are said to lower the uric acid level in the blood.

MOTHERWORT (*LEONURUS CARDIACA*)

Part Used: Aerial parts

Constituents: Bitter glycosides, including leonurin and leonuridine; alkaloids, including leonuinine and stachydrene; volatile oil; and tannin

Motherwort has been used historically to help manage rapid heartbeat due to anxiety, worry, and tension. It has been useful in disturbed sleep, spinal irritation, neuralgia, and nervousness from irregular menstrual activity and/ or menopause. It is helpful with spasms and palpitations of the heart. It can be useful for women who are affected by weaknesses in the pelvic and lumbar regions. It works well in combination with Hawthorn. Motherwort is found to have sedative and antispasmodic properties. Traditionally, it is used for cardiac weakness and nervousness.[25]

FLOWER ESSENCES USED IN HAWTHORN/HOLLY BLEND

- HOLLY (*ILEX AQUIFOLIUM*)
- BLEEDING HEART (*DICENTRA FORMOSA*)
- BORAGE (*BORAGO OFFICINALIS*)
- DOGWOOD (*CORNUS NUTTALLII*)
- ALOE VERA (*ALOE VERA*)

This synergistic blend of flower essences addresses the psycho-emotional themes of the human heart. These essences support the base of the heart chakra to energetically stabilize the heart. Holly opens one to feelings of compassion, love, and peace. Borage lightens and frees the heavy heart. Bleeding heart develops a greater range of emotional sensitivity and objectivity in the heart simultaneously. Aloe Vera revitalizes the heart center from effects of burnout, emotional exhaustion, grief, loss of a loved one, and separation. Dogwood allows grace and gratefulness to grow in the heart.

2. Passionflower/Lavender Blend: A Tonic for the Nervous System

Primary Colors: Violet and Blue

BOTANICALS USED IN THE PASSIONFLOWER/LAVENDER BLEND

PASSIONFLOWER (*PASSIFLORA INCARNATA*)

Part Used: Leaves

Constituents: Alkaloids, including harmine, harman, harmol, and passiflorine; flavone glycosides; sterols

Passionflower is an herb known for its sedative and antispasmodic properties. These responses are associated with the indole alkaloids and flavone glycosides present in the plant. Passionflower is also found to have sedative and analgesic properties. It helps lower motor activity often associated with twitches and spasms. It beneficially influences the heart, liver, and lung meridians, thus balancing and supporting the cardiovascular system, central nervous system, kidneys, and lungs.[26]

Passionflower has been effective in nerve pain, such as neuralgia and shingles, as well as being an effective antispasmodic. It assists in the transition into restful sleep without any narcotic hangover.[27]

The harmala chemicals in Passionflower dilate the coronary arteries, assisting in the prevention of heart disease.[28] Passiflora extracts have been shown to reduce locomotor activity and prolong sleeping time, and they are traditionally used to reduce excitability in cases of heart palpitations and sleep disorders. They also have a calming influence in adults and children.

They have historically been used for nervous restlessness, sleeplessness, and gastro-discomfort of nervous origin.[29]

Medical literature contains no reports of harm from Passionflower used properly. However, because the harmala compounds in Passionflower are uterine stimulants, excess dosages are to be avoided by pregnant women.

SKULLCAP (*SCUTELLARIA LATERIFLORA*)

Parts Used: Aerial parts

Constituents: Flavonoid glycoside, including scutellarin and scutellarein; trace of volatile oil; bitter

The therapeutic action of skullcap acts as a nervine tonic, antispasmodic, and hypertensive. Skullcap relaxes nervous tension and fortifies the central nervous system. It is also found to be helpful with nervous exhaustion and depressive conditions. It is indicated for nervous irritation of the cerebrospinal nervous system, restlessness, insomnia, nightmares, and general irritability.

It may be used for nervous symptoms associated with irregular muscular action, such as twitching, tremors, or lack of coordination.[30] The calming effect of skullcap has been attributed to the volatile oil scutellarein. Skullcap enters the heart and kidney meridians, influencing the autonomic and central nervous system, brain, and spine.

No health hazards have been reported with proper use.

WILD OAT (*AVENA SATIVA*)

Part Used: Oats

Constituents: Proteins, C-glycosyl flavones, avenins avenacosides, fixed oil, vitamin E, starch

Wild Oat is known to build nervous system reserves to assist in overcoming nervous excitement, cardiac weakness, insomnia, and mental weakness. Wild Oat addresses muscular debilitation. It is high in minerals, particularly calcium, and therefore provides nutrition to the nervous system.[31]

GOTU KOLA (*CENTELLA ASIATICA*)

Part Used: Whole plant

Constituents: Glycosides, brahmoside and brahminoside, saponin, and asiaticoside

Gotu Kola is known as the *brahmi* (supreme reality) herb in Ayurvedic medicine. It is one of the most revered herbs of India and is used to rejuvenate both body and mind. It has been used for centuries to increase intelligence, longevity, and memory, and it reduces premature aging and senility. It has also been used to strengthen the adrenal glands and purify the blood.

In Ayurvedic medicine it inhibits *vata*, thus calming the nerves. Yogis in the Himalayas use Gotu Kola as a food for meditation. It balances the left and right hemispheres of the brain and opens the crown chakra.[32]

Studies in India reveal that Gotu Kola can be used to increase powers of concentration and attention, thus increasing IQ and producing shifts in general behavioral patterns, from shy and withdrawn to communicative and cooperative.[33]

Gotu Kola has been shown to stabilize blood sugar levels in association with mood swings, fatigue, and depression.[34]

Gotu Kola is shown to be high in B-complex vitamins, including B-1 (thiamine), B-2 (riboflavin), and B-6 (pyridoxine). B-complex vitamins are responsible for normal functioning of the nervous system and its healthy effects on the brain.[35]

This herb is thought to be completely safe with proper use.

LAVENDER (*LAVENDULA OFFICINALIS*)

Part Used: Flowers

Constituents: Volatile oil that contains linalyl acetate, linalol, geraniol, cineole, limonene, and sesquiterpenes

Lavender is primarily known for its effectiveness in clearing depression, headaches, and nervous exhaustion. It has been found to be a strengthening tonic for the nervous system.[36] Lavender has been historically used as a mild sedative for cases of excitement, nervous exhaustion, and disturbances of sleep. It has been used in cases of restlessness, sleeplessness, lack of appetite, irritable stomach, and nervous discomfort of the intestines.

Lavender has been demonstrated to possess antispasmodic, carminative, diuretic, sedative, tonic, and stomachic properties. Conditions for which it is used include spasms, nervous headache, neuralgia, nausea, flatulence, sprains, and colic.[37]

FLOWER ESSENCES USED IN THE PASSIONFLOWER/ LAVENDER BLEND

- LAVENDER (*LAVENDULA OFFICINALIS*)
- CHAMOMILE (*MATRICARIA CHAMOMILLA*)
- ALOE VERA (*ALOE VERA*)
- MORNING GLORY (*IPOMOEA PURPUREA*)
- CHERRY PLUM (*PRUNUS CERASIFERA*)
- CLEMATIS (*CLEMATIS VITALBA*)
- IMPATIENS (*IMPATIENS GLADULIFERA*)
- STAR OF BETHLEHEM (*ORNITHOGALUM UMBELLATUM*)
- ROCK ROSE (*HELIANTHEMUM NUMMULARIUM*)

This blend of essences complements the herbs to address the primary energetic stresses that are held in the emotional body. These stresses are imprinted into the nervous system due to genetically inherited dispositions, habitual conditions of mind, or long-held shock or trauma. As the herbs bring healing into the physical domain of the body, the flower essences are empowered to dissolve the layers of patterned stress taken on by the nervous system and acted out through the emotional and mental bodies. Deep-rooted stresses are released, and energy and alertness are enhanced.

Chamomile increases the ability to remain objective in stimulating, stressful situations. Lavender grounds high-strung, nervous energy. Morning Glory balances the natural rhythms of sleeping and waking. Aloe Vera rejuvenates vital life energy depleted due to burnout, stress, or exhaustion.

The last five flowers in the above list, known as the Five Flower Remedy or Rescue Remedy, facilitate emotional balance, releasing tension and irritability.

Together, the formula produces an overall calming and stabilizing effect on body, mind, and emotions.

3. Gotu Kola/Peppermint Blend: Awakening the Higher Mind, Memory, and Cognitive Function

Primary Colors: Green, White, and Yellow

BOTANICALS USED IN THE GOTU KOLA/PEPPERMINT BLEND

GOTU KOLA (*CENTELLA ASIATICA*)

Parts Used: Whole plant

Constituents: The glycosides brahmoside and brahminoside, saponin, and asiaticoside

(See Gotu Kola description in Passionflower/Lavender Formula, previous section.)

BASIL (*OCIMUM LABIATAE*)

Parts Used: Aerial parts

Constituents: Essential oil, estragol with linalon, linerol, and camphor

Basil is a primary herb considered sacred in India. It is an herb whose properties have a beneficial influence on the nervous, respiratory, and digestive systems. It is a primary herb considered sacred in India. In Ayurvedic medicine, it is thought to open the heart and mind to the experience of love and devotion, bringing faith, compassion, and clarity. It is seen to be cleansing to the aura (the electromagnetic field surrounding the body), as well as strengthening to the immune system.

Basil absorbs positive ions from the environment and generates negative ions, which are beneficial to the physiology and to the vitality of the mind/ body. Basil has been used to open the lungs, thus increasing *prana* (life-force energy) and promoting sensory acuity. It strengthens the nerve tissue and increases memory. It is used in India to promote clarity of mind and the quality of *sattva* (purity of mind/body/spirit).[38] Basil is also used to increase blood circulation.

Basil has been used historically as an antidepressant, antiseptic, antispasmodic, carminative, and nervine. Basil supports the body in conditions of fatigue, cold, depression, and respiratory weaknesses.[39]

GINGKO (*GINGKO BILOBA*)

Parts Used: Leaf

Constituents: Gingko glycosides (bioflavonoids); terpene lactones gingkolides and bilobalide; flavone glycosides quercetin, kaempferol, and isorhamnetin

Gingko has historically been used to increase circulation to both the brain and the extremities of the body. Studies have shown that it inhibits platelet stickiness and regulates tone and elasticity of the blood vessels. Gingko increases circulation to both arteries and capillaries, indicating that it is effective with circulatory problems in the elderly and in the early stages of Alzheimer's. The gingkolides are the factors that improve circulation; they have platelet-activating factor (PAF)–inhibiting properties.

The bioflavonoid group provides antioxidant activity, as well as the ability to inhibit platelet aggregation, thus improving cardiovascular capacity as well as protecting nerve cells in the central nervous system (CNS) from damage due to lack of oxygen to tissues in the body.

Research has indicated that gingko improves cardiovascular capacity and reduces memory loss, depression, tinnitus, and hardening of the arteries. Gingko reduces free-radical damage in the brain associated with aging.

Gingko stabilizes the blood-brain barrier (BBB), lowering swelling (edema) in the brain—one of the most significant causes of aging. This stabilization occurs directly through action on the ionic potential across the membranes and indirectly through action on intracellular (mitochondrial) respiration.

Gingko biloba extract significantly increases the synthesis of dopamine (a critical neurotransmitter) and inhibits histamine by influencing the muscular receptor sites. It has been shown to have a profound effect on the glandular, cardiovascular, and nervous systems.[40]

Gingko is essentially devoid of serious side effects. Some persons indicate sensitivity, including mild gastrointestinal problems or mild headache. Gingko is not recommended during pregnancy or lactation, for epileptics, or for those using blood thinners.[41]

ROSEMARY (*ROSMARINUS OFFICINALIS*)

Parts Used: Leaves and twigs

Constituents: Volatile oils, flavonoids, phenolic acids, rosmaricine and isoromaricine, triterpenic acids. The volatile oil is made up of alpha-pinene, camphene, cineole, and borneol.

Rosemary acts as a circulatory and nervine stimulant that has a toning and calming effect on the digestion, particularly in cases where psychological tension is present.[42] Rosemary has antispasmodic and antidepressant qualities. It is also a carminative. Carminatives are rich in volatile oils and by their action relax the stomach and stimulate peristalsis of the digestive system.

Borneol is the source of rosemary oil's antimicrobial (bacterial and anti-fungal) properties. The flavonoid diosmin is seen to be an effective factor in decreasing capillary permeability and fragility. Rosemary extract is known to have antioxidant properties. Rosemary enters the lung, spleen, heart, and liver meridians, influencing the brain, nerves, heart, lungs, intestines, uterus, and urogenital organs. Historically, it has been used for nervous disorders, headaches, colds, cholic, and menstrual problems.[43]

Rosemary is an excellent remedy for people with weak circulation, either constitutionally or from weakening conditions. It is an ideal tonic for elderly people and atonic conditions of the stomach.

Rosemary is said to be useful in the treatment of nervous headaches and to have beneficial influences on the brain, improving memory with long-term use.[44]

No records of toxicity are mentioned in the literature when Rosemary is used properly.

SCHIZANDRA (*SCHISANDRA CHINENSIS*)

Parts Used: Berry

Constituents: Lignans

Schizandra belongs to a class of herbs called *adaptogens*, which act to regulate processes that affect all body systems. Schizandra is known as an adapto-genic herb, an herb that brings homeostasis to the organs and systems of the body. Adaptogens correct imbalances at a cellular level by encouraging the body's inherent capabilities to repair and regulate itself. When the body incurs stress—such as depression, hard physical labor, infections, environmental toxins, or psycho-emotional challenges—its ability to regenerate is decreased. Adaptogens support the RNA and DNA molecules to rebuild cells and tissues, initiating a self-regeneration process.

Schizandra is a mild stimulant to the gastrointestinal tract and supports the immune system, nervous system, lungs, liver, and long-term memory, as well as other mental functions. Schizandra extract aids the body's ability to utilize oxygen and assists with respiratory problems. It is also used in the treatment of chronic viral conditions.

Studies show Schizandra to have positive effects on mood and emotional stability. It stimulates portions of the central nervous system, strengthening and quickening reflexes, and it increases efficiency in stress-related tests. The Chinese see this herb as a tonic for both yin and yang, a balancer for the whole system. It contains all five tastes from Chinese medicine; this characteristic imparts the energy of all five elements in a balanced and profound manner.

Seventy to eighty percent of all illnesses are stress related. Adaptogens aid the individual to overcome stress and gain flexibility in his or her life. They create a stress shield in the body to help prevent degenerative processes.[45]

Tests on Schizandra use show improved concentration and positive results for conditions such as insomnia, mental fatigue, and poor memory. Schizandra is also renowned as a longevity herb. It has a nourishing action on the liver and increases the chi energy of the kidneys and adrenal glands.

Long-term benefits include the strengthening of the general constitution and the ability to resist stress due to chemical, emotional, or physical conditions. Schizandra is known as a regenerative and detoxifying herb for the liver, increasing hepatoglycogen content and relieving fatty degeneration of the liver.[46]

Studies on cardiovascular effects have shown that Schizandra is beneficial in the normalization of blood pressure. It is also considered an antioxidant and helps to improve brain efficiency and increase endurance.[47]

This herb has no toxic or adverse side effects and has a positive, cumulative effect.

PEPPERMINT (*MENTHA PIPERITA*)

Parts Used: Aerial parts

Constituents: Volatile oil containing menthol, menthone, and jasmone

Peppermint is a carminative (aids in digestion), antispasmodic, and nervine. As a nervine tonic, peppermint eases anxiety, nervous tension, and hysteria. It can also relieve pain and reduce cramping. Peppermint is effective at treating migraine headaches that are associated with digestive disturbances. As a carminative, it relaxes the visceral muscles, working as an anti-flatulent and stimulating the secretion of bile and digestive juice.[48]

The essential oils present in Peppermint help prevent congestion of blood supply to the brain, thus helping to clear circulatory congestion. They stimulate circulation and strengthen and calm the nerves, improving the powers of concentration.[49]

In Ayurvedic medicine, Peppermint is used to relax the body and clear the mind and senses. Mints contain large amounts of the element of ether, which promotes a soothing, cooling, clarifying, and expanding influence. The ethereal nature of mints helps to relieve mental and emotional tension and congestion.[50]

FLOWER ESSENCES USED IN THE GOTU KOLA/PEPPERMINT BLEND

- PEPPERMINT (*MENTHA PIPERITA*)
- WHITE CHESTNUT (*AESCULUS HIPPOCASTANUM*)
- MADIA (*MADIA ELEGANS*)
- SHASTA DAISY (*CHRYSANTHEMUM MAXIMUM*)
- NASTURTIUM (*TROPAEOLUM MAJUS*)
- MORNING GLORY (*IPOMOEA PURPUREA*)

This group of flower essences enhances the higher functions of the mind. They catalyze a shift in perception, enabling an integrative whole-brain functioning. Use of this formula heightens one's ability to organize and synthesize information.

This herbal blend nourishes the brain, nervous system, and senses, promoting clarity and neural conductivity and strengthening mental faculties. The flower essences in this formula feed the subtle mental field to create a self-regenerative feedback loop between the mind/body and cosmic intelligence.

Peppermint increases mental alertness and mindfulness. White Chestnut reduces worry, repetitive thoughts, mental agitation, and anxiety. Madia increases focus, concentration, attention to detail, organizational ability, mental clarity, and mental repose. Shasta Daisy allows the mind to be more receptive to impulses of higher intelligence and enhances the ability to synthesize information. Nasturtium vitalizes and clears the mind fields, creating a renewed state. Morning Glory allows the mind to lift free from old patterns, thus gaining in its ability to perceive from a new vantage point.

4. Dandelion/Solar Blend: A Vitalizing Liver-and-Digestive Tonic

Primary Color: Yellow

BOTANICALS USED IN THE DANDELION/SOLAR BLEND

DANDELION (*TARAXACUM OFFICINALE*)

Parts Used: Root, leaf, and flower

Constituents: Glycosides, triterpenoids, choline, taraxacerin (an acrid bitter resin), inulin (25%), phytosterols, saponins, glutin, gum, potash, up to 5% potassium

Dandelion is seen as a hepatic, an herb that tones and strengthens the liver, increasing the flow of bile. It is also an alterative commonly used as a blood cleanser, as well as a diuretic and deobstruent. Dandelion roots are known to be an excellent blood cleanser, specific to the liver, with a mild laxative influence.[51]

Dandelion is one of the best natural sources of potassium. For this reason, it is an ideally balanced diuretic that can be used safely in cases of water retention. Dandelion reduces inflammation and congestion of the liver and gallbladder.

Inulin, which accounts for 25 percent of the chemical constituents of dandelion, is being studied for its immuno-stimulatory function. It is also found to strengthen the kidneys and support the pancreas. The juice of dandelion root is used in Europe in cases of pancreatic and liver issues. It is considered one of the best herbs for building the blood and preventing anemia. Dandelion contains high amounts of vitamins A and C, which act as antioxidants, helping prevent cell damage. According to Chinese medicine, dandelion enters the spleen, liver, and gallbladder meridians, influencing the liver, gallbladder, spleen, intestines, kidneys, blood, and interstitial fluid.

Dandelion should not be taken in conjunction with other diuretics.

MILK THISTLE OR SILYMARIN (*SILYBUM MARIANUM*)

Parts Used: Seeds

Constituents: Flavones, silybin, silydianin, and silychristin

The extract obtained from Milk Thistle seed was originally termed silymarin; it represented a mixture of several complex compounds, which were later identified as the flavolignans silybin, dehydrosilybin, deoxysilydianin (silymonin), silydianin, silandrin, silychristin, and silybinomer.[52]

The primary use of Milk Thistle is to protect and regenerate the liver in cases of hepatitis, alcoholism, and damage from drugs and environmental toxins and poisons. It is also used to support the damaged liver and reduce associated conditions such as fatigue, depression, food allergies, and candidiasis.

Studies reveal that silymarin (the generic name for Milk Thistle) is effective with hepatic stress and toxic metabolic liver damage (fatty liver, drug-induced liver damage, and poisoning). Silymarin alters the structure of the outer cell membrane of hepatocytes, rendering liver poisons unable to penetrate the interior of the cell.

Silymarin also effects cellular lipid metabolism and acts as a free-radical scavenger. Silymarin is absorbed primarily through the intestines, entering the enterohepatic loop, recycling through the liver.

European research also indicates the effectiveness of Silymarin in reducing enlargement of the spleen and restoring liver enzymes to normal or nearly normal, usually within approximately thirty days.[53]

GENTIAN (*GENTIANA LUTEA*)

Parts Used: Dried rhizome and root

Constituents: Gentiopictin, gentiamarin, and amarogentine

Gentian is the most important of all European bitters. It is known as a "pure bitter"; the bitter taste persists even in a dilution of 1:20,000. Gentian becomes active as soon as it is absorbed by the mucous membranes of the mouth. Gentian root does not contain tannin, so there is no astringent or irritant effect.

Gentian is known for its bitter and gastric stimulative actions, which influence the general release of digestive juices. It also promotes the production of saliva, gastric juices, and bile, thus accelerating the emptying of the stomach. It is used effectively in cases where there is a lack of appetite and sluggishness in the digestive system.[54]

In Ayurvedic medicine, Gentian is revered as a bitter tonic that is used for fevers, jaundice, enlargement of the liver and spleen, and debility after prolonged illnesses. It is an herb that destroys *ama* (toxins, undigested food, or uneliminated waste materials) in the case of fever and inflammation. In Ayurvedic medicine, it is used for sedating hyperactivity of the liver and spleen and is useful for the stomach and small intestines. It is one of the best *pitta*-pacifying herbs, reducing excess heat.[55]

Contraindications would be irritable stomach, excess acid, and ulcers.

OREGON GRAPE (*BERBERIS AQUIFOLIUM*)

Parts Used: Root

Constituents: Berberine, oxyacanthine, berbamine

The Eclectic doctors, who prescribed herbal medicine in the twentieth century, often prescribed Oregon Grape root for easing painful digestion and loss of appetite. The alkaloid berberine has a cooling, anti-inflammatory, heat-clearing effect. The bitter taste stimulates the production of hydrochloric acid in the stomach, along with the production of digestive and liver secretions in general.

The influence of Oregon Grape is on the entire glandular structure of the intestinal and digestive tracts. It stimulates digestion and absorption, thus improving general nutrition. It has been found to be useful in cases of sluggish bowels, improving muscular strength.

Oregon Grape has been used to improve skin complexion in cases associated with blood and digestive stress. It is one of the most effective blood cleansers for the treatment of skin conditions and has been used in cases of eczema and psoriasis.[56] Oregon Grape has been found to be effective in cases of liver malfunction of a constitutional or chronic nature.[57]

Studies on Berberis alkaloids reveal high activity against Staphylococcus epidermidis and other bacteria. Some reports state that berberine is amoebicidal and anticonvulsant; it also exhibits sedative activities. The berbamine test results indicate it to be an immunostimulating agent. The root preparation is primarily used as a bitter tonic.[58]

Oregon Grape is used for liver fire (overheated liver), liver toxicity, low stomach acid, infections, and irritation in the intestines. It has also shown, when combined with other herbs, to be helpful with intestinal parasites, such as giardia.[59]

FENNEL (*FOENICULUM VULGARE*)

Parts Used: Seeds

Constituents: Volatile oil that includes anethole and fenchone; fatty oil

Fennel is carminative, aromatic, antispasmodic, and a mild expectorant. The carminative action of fennel works to relieve intestinal spasms, flatulence, and colic, while at the same time stimulating digestion and appetite.

Fennel tea has been used to treat dyspepsia and diarrhea in infants. In Ayurvedic medicine it is considered to be tridosha, balancing all elements. It is primarily indicated for indigestion, low agni (biological fire governing metabolism), abdominal pains and cramps, and colic in children.

Fennel seeds are considered to be one of the best herbs for strengthening *agni* without aggravating *pitta* (bodily fire element). Fennel seed is used for weak digestion in both children and the elderly. It also exhibits a calming influence on the nerves, and the aroma acts upon the mind, promoting alertness. Fennel is considered a good general herb for all constitutions (body types).[60]

FLOWER ESSENCES USED IN THE DANDELION/SOLAR BLEND

- DANDELION (*TARAXACUM OFFICINALE*)
- OREGON GRAPE (*BERBERIS AQUIFOLIUM*)
- CHAMOMILE (*MATRICARIA CHAMOMILLA*)
- BEE BALM (*MONARDA DIDYMA*)
- DILL (*ANETHUM GRAVEOLENS*)
- SUNFLOWER (*HELIANTHUS ANNUUS*)

This group of flower essences harmonizes the solar forces in the stomach center, facilitating emotional balance and calmness. It enhances digestion and the assimilation of nutrients on the level of both the mind and body. Oregon Grape increases one's ability to trust and receive love. Bee balm helps transform hostility, aggression, and anger into creative expression. Chamomile releases emotional and mental tension, especially from the stomach. Dandelion allows energy and vitality to flow fully and freely through the body. Dill supports consciousness to digest life's experiences calmly and intelligently. Sunflower harmonizes the personality with the radiant force of the higher Self.

5. Echinacea/Self-Heal: Immune-Potentiating Extract

Primary Color: Pink

BOTANICALS USED IN THE ECHINACEA/SELF-HEAL BLEND

ECHINACEA (*ECHINACEA AUGUSTIFOLIA AND ECHINACEA PURPUREA*)

Parts Used: Root (augustifolia), flowers, and seeds (purpurea)

Constituents: Echinacea augustifolia—polysaccharide echinacin B, glycosides, echinacein, volatile oil, polyacetylenes, phenols; Echinacea purpurea—polysaccharides (arabinogalactan, xylose, and galactose), echinacin B, polyacetylenes, volatile oil

Echinacea augustifolia is primarily a wild-crafted herb that is difficult to cultivate. For this reason, it is not used extensively. Both *E. augustifolia* and

E. purpurea species are powerful alterative (blood-cleansing) herbs. The glycosides in E. *augustofolia* possess antibiotic activity; at 6 mg, *E. augustofolia* is equivalent to one unit of penicillin. A component of *E. purpurea* has been found to have a cortisone-like activity and inhibits hyaluronidase enzyme activity associated with wound inflammation and swelling response.[61]

The most important part of the chemistry of Echinacea of both varieties is a mixture of several polysaccharides. These are complex sugar molecules that safely activate the immune system. (The polysaccharides are completely nontoxic.) The polysaccharides affect the surface chemistry of body cells, inhibiting the spread of viruses in ways similar to interferon. These polysaccharides are known to form complexes with hyarluronic acid (the gel that surrounds tissue cells), preventing bacteria-produced hyaluronidase from breaking it down and gaining easy access to tissues, as well as easing swelling and infection.[62]

The roots and seeds of both plants contain a highly pungent essential oil that, when ingested, lends the distinguishing characteristic of a tingling sensation. This oil contains a compound called echinacein, which has anti-insecticidal properties. This oil is also antibacterial.[63] There is an aromatic glycoside in *E. augustofolia* called echanoside that reinforces its antibacterial action. In 1973, a team of German biochemists reported findings that indicated Echinacea had antiviral activity.[64]

Further study reveals that a high-molecular-weight polysaccharide found in the leaves, flowers, and seeds of *E. purpurea* exhibits a pronounced immune-stimulating activity. Tests reveal a high degree of stimulation of macrophages (waste removal cells). Macrophages are concentrated in lymphatic tissue, especially in the colon (Peyer's patches and other areas), respiratory tract, and urinary tract. For this reason, Echinacea works as a protective agent against virus, bacteria, or candida invasion or overgrowth.[65] Studies suggest that the polysaccharide blocks the virus receptors on cell surfaces and thereby prevents incorporation of the viral particles.[66]

E. augustofolia and *E. purpurea* bind to carbohydrate receptors on the cell surface of T-lymphocytes. These lymphocytes trigger the activation of the macrophages and natural killer cells that in turn help eliminate bacteria and tumor cells. Antiviral properties of echinacea appear to be directly related to release of interferon by T-cells. The interferons bind to cell surfaces, simulating the synthesis of intracellular proteins that block the transcription of viral RNA, preventing viral infection.[67]

In summary, Echinacea has been used in the management of chronic infections, lymphatic swelling, poisonous insect bites, and various immune deficiencies.

Echinacea is best used in high dosages from 40 to100 drops of liquid extract, for five to ten days and as often as every two hours (check with your health professional for proper use). It can also be used in low doses for clearing the lymphatic system or as a preventive measure as an extract of 10 to 40 drops three times a day. Echinacea should be used in ten-day cycles, with a rest of five to seven days between cycles. Echinacea's effectiveness is dose dependent; however, it has no toxic effect in high doses.

Individuals with autoimmune illnesses and other progressive systemic diseases should not use echinacea.[68]

FLOWER ESSENCES USED IN THE ECHINACEA/ SELF-HEAL BLEND

- SELF-HEAL (*PRUNELLA VULGARIS*)
- ECHINACEA (*ECHINACEA PURPUREA*)
- RED CLOVER (*TRIFOLIUM PRATENSE*)
- PINK YARROW (*ACHILLEA MILLEFOLIUM*)
- WHITE YARROW (*ACHILLEA MILLEFOLIUM*)
- GOLDEN YARROW (*ACHILLEA FILIPENDULINA*)
- NASTURTIUM (*TROPAEOLUM MAJUS*)
- OLIVE (*OLEA EUROPAEA*)

This group of flower essences builds and maintains a healthy core identity structure and immune system. It enhances the mind/body's self-regulating intelligence. Echinacea is a powerful flower essence that strengthens and maintains the core integrity of the Self. Red Clover helps to establish one's awareness of one's own unyielding center. The yarrows generate radiant inner light, infusing vitality and strength into the etheric body and auric field as a whole. They maintain healthy boundaries, allowing healing energies to enter while deflecting influences injurious to the integrity of the Self. Nasturtium

71

and olive revitalize the physical and subtle bodies. Self-heal promotes a profound experience of self-love and acceptance, the most important ingredients for a healthy immune system.

GEMS IN THE LIGHT OF HEALING

Accessing Cosmic Intelligence

You are a divine being. You matter, you count. You come from realms of unimaginable power and light, and you will return to those realms.

—Terence McKenna

Gems are composites of frozen interstellar light. Though gems are created on Earth, they resonate with stellar points of origin throughout the galaxy, interfacing with energies that empower their healing properties. The gem is part of an extended influence of stellar light that forms the pathways for specific waves of creative intelligence to bring each celestial pattern into form.

Due to the powerful ability of gems to act as transformers for interstellar intelligence, they are utilized to deposit information into the earth plane of existence. In the Vedic tradition, the gem is viewed as a deity in its own right. Its divine identity is composed of harmonic bandwidths that act as reference points for a bio-spiritual harmonic grid. These blueprints have both physical and nonphysical components.

Gems communicate in grid patterns throughout the infrastructure of the Earth. This sets up a field-matrix system in which the gems can focus their operational systems. The field-matrix system is governed by the dictum "as above, so below," implying that the gems function as locator points between this planet and the heavens. They align the flow of energy between the subatomic, molecular, and originating levels of reality.

The bio-spiritual harmonics between human and mineral forms interface with perfect alignment in a waveform governed by the "law of similars." **When a gem or gem elixir interfaces with the human auric field, it resonates with the originating plane of existence.** This originating plane is the birth space of creation, where the blueprints for the manifest plane are born. The seat of higher consciousness lies in this causal plane, where consciousness is patterned and where the Divine breathes life into every facet of existence.

Ingesting a potentized planetary gem elixir imprints a pathway of patterned energetic expression from the subtle level of life to the outermost level. The gem elixir enters the physical and subtle bodies, is taken into the originating plane of awareness, and then permeates the dimensional levels of the DNA. Here, the transformation of the karmic cycle takes place.

Over time, the transformative properties of gem elixirs serve to bridge awareness between the subconscious, conscious, and superconscious minds. This frees the divine blueprint of the soul to express and manifest its full range of intelligence and wholeness.

Planetary gem elixirs offer a macrocosmic and microcosmic approach to enlivening wholeness of the heart, mind, body, and spirit. They clear and balance the electromagnetic fields, resolving discordant ancestral energies. They provide a vibrational "meta-cine" (metaphysical medicine) system that complements many other approaches to natural healing.

In this chapter, we will discuss how gem elixirs work through the chakra system and subtle bodies, their historical use, how gems enhance the light within our electromagnetic body, how they're made, and how to apply gems as color/light therapy. We will also discuss gems and gem elixirs as astrological remediation.

TAPPING INTO THE CAUSAL LEVEL

It is the function of the nervous system to keep the mind/body consciousness in tune with the natural forces of creation. Gem elixirs allow the articulation and adjustments of the karmic, spiritual, psychic, mental, and physical dimensions of life to cascade down from above to below, from the higher, subtler levels into the denser levels of definition.

The first changes that occur as a result of imbibing a gem elixir will be sensed in the auric cranial field. Subtle impulses fluctuate in the brain, altering brain respiration and the patterning of the cranial field, the cerebral spinal fluid, and ultimately, the sacrum. These adjustments modulate the light frequencies and pranic patterns that enter the system through the gem elixir, expanding awareness and creating a liberating experience for the soul.

The cranial field holds the formative patterns of life. As the energetic living intelligence of the gem elixir interfaces with the auric field, it begins to dissolve any discordant energies within those patterns.

This profound process is based on the subtle anatomy of the holographic body. The subtle nervous system is composed of two intertwining currents of energy that originate out of the causal level. Physiologically, these pathways begin in the brain and end at the base of the coccyx. These two currents of energy, referred to in the Vedic tradition as the Ida and the Pingala, are represented symbolically as two serpents crossing over the spine. These currents constitute the electromagnetic principles of creation in their male/female, solar/lunar values.[1]

These solar/lunar principles are represented in the ancient medical symbol of the caduceus, also known as the staff of Hermes. The caduceus is depicted as two serpents creating a helical pattern along a central staff, with two wings topped by a golden headdress.

The top of the head represents the crown chakra, the seat of Supreme Consciousness. The central shaft, which represents the etheric level of the spine, is a hollow vortex that conducts the ultrasonic core energies, giving rise to the governing principles of creation and manifestation. The two serpents are the polarizing dual currents that govern manifest creation. The golden ball that sits on top of the central staff of the caduceus represents the pineal gland. When it is activated, the inner light of illumination is released, creating the divine nectar of immortality that permeates every cell to the core of being. The two wings represent the two hemispheres of the brain as whole-brain functioning.[2]

Through ingestion of the gem elixir, the vital etheric and physical nervous systems are cleared. Karmic patterns of the mind, emotions, and physiology are addressed.

AFFINITY WITH THE CHAKRAS

The gem elixir harmonically resonates with the values of light, color, and ultrasonic sound, which travel from the originating or causal levels into the cranial field. The vibration of the gem elixir activates and conducts information along the two currents of the nervous system described above. **Depending on the gem's color, crystalline pattern, and stellar sonic frequency, the gem will have a specific affinity for one or more of the chakras.**

The chakras are energetic interdimensional vortices that govern the physical, mental, and emotional levels of existence. They form a holographic lattice that flows along the central shaft of the spine and overlays a 360-degree span that governs the entire energy matrix. These wheels of light-energy vortices are created when the two currents, Ida and Pingala, cross over each other at specific junction points, precipitating change in the electromagnetic frequencies that open at different dimensional portals of existence.

The chakras, or wheels of light, are also energetic configurations that build the reality of how we think, perceive, feel, and mentally process energy/ information. They house the life force that enables physical and subtle levels of existence to regenerate and sustain spiritual nourishment.

When ingested, the gem elixir bridges the originating, or causal, plane with its resonant chakra, influencing the endocrine system, specific organs, and specific tissues. The elixir elevates the vibrational frequency and enhances the symmetry of the chakra. This process catalyzes the clearing of blockages, the balancing of the elements, and the harmonic attunement to a higher order of intelligent functioning.

This enhanced functioning activates the dissolution of thoughts, belief structures, and energies that inhibit the positive manifestation of potential soul qualities in the individual. Ultimately, the emotions are refined to a point of subtle, neutral feeling, activating the higher mind and developing a unifying value at the level of the heart.

As the shift occurs on the level of the chakras, one may have a direct cognition of the subtle and physical action of the gem elixir. One may be able to see its originating point, as the vital influx of chromatic light filters into the glandular system, into the nervous system, and throughout the organs of the physical body.

The geometric design of liquid light that forms the blueprint of the gem elixir activates the supersonic currents of the nervous system, directly infusing light into the pineal gland (the gland of illumination). The liquid light flows down the etheric spine through the *shushumna*, or central shaft. The whole nervous system and subtle physiology is infused with this light/chromatic information, which enhances the blueprint for an advanced divine design.

Planetary gem elixirs have the capacity to transmute discordant energies, facilitating the expansion of consciousness through the chakra field. They increase the vitality of the physical and subtle bodies. A specific geometric form, overseen by devic intelligence, characterizes the signature of the gem. The gem's spectral color ray, planetary affiliations, elemental composition, density, and place of origin play key roles in its unique vibrational character and healing potential.

Gem elixirs have the capacity to stabilize transformational changes in the field of consciousness, anchoring those changes into the physical reality of everyday life.

THE BIRTH OF GEMS

The Earth has its own soul or spiritual signature, which is endowed with innate qualities that identify its galactic power. Rays of information are transmitted into the Earth's subterranean levels, penetrating the planet's soul body. The organizational forces of nature magnetically attract primordial elemental minerals to a space/time locale in the womb of the planet. Earth herself predetermines and sets up these fertile birthing conditions.

Gems are formed through the process of the universal light information being deposited into these primordial elements. The Earth meets the cosmos through this symbiosis, translating cosmic information and configuring it so as to form compressed modules of stellar frequencies. These precious stones serve as communicators of detailed celestial information.

Gems are the repositories for stellar time-coded information to be deposited into the collective consciousness. Through the interface between astrological gem elixirs and the human auric field, vibrational information is fed to the subconscious, conscious, and superconscious fields of awareness.

The stars of our galaxy and the cosmic rays that permeate their celestial territory empower gems to act as ambassadors of divine awareness. Gems possess a unique capacity to reflect this chromatically coded light in physical form, bridging Earth and the cosmos.

GEMS AND THE ANCIENTS

The power and potency of gems have been greatly valued, at times even fought over, by the greatest rulers of the world. For example, some modern researchers believe that in ancient Egypt, gems and sound vibration were used to activate subtle forces of nature necessary for the moving of stone in the building of pyramids and for initiatory rites in temples.

Ancient India, Egypt, Greece, and China are among the many cultures that had healing traditions that used gems to restore psycho-emotional and physical health. These societies utilized gems for their dazzling beauty, as well as their ability to calm, uplift, energize, and empower. Modern sciences such as ophthalmology, Ayurved, naturopathy, and colorpuncture are some of the modalities benefiting from the ancient understanding of gem therapy.

When utilized properly, with the intention of healing and the elevation of consciousness, gems are a source of blessings, unveiling the powers of the soul to guide an individual or an entire civilization. The exalted use of gems to alter and clear karmic patterns can aid in the development of what Sri Aurobindo refers to as the "supramental body," or the diamond body of light. **An alliance with the appropriate gem in space and time ensures an unhampered destiny.** The gem aids not only individual liberation, but also the unfoldment of planetary consciousness.

Historically, the use of gems was limited to members of the royal court or the elite strata of society. However, planetary gem elixirs convey the same noble caliber for use by people in all walks of life. Astrological gem elixirs are founded on the ancient and modern scientific understanding of the effects of color and geometry and the relationship of biological and cosmological frequencies on the human energy matrix. Grounded in ancient knowledge, the elixirs instill a heightened sensitivity to the causal level of the human physiology. Receptivity to gem elixirs enhances the inner healing network that serves as a foundation for the mechanics of human consciousness.

The soul communicates holographically through the imagery of color, light, and geometric designs, which in many traditions are seen as an outgrowth of transpersonal states. Ayurved, colorpuncture, psycho-spiritual development, body-centered therapies, healing music and art, flower essences, etc., all offer color as a vehicle for therapeutic application. Inherent in the very idea of color and geometry is a world of possibilities for the human evolutionary process. Planetary gem elixirs extend this wide range of applicability to existing and original therapies.

GEO-CHROMATIC THERAPY

One of the most powerful healing attributes of a gem elixir is its ability to feed the energy body with its specific color spectrum. Color is a universal language found in nature. Animals, plants, and peoples adorn themselves with color as a reflection of their interior and exterior worlds.

When the color frequency of a gem elixir is introduced into the energetic pathways of the body, the nervous system is able to use that frequency for its vital nourishment and regeneration. One becomes attentive to those areas of the mind/body where a weakening or misidentification of the proper neuro-chemical pathways has occurred. This facilitates psychological growth that reflects a greater synthesis of the chromatic frequencies needed to restore the essential building blocks of life.

Each gem and its inherent planetary and color emission is correlated with a sign in the zodiac. A planetary gem elixir reawakens the clarity, strength, and stability of our subtle and dense physiologies. The psycho/physiology opens to the subtle experience of how personal attributes—such as courage, resilience, beauty, and compassion—are cultivated by the language of color.

Our visual sensory input provides a rainbow of impressions that feed our bodies with knowledge and insight. Through color, we acclimate to our surroundings, learning how to model our emotions and behavior to more accurately reflect the multimodal world of light-sensitive intelligence. As beings of light, all members of the human family have a responsibility to themselves to develop pathways of knowledge that will uphold the innate light value of humanity as an evolving species.

Therapeutic studies and research have been conducted on the use of superior, prescriptive-quality gems on the human energy matrix. Researchers are using tools such as Kirlian photography and other forms of energy emissions analysis to document the effect of gem elixirs' chromatic resonance on the mind/body field.

The color-coded frequencies that travel from the planets of our solar system and infuse themselves into the natural landscape of Earth are filled with interstellar intelligence. Planetary gem elixirs attune us to this stellar intelligence, which provides the geo-chromatic information for the restructuring and integration of our human potential. The elixirs focus and concentrate light and color frequencies, simultaneously enhancing the geometric patterns of our blueprint. Gem elixirs infused with a sacred intent bring the light of the cosmic world into the everyday activities of modern life. The knowledge that gem elixirs bestow transcends our psychologically based perception of mind and matter and extends into the holographic realm.

The Role of Light in Geo-Chromatic Therapy

Humans utilize light as a form of stabilization and nourishment for the mind/body unit, and thus, humans can be deleteriously affected by light deprivation.[3] In ancient times, the physician would prescribe color as a means of healing and rejuvenation. As late as the 1900s, individuals were often sent to sanitariums or outdoor facilities and exposed to natural light and sun, which were seen as essential to the restoration and maintenance of health.

During periods when subtle perception was livelier in collective consciousness, variations in the shade and fabric of the human aura could be documented through direct perception. The science of viewing the human energy system and the development of higher states of consciousness is presently documented using Kirlian photography, EEG technology, Gas Discharge Visualization (GDV), and heat-sensitive photographic systems.[4]

On the whole, the human body is an intricate receptor site for light. The skin, the largest organ of the body, defines the boundaries of the physical form and is highly photosensitive, with receptor sites spread throughout its field. Photoreceptors, when activated at the molecular/cellular level, cause a cascade of biological action, including DNA/RNA synthesis. This results in regeneration and normalization of cellular functions and tissue healing.[5]

Peter Mandel, in his system of Esogetic Colorpuncture, integrates a thorough understanding of modern physics and spectral mechanics. Colorpuncture is revolutionary in its application of color to the human energy system for the purpose of healing and the ascension of higher consciousness.

Mandel's therapy consists of the application of specific frequencies of colored light through a geometrically cut crystalline glass rod that is applied to the acupuncture points, meridians, and body zones along sacred geometric grid lines. The points of contact are gateways into the unified field of the holographic light body. **Light is an information system that enhances cellular communication at the subatomic level.** So color therapy is also cell therapy. Light creates a coherent fluid bond between body, soul, and spirit.

Through the uptake of light in chromatic therapies, new neuro-synaptic pathways are formed. Light travels through these pathways. As the subtle energetic system is fed by the chromatic lightwave, there is the possibility of greater complexity and increased articulation between the chakras. The solid or viscous light that is generated through such color therapy is stored in energy conduits in the brain and central nervous system. The successful utilization of this light information leads to a more efficient holographic distribution of intelligence throughout the mind/body complex.[6]

Einstein theorized that light is composed of both a wave and a particle.[7] We are beings of light whose existence is based on the composition of light particles and specific wavelengths that are organized from the atomic level. The theoretical foundation of modern quantum physics suggests that light, at the deepest level of subatomic reality, is the fabric of what and how we are made.

In 1922, Einstein won the Nobel Prize for his contribution to physics and the explication of the mechanics of light. He observed that the motion of light through space could only be explained through the understanding that light is both a wave and a particle in its nature and function. Einstein coined the term *photon* to describe the subatomic light bundles that, when organized in a coherent but random fashion, present themselves as waves. These waves differentiate through the electromagnetic spectrum, becoming heat sensitive and formulating the chromatic frequencies with which we are familiar.

Energies of a higher frequency, such as ultraviolet light, have a greater capacity for energetic conductivity than do energies of lower frequencies, such as infrared light. In the case of higher light intensity, there is a greater density of photon activity that escalates the discharge of electrons in photo-sensitive conditions. This type of light creates an increased standardization of light capacity, speeding up the transmission of energy and inducing a higher level of transference to the electrical medium, whether it be physical or nonphysical in nature. World-renowned physicist Max Planck concluded that matter is created and maintained by forces that cause atomic particles to vibrate.[8]

Referring to the work of American physicist Arthur Compton, the "Compton Effect" theorizes that one of the main differences between photons and particles of matter is the factor of "rest mass." Photons are massless and therefore continuously travel through empty space at the speed of light, while other elementary particles, because they possess mass, move at slower speeds. Photons interrelate with matter and are capable of penetrating it, transmitting energy to all electrically charged particles. Photons act as energy carriers.[9]

World-renowned physicist David Bohm theorized that matter is condensed or frozen light. Matter of any mass is actually composed of highly condensed light, existing at speeds that are less than the speed of light. This implies that matter simply appears solid. In the context of the electromagnetic color spectrum, the frequency of each color corresponds to a specific electromagnetic wavelength. Light involves the constant oscillation of these color waveforms.

THE BODY'S RESERVOIR FOR GEM INTELLIGENCE

The efficacy of the healing power of gem elixirs is further understood in the knowledge that the human body is 80 to 90 percent water, which causes the body to act as a fluid, receptive medium for the translation of light into energy.

Water in its natural state is highly structured and charged. **The structure of water is crystalline, composed of geometric fractals capable of storing**

memory and viable for the communication of information. These dynamic fractal forms function like computer chips, regulating frequency transmission on an intracellular and intercellular level throughout the physical and subtle bodies. Biologically resonant gem elixirs are a fluid preparation of rare and precious Vedic-quality gems, thus serving as an effective conduit for light-coded information to reach the cells.

The theoretical foundation of this idea of light-coded information is based on the work of Dr. Fritz-Albert Popp, a German biophysicist who proved that the cells of all living things radiate light, which he called "biophoton emission." His research clearly indicates that light is the language of the cell. Popp states that normal living cells emit streams of photons. **Light, originating in the cell, can be understood as the language of life.**

Light, sound, and water naturally form highly regular crystalline structures. All form may be understood as geometrical, affirming at its most fundamental level the interaction of vibration, resonance, and frequency. Geometry serves as a portal into the implicate organizing principle of Nature. Sacred forms reveal their practical application through the revelation of self-generating patterns and processes. The harmonic orchestration of these forms may be found in the mineral world, where gems reflect sacred geometric patterns of symmetry.

The energetic uptake of a bio-resonant gem elixir elicits a response from the internal light matrix of the individual, thus enhancing a natural geometric level of higher organization. The body functions as a resonance chamber, equipped with the capacity to translate the cosmic order of creation from the macro to the micro level of conduct. The blood, bones, nerve plexus, and sheathing all reflect this crystalline organization.

Planetary gem elixirs draw on the innate intelligence of the crystal water body to conduct vibrational information. The elixirs stimulate the mind/body to regenerate, maintain, and enhance its cellular energetic potential. Gem elixirs rely on the mechanics of space, time, and motion that govern the relationship between dimensions.

GEMS SPEAK THE LANGUAGE OF LIGHT

When one ingests a gem elixir, one literally ingests the chromatic light ray of that specific gem. Light is the language of life. Light is energy, information, content, form, and structure. **Gems, as well as the whole human body, are a composite of light organized into atomic patterns.**

It is helpful to understand how gem elixirs function as light conduits for higher consciousness. Light has the intelligence to differentiate between subtle levels of vibration, as well as the ability to function as a carrier wave for new avenues of spiritual/technical information. Regenerative light technologies utilize the capacity of the individual to synthesize both aspects of functioning so as to promote a full unification of mind and body.

The challenge people now face is to accept responsibility for the transmutation of the physical, emotional, and mental bodies so that they can function as both high-frequency light conductors and way stations for grounded, practical functionality in the world.

Light flows downward from above the crown chakra and upward from the lower chakras. The interwoven pathway this creates requires incremental knowledge of unification at each stage of the cross-section. Holographic insight makes it possible for the individual to find his or her way through each subtle intersection. Understanding of these energy flow patterns encompasses both psycho-spiritual and physical realms.

During this process, there are times when one is held temporarily in abeyance, awaiting the next "turn signal." This is when one learns to pierce the veils of false perception and see with clearer, more honest eyes the truth of what is being presented. When light is rushing in, it often takes time to assimilate the magnitude of the information it presents. The assimilation of light at these higher ranges of frequency challenges the capacity for information storage as well as the capacity for interpretation.

Transformation involves a change in the scope of knowledge about who one is and where one is going. This expanded perception must be combined with a laser-like self-examination of personal agendas, beliefs, traditions, and cultural identity structures, which have imprinted the mind field and clouded the lens of innocence.

When the dense light unpacks its stored information, the resultant spiral of knowledge illumines both the physical and subtle bodies. As the light is increasingly sourced from one's own field of consciousness, the potential expression from the soul level is infinite. Out of this state, a loving Presence fills one's awareness, revealing the godliness within.

To awaken the holographic psyche, the ego or personal self is metabolized by the fire of light and transmuted into the higher Self. Higher consciousness scans the inner landscape of the psyche, identifying and releasing aspects of the personality that no longer serve the soul. In other words, silent intelligence digests life, emotions, and thoughts, metabolizing and transmuting them into higher ranges of life-force energy.

In this clear state of intuitive discrimination, the solar chakra/digestive system creates a refined nectar called *ojas*. Ojas is the substance that lives in the gap between consciousness and matter. It holds the information that sustains the mind/body field of consciousness, yet the seat of ojas is in the heart.[10] The role of the subtle digestive system is ultimately to create ojas, whose influence expands the heart toward unlimited and unconditional love. Ojas is the nectar that generates, sustains, and maintains one's mind/body in a state of radiant being.[11]

Ojas gives the physical body a state of glowing vitality and promotes a state of harmony and bliss in the emotional body. The mind gains a steady state of peace, silence, and positivity through the abundant and continual production of ojas. The whole mind/body field is bathed in liquid light, creating a superfluid style of functioning in the physiology, giving rise to *bala*, immortal strength. The experience of the soul dwells within the heart. The contraction or expansion of the heart predicates the conditions in which ojas is gained or lost.

As one begins living the holographic psyche, the body gains the capacity for frictionless or superfluid conductivity, in which the life-force currents can flow without losing energy or encountering resistance. The life force is transmitted through *kundalini*, an electrical blue flame of light housed at the base of the spine.[12] Spiritual energy moves through the chakra system from the base of the spine; up through the sacral chakra; up through the solar plexus; into the heart center, throat, and third eye; and then up through the crown, merging with the cosmos. This *kundalini shakti* has its own powerful innate intelligence, which configures to fit both material and spiritual circumstances.

Planetary gem elixirs activate the flow or movement of this life-force energy.

CAPTURING THE LIGHT: HOW PLANETARY GEM ELIXIRS ARE PREPARED

A planetary gem elixir is prepared according to ancient Vedic tradition, particularly knowledge of benefic astrological times, to maximize the power of the resonant frequencies of a specific gem. Each gem elixir is infused with its specific Sanskrit mantra (sacred sound), yantra (sacred symbol), divine purpose, and prayerful intent. The yogic discipline of performing alchemical processes is an art and science of Spirit.

Planetary gem elixirs are ideally prepared from rare and superior quality gems—hand selected to ensure that they are natural, untreated, visually perfect, and virtually free of flaws—so as to reflect a refined geometric cut to optimize the full radiance of light and color.

In selecting the medium and process for the preparation of gem elixirs, one must be aware that the absolute highest level of purity is necessary. All materials, including the vessels used to prepare the gem elixirs, must be selected for their ability to vibrate at clear, elevated frequencies, in order to maintain the gem elixir's potency at all ranges of dimensional experience. The proper vessels and materials have a profound ability to ground divine energy and the integrity of the gem's imprint.

A planetary gem elixir is both a solar and a lunar light infusion of the gem's pure original blueprint into a highly charged receptive liquid medium. The result is living liquid light that acts as a carrier wave to deliver the gem's stellar intelligence, the celestial energies of its resonant planet and specific chromatically coded information.

Phase one of preparing a planetary gem elixir involves 18–24 hours for full-spectrum solar/lunar imprinting. A phase-two process is activated over a three-day span to fully stabilize the frequencies and imprinting. This time is referred to as "being in the gap," a silent, timeless space out of which the evolutionary dimensional imprints can fully manifest and ground in the liquid medium.

Gems have traditionally been used in Vedic astrology for ameliorating astrological imbalances and afflictions in an individual's planetary chart. The sacred intention embedded in the planetary gem elixirs clears distortions and anomalies in the electromagnetic fields and strengthens the integrity of the life-force matrix. This opens the pathways to restore chromatic frequencies in the auric fields and remove discordant ancestral imprints.

The spiritual practice of preparing astrological gem elixirs requires a pure state of witnessing consciousness and an unbounded, coherent heart. One engages in a time-honored meditative process that unites individual identity with the inner configuration of the radiant God-light of the gem. Viewed from the standpoint of traditional yogic practice, the process involves the science of unifying one's consciousness with a given object: I AM THAT. The yogic model practitioner functions in the historical context of High Priestess, performing a sacred ceremony involving the mechanics of consciousness and the transformational elements of creation.

Maintaining a sacred space opens dimensional portals that activate the alchemical process to infuse the intelligence of the gem into a liquid medium that is ingestible. It is important to place this sacred tradition within a contemporary practical and historical context. However, by its very function and depth of feeling, the process is intensely mystical in nature.

The intent and inner preparation for entering this process begins in consciousness, days, weeks, and months before the actual physical mechanics are initiated. One invites and acknowledges the spirit of the gem into the auric field and awakens its energetic patterning, creating a spiritual confluence. One must maintain a vigilant alertness as to the influx of information that is presented during this process of communion. This involves the superconscious mind, a place in awareness where, through an intuitive cognitional interplay, the mind is stripped of its usual psychological content and enters into a more absolute stance.

There is a living intelligence of the gem known as "devic intelligence." Within all of nature there is a divine organizing principle. Spiritual traditions acknowledge this "overlighting" force and refer to it as the *deva* of the object. The practitioner preparing a gem elixir must open his or her awareness to the devic aspect of consciousness within the gem. He or she will perceive this intelligence to be a direct expression of the Light of God.

The devic intelligence knows the purity of heart, quality of soul, and specific intentions of the practitioner for preparing the sacred gem elixir. The spiritual process of interfacing with the devic intelligence of the gem determines the degree of potency and complexity of information that is downloaded into the individual and the gem elixir. Knowledge is structured in consciousness. **The intelligence of the gem will meet you where you are.**

According to ancient Ayurvedic understanding, gems are more than just terrestrial in nature. Although gems are created in the earth, they resonate with stellar points of origin that define and empower their healing properties. Gems are part of an extended influence of stellar light that forms the pathway for a specific wave of creative intelligence that brings each celestial pattern into form. This forms the basis for the use of the gem as a keeper of the archetypal celestial information.

HOW TO USE PLANETARY GEM ELIXIRS

The healing properties of the gems can be ingested through several time-honored processes. The first, visual interaction, involves the absorption of the gem's celestial light through the physical eyes. In ancient times, articles of clothing, armor, jewelry, the crowns of royalty and leaders, or other accoutrements were encrusted with gems as a means of receiving the gems' power and blessing.

The second means involves the ingestion of the gem as living liquid light. The value of the planetary gem elixir lies in its ability to be taken at frequent intervals, infusing the physiology with its transformative properties over time.

Planetary gem elixirs are both subtle and powerful. Seasonal, environmental, astrological, and life cycles are key factors in determining the use of one or more gem elixirs. The general recommendation for initial introduction of a gem elixir is 4 to 12 weeks. Restoration of chromatic frequencies and saturation usually occurs during this period of time. Ideal suggested use is 5 to 10 drops directly under the tongue or in 2 to 3 ounces of pure water, 3 to 5 times daily or as recommended by a health professional or astrological advisor. Maintenance recommendations are then one to two times per day or as needed.

Daily use of an elixir can be an act of sacred repetition that represents a conscious action of self-love and a soul-level affirmation to embrace the light of wholeness within. When the user infuses his or her divine intent into the process, the subtle power of choice overcomes any psycho-spiritual resistance that would impede the light of transformation.

Upon ingesting the gem elixir, awareness and intent empower the soul/spirit to actualize new dimensions of life—perceptions, behaviors, and attitudes. The living liquid light of the gem guides the process, determining the dosage and frequency. Many feel they crave the elixir like food. **A planetary gem elixir, in essence, is a nutrient of spirit that feeds body, mind, and soul.**

Gems are ambassadors of light that illuminate consciousness and bring one closer to knowing the Self. Gems are celestial gifts from the gods that ground our true nature. They are not meant as a quick fix or a means for bargaining with God to change one's circumstances in life. Gems are vehicles that illuminate one's field of consciousness and generate self-awareness, which facilitates positive, responsible change. Planetary gem elixirs awaken the individual to conscious, spiritually mature avenues of choice.

COLORS AND INDICATORS FOR PLANETARY GEM ELIXIRS

The following section contains a list of the principal colors and indicators that form the palette for planetary gem elixirs. The information is presented in an abbreviated format for the sake of clarity and quick reference.

Red

Gem Elixir—Ruby

Vedic Planetary Indicator—Sun (Surya)

Inherent Meaning—Rejuvenates physical and subtle bodies, builds vitality and courage, promotes stability, establishes grounding, builds positive self-esteem, creates integration of core identity and the solar soul-force presence, uplifts one's spirit, encourages outward expression, increases confidence, strengthens integration of archetypal masculine energy on inner and outer levels, creates an aura of self-empowerment, establishes inner authority, attracts wealth and abundance

Positive Key Words—Yang, tonifying, warming, heating, supports sensory nervous system, penetrating, vitalizing, grounding, stabilizing, builds security, strength, courage, activates the will

Stress Imbalances or Deficiencies—Insecurity, apathy, numbness, survival consciousness, mistrust, low self-esteem, lack of confidence, fatigue, weakness, anger issues, low libido, sexual issues, risk-taking issues, sadness, insufficiency conditions

Spinal Correlations—Coccyx, sacrum, lower lumbar 3, 4, 5

Physiological Correlations—Reproductive system, kidney/adrenal, heart, lungs, muscles, circulatory system, blood deficiencies and conditions, lower back, excess cold and moisture in body, anemia, chronic cough or congestion, decreases Vata and Kapha

Chakras—Heart, solar plexus, and root

Red/Orange

Gem Elixir—Red Coral

Planetary Indicator—Mars (Mangala)

Inherent Meaning—Balances fiery temperament; generates courage, strength and vitality; balances sexual forces; clarifies energetic direction and focus in life; inspires constructive endeavors and activities; ensures follow-through of commitment to completion; uplifts the creative spirit; cultures positive, self-affirming thoughts and happiness; encourages decisive action without judgment; brings the courage to overcome fears and procrastination; strengthens self-determination; enhances concentration; balances the male/female energetic axis; brings improvement to finances

Positive Key Words—Yang (medium warm), balances fire/water elements, strengthening, focus, direction, commitment, stamina, responsibility, instinctive wisdom in action, creative joy in life, confidence, strengthens mental clarity and focus, reduces worry, stabilizes emotions

Stress Imbalances or Deficiencies—Mistrust, weak physically and emotionally, lacks focus and follow-through, absence of joy, procrastination, fear, sadness, history of abuse, depression, lack of groundedness, worry, lack of self-love, guilt, shame, inhibition

Spinal Correlations—Lower lumbar 2 and 3

Physiological Correlations—Intestines, stomach, digestion, metabolism, heart, circulation, blood, enhances fertility, balances the water and fire elements in the physiology, increases stamina and vitality, strengthens mental powers of focus and concentration, decreases Vata and Kapha

Chakras—Sacral, root

Orange /Gold

Gem Elixir—Hessonite (an Orange/Gold Garnet)

Planetary Indicator—Moon's North Node (Rahu)

Inherent Meaning—Illuminates the subconscious mind to transform obsessive desires and addictive tendencies; reduces confusion in the mind field and assists in developing a creative imagination that can be applied constructively; magnetizes potential for wealth, fame, and success; instills a strong, centered foundation and self-confidence for rapid and unpredictable change; increases ability to discern the truth; helps build a protective auric field; assists the psyche to be in the now; provides clarity and ambition to fulfill worldly desires

Positive Key Words—Warmth, deep insight, clarity of mind, creative imagination, joy, bliss, fulfillment, self-confidence, self-introspection, integrity, ambition, assertiveness, self-love

Stress Imbalances or Deficiencies—Obsessive, addictive tendencies; attached and dependent behaviors; tendency to exaggerate; grief; trauma; accident prone; controlling; hidden and secretive; feelings of inferiority; passivity; depression; discontentment; pessimism; depression; aloofness; fear

Spinal Correlations—Thoracic 10–12

Physiological Correlations—Reduces overheating, fever, hyperacidity, insomnia, excessive sexual desire; good for glandular weakness, digestion, lymph, intestines, heart, immune system; stabilizes nervous system and mind field; decreases Vata and Pitta

Chakras—Sacral, solar plexus

Yellow

Gem Elixir—Yellow Sapphire

Planetary Indicator—Jupiter (Brihaspati)

Inherent Meaning—Generates bright and positive perspectives; sparks inspiration and joy; cultures reverence for life; inspires devotion to spiritual and mystical interests; expands awareness into the higher mind; strengthens faith and purpose; cultures practical wisdom and divine knowledge; spurs philosophical ideas and thinking; improves comprehension and objective understanding; creates contentment; clears vision; opens spiritual insight; sharpens clarity and continuity of thought; deepens soul alignment to divine guidance and supreme source; creates optimism, peace, and happiness; develops trust; helps to overcome doubts; reveals new possibilities and light; magnetizes wealth, prosperity, good fortune, and support of nature; strengthens core self

Positive Key Words—Warmth, joy, happiness, acquired knowledge, illumination, optimism, trust, faith, insight, brightness, positive perspective, uplifting, integrative, mental clarity, good fortune, expansive, hopeful, empowering, easygoing, flexible, spiritual insight

Stress Imbalances or Deficiencies—Depression, fearful, dull intellect, poor memory, lack of foresight, contracted, mental confusion, anxiety, nervous tension, panic, helplessness, control and power issues, resentment, frustration, seasonal affective disorder (SAD), egotistic

Spinal Correlations—Thoracic 4–9

Physiological Correlations—Helpful with bodily cavities, fat systems, and imbalances of the glands; strengthens endocrine system and fortifies nervous system, liver, stomach, spleen, pancreas, assimilation, vision, eyesight, cranial field, learning, and comprehension; relates to the akashic element and one's ethereal nature; decreases Vata

Chakras—Solar plexus, third eye, crown

Green

Gem Elixir—Emerald

Planetary Indicator—Mercury (Buddh)

Inherent Meaning—Powerful influence on the range of intelligence; enhances and refines all forms of communication; greater articulation in speaking and writing; sharpens memory and linguistic abilities; accelerates learning and broadens interest for knowledge; encourages a youthful, fun-loving disposition; sparks enthusiasm; may activate psychic abilities; stabilizes the nervous system; promotes dexterity and discernment; optimizes ability to love self and others; cultures kindness and generosity; attunes one to Divine Mother earth energies; inspires communion with nature; fosters feelings of abundance and gratitude; expands the heart

Positive Key Words—Neutrality, equilibrium, love, harmonizing, balancing, renewal, regeneration, nourishing, communication, speaking, writing, earth energy, abundance, prosperity, gratitude, enthusiasm, decisive, clear, integration, inspiration, affection, intuitive, kind, generosity, heart-centered, balances emotion/intellect

Stress Imbalances or Deficiencies—Grief, loneliness, loss, ungroundedness, lack of love or affection, needy, disconnected from earth, envy, jealousy, weak speech, indecisive, poor discrimination, alienation, disassociation, lack of gratitude

Spinal Correlations—Thoracic 2–3

Physiological Correlations—Nervous system, reduces stress, equilibrium, pituitary gland, rebuilds muscle and tissue, disinfectant, antiseptic, lung, bronchial, heart, ulcers, cysts, eyes, improves physical dexterity and motor coordination, decreases Pitta

Chakra—Heart

Blue

Gem Elixir—Blue Sapphire

Planetary Indicator—Saturn (Shani)

Inherent Meaning—Aligns personality and subtle bodies with soul purpose; creates focus on task at hand; strengthens virtues of compassion and selfless service; develops character traits of loyalty, honesty, impeccability, balanced responsibility; fosters a contemplative nature; cultures a state of calmness, tranquility, and peace; stabilizes and strengthens the nervous system; expands and slows down the experience of time, giving rise to a transcendent view of reality; enhances intuitive psychic perception and meditative states; offers a protective influence in the auric field; strengthens faith and commitment to spiritual dimensions of life; cultivates self-love, acceptance, tolerance, and non-attachment; grants objectivity or a witnessing state in life; enhances lucid dreaming

Positive Key Words—Yin, cooling, inner peace, calming, tranquil, creative, communication, sedating, intuitive, contemplative, loyal, honest, compassionate, on purpose, faith, acceptance, tolerance, selfless

Stress Imbalances or Deficiencies—Agitated, impatient, selfish, tension, anxiety, stress, insomnia, worry, fears, difficult communication, lack of nurturing, exaggerated extroversion, dependent, unhealthy bonding, issues with verbalization, grief

Spinal Correlations—Thoracic 1, cervical 3–6

Physiological Correlations—Nervous system, thyroid gland, pituitary gland, endocrine system, supports structure, relieves contraction or muscle spasm, hyperactivity, insomnia, reduces pain, decreases Pitta

Chakras—Throat, third eye

Violet

Gem Elixir—Amethyst

Planetary Indicator—Saturn (Shani)

Inherent Meaning—Aligns and fuses personality with soul; expands crown chakra; strengthens character; develops a deepening sense of ease and surrender to what is; cultures loyalty and honesty; fosters a contemplative nature; cultures a state of calmness, tranquility, and peace; stabilizes and strengthens the nervous system; expands and slows down the experience of time, giving rise to a transcendent view of reality; enhances intuitive psychic perception and meditative states; offers a protective influence in the auric field; strengthens one's faith and commitment to spiritual dimensions of life; cultivates self-love, acceptance, tolerance, and nonattachment; grants objectivity or a witnessing state in life; helps one let go of old patterns and conditioning

Positive Key Words—Yin, cooling, calming, peace, stillness, tranquilizer, higher consciousness, increases awareness, meditation, sedating, soothing, spiritual nature, selfless service, spiritual guidance and leadership, deep transformation, healing, trust in spirit, faith, purification, uplifting, wisdom, intuition, emotional balance

Stress Imbalances or Deficiencies—mistrusting, anxious, nervous, hypersensitive, aloof, arrogant, self-centered, dissociative, need to control, cut off from inner nature or true self, fiery temperament

Spinal Correlations—Cranial and coccyx

Physiological Correlations—Nervous system, lymphatic, spleen, pancreas, pituitary, optic and auditory nerves, mastoid bone, whole brain, cerebrospinal fluid, hypothalamus orchestrates the entire endocrine system, helps process information (internal and external)

Chakra—Crown

Clear Pure Light (Prismatic)

Gem Elixirs—Diamond and White Sapphire

Planetary Indicator—Venus (Shukra)

Inherent Meaning—Creates a charismatic auric field; increases artistic abilities and deepens the feeling level of appreciation and beauty; fuses spirit into matter; leads the individual to move physically through life with grace, ease, coordination, and fluidity; enhances sensual nature; restores freedom to express oneself in a refined style; teaches the distinction between love and lust; increases ability to attract wealth, beauty, comforts, relationships; cultures feelings of passion and devotion; has a unifying effect on the positive/negative electromagnetic polarity currents; opens and cleanses the third eye; enhances clear vision and insight; strengthens the energetic matrix of the human light body; amplifies and broadcasts energies

Positive Key Words—Yin/yang balance; purifies; clarity; strengthens cognitive and whole-brain functioning; illumination; intuition; unification of light;

deepens devotion and love; intensifies other gems or colors; universal truth; knowledge gained from within; aligns personal will with Divine; amplifies inner light of invincibility; creative life force; visionary insight; stores, transforms, broadcasts, and amplifies energy; attracts life-force energy as the full spectrum of color; aligns with true self

Stress Imbalances or Deficiencies—Impure intent, negative thought patterns, lack of focus and clarity of thought, instability, scattered, blockage or stagnation on any level, emotional extremes, lack of spiritual strength and stamina

Spinal Correlations—Cervical 1–2, atlas

Physiological Correlations—In Ayurved, possesses the virtue of tridosha (i.e., containing all three doshas in balance: Vata (air), Pitta (fire), Kapha (water)); amplifies crystalline structures of physical and subtle bodies; adjusts cranial plates and enhances whole-brain function; balances function of pineal, pituitary, mid-brain, cerebellum, medulla oblongata, temporomandibular joint disorder (TMJ); clears miasms (collective ancestral discordant energy patterns); clears thick conditions of the body/mind; balances all elements

Chakras—Crown, third eye, heart

White

Gem Elixirs—Pearl and Moonstone

Planetary Indicators—Moon (Chandra)

Inherent Meaning—Clears emotional attachments and associated mental stress and anxiety; reveals the inner constructs of the psyche; enhances lucid dreaming and recall; promotes conscious awareness of creating reality from within; fosters qualities of receptivity, softness, sensitivity, love, nurturing, sensuality, grace, creativity, intuition; calms and pacifies the excitability of the emotional/mental body; reduces stress; promotes feelings of peace; enhances harmonic resonance with the feminine energy force within and the outer Mother principle, enhances appreciation for creativity and the arts

Positive Key Words—Wholeness, integration, deep insight, purification of emotional/mental body, devotional love, feminine nature, creativity, sensitivity and grace, calms and soothes emotions, contentment, appreciation, nurturing

Stress Imbalances or Deficiencies—Dependency, attachments, anxiety, emotional reactiveness, resists self-examination, lack of commitment to life's responsibilities, difficulty with feminine energies

Spinal Correlation—Sacrum

Physiological Correlations–Assimilates nutrients, enhances fertility and pro-creative energies, stimulates pineal gland, balances endocrine system, clears lymphatic congestion, aids in the absorption of calcium, reduces excess heat in the heart and brain, decreases Pitta and Vata, increases Kapha

Chakras—Sacral, heart

White/Yellow/Gold

Gem Elixir—Cat's Eye

Planetary Indicators—Moon's south node (Ketu)

Inherent Meaning—Facilitates penetrating insight into the fear of death, both physical and egoic; activates creative psychic energies; aids in the release of emotion, tension; reduces worry; neutralizes fevers of the spirit that lead to fanaticism; increases intuition and heightens perception; elevates the power of discrimination; magnetically creates an energetic field of protection; increases good fortune and luck; increases interest in mystical aspects of life; activates a "living-in-the-now" presence

Positive Key Words—Enhances intellectual faculties, strengthens the nerves, transformation, elevates consciousness, penetrating insight, heightened intuition

Stress Imbalances or Deficiencies—Survival fears, fear of death, anxiety, worry, clinging

Physiological Correlations—Reduces fever, alleviates survival fears, anxiety, and fear of death; transforms worry; diminishes clinging to the past; may assist in reducing intestinal disorders; strengthens eye sight and concentrative abilities

Chakras—Root, third eye

Pink

Gem Elixir—Rose Quartz Crystal

Planetary Indicator—Venus

Inherent Meaning—A universal heart harmonizer; balances the emotional body and soothes deep-seated scars and traumas; assists the heart chakra to open to the universal flow of giving and receiving love; resolves issues of anger; facilitates clarity and integration on all levels; teaches the highest form of Love

Positive Key Words—Unconditional love; emotional fulfillment; expansion of love; unifying heart connections; promotes feminine creative principle; develops feeling and sensing intuition; calms and soothes anger; emotional self-sufficiency; cultivates gentleness, self-love, and self-healing; appreciation for beauty

Stress Imbalances or Deficiencies—Lack of self-love; feeling empty, hopeless, or separate; emotionally needy and demanding; self-centered; difficulty connecting with others; fear of love and sense of unworthiness; creative blocks; lack or denial of feminine energy; smothering; unresolved childhood traumas and issues; anger

Physiological Correlations—Supports and balances the heart and circulatory system; supports and balances the reproductive system; calms excess liver heat; supports kidney chi

Chakra—Heart

5

SACRED GEOMETRY AND THE MYSTICAL POWER OF GEMS

The harmony of the world is made manifest
in form and number, and the heart and
soul and all the poetry of natural philosophy
are embodied in the concept
of mathematical beauty.
　　　　—Sir D'Arcy Wentworth Thompson

Sacred geometry is a mathematical language that reveals information about how creation unfolds. It was understood by the ancients to be the "language of the Godhead." **Gems are composed of minerals that organize themselves using this language of geometry.** They are precise mathematical formulations that reveal a profound depth of meaning about the creative forces that govern life and our universe.

In this chapter, we will discuss the primary organizing patterns of the manifest world known as the Platonic solids and how each of these evolutionary mathematical progressions is directly expressed through gems.

CRAFTING GEMSTONES INTO VEHICLES OF LIGHT

In approaching a raw gemstone, one skillfully intuits how the gem wishes to unveil its multifaceted light potential. The art of precision cutting reflects both the technical and aesthetic sensibility of the craftsperson. A master gem cutter observes all the angles of refraction, considering the degree of luminosity and the density of the light moving through the gem. He or she evaluates the cut of the gem to reflect its most prominent celestial characteristics, its effectiveness as a conductive medium, and its capacity to highlight the stone's divine beauty. Such chromatic symmetry gives rise to the luminosity and purity of the gem, a gift to both the beholder and the environment.

A panoramic cosmic blueprint emerges through the enhancement of the gem's sacred geometry, reflecting its unique features. **The symmetry and precise angularity of cut reflect an inner panoramic viewpoint that emulates the patterns of the heavens in each stone.** When a craftsperson has a comprehensive understanding of the mechanics of creation and the yogic powers of inner sight, he or she is able to cut gems that emulate royal talismans.

Such a beholder of gemstones is able to gaze deeply into the fabric of creation, finding himself or herself traveling down corridors of light that catalyze and promote a superconscious state of awareness. Here is beauty in its absolute yet material form. The intellect is temporarily suspended, and the beholder is entranced to a point of inner stillness. The gem becomes a yantra, or visual meditative tool.

SACRED GEOMETRY: THE PLATONIC BUILDING BLOCKS OF GEMS AND CRYSTALS

Gems are a type of mineral crystal. When we look into infinity turning back on itself (through inner vision), the pure crystalline structures of perfect form appear. The impulse of pure intelligence stirs the void within space, creating a cohesive order of interrelationship. Awareness brings to light the fundamental crystalline structure. Its meaning, function, and elemental consciousness are expressed as form within space.

The Greek philosopher Plato and the mystery schools identified the five perfect divisions of a sphere, known as the Platonic solids. The Platonic solids are the five basic fixed forms in nature that constitute the building blocks of creation. These sacred forms are the embodiment of the natural structures of the cosmos from which the five elements—earth, water, fire, air, and ether—are derived.

In the book *Advanced Light Language*, Star Fuentes and Shirley A. Resler write, "The Platonic solids are the ideal primal models and crystal prototypes that occur throughout the mineral world and in nature."[1] The basic five Platonic solids are the tetrahedron, cube, octahedron, icosahedron, and dodecahedron. They are the only five solids that are regular polyhedra, meaning that they are both equilateral and equiangular. A polyhedron is defined as three or more planes that intersect and form a common vortex.

It takes three lines to construct an enclosed space. The number three represents the triangle or Trinity. Four lines enclosing space define the square, representing Manifestation. Five lines enclosing space define the pentagon, representing the principle of Resurrection. These three shapes—triangle, square, and pentagon—are irreducible; one cannot be created from any combination of the others.

Form is the expression of a geometric continuity that gives meaning to the world of space. Sacred forms, when approached with conscious awareness, reveal their functional value in both relative and absolute terms. **Sacred geometry bridges matter and spirit; it is the mathematics of mysticism.** The Platonic solids are the perfection of form that brings the mind into the realm of pure intelligence. The journey into sacred geometric form leads the traveler into multilayered fractals that illustrate the interconnectedness and union of all creation.

A gem, being of the mineral world, enters into form and vibrates the harmonic frequencies of its innate geometric patterns. The geometric configuration inherent in a gem determines the type of resonant stellar frequencies it receives, as well as the electromagnetic emanation it transmits. Gems function as harmonious orchestrators of the cosmos's self-generating patterns and processes.

The three-dimensional configuration of gems exemplifies the language of spirit and the manifestation of profound spiritual principles. **Encoded in the organization of these fundamental geometric containers of space/ time are precise, mathematically ordered shapes provoked from an unseen level of pure intelligence.** The geometric structures resonate with the double-helical structure of DNA.

DNA compresses or unpacks information according to its operative processes in time and space. As one uses gems, gem elixirs, or gem therapies, one experiences the interception of space/time planes at deeper levels of consciousness.

Within the geometry of the gem lie the archetypal patterns of creation, expanding from the subatomic levels to the human, planetary, solar, galactic, and universal levels of creation. The divine God-metric blueprints are the fabric of a unified field of consciousness.

GEOMETRIC FORMS AND CONSCIOUSNESS

Geometric forms create a portal into specific realms of reality that display unique natural laws and are inhabited by inner-dimensional beings. These holographic forms serve as conduits for the flow of consciousness in the human energy system. As one moves into higher states of consciousness, one enters a hyperspace reality. This reality involves more complex geometric systems embedded within each other that define the implicate order of space/time. It is through these sacred forms of creation that one's personal experience of life is structured.

Gems and crystals manifest into the world as a seven-step process. Each step is an independent stage of the whole. The steps of manifestation correspond to a mathematical set of interval relationships that express vibration, color, and form. This is a precise energetic language of creation that involves light, vibration, and pure consciousness stepping off the platform of the absolute and into the relative field of life.

Mathematicians have determined that this seven-step process completes a whole level of creation. At the point where an octaval, or dimensional shift, occurs, crystals become repositories of frozen sound. The function of a crystal is to hold a precise proportional formula expressed through its corners, edges, and faces.

As atoms cool to form minerals, the rate of vibration slows down to allow a fixed pattern. These molecular patterns give rise to the crystalline structure through symmetrical repetition at regular intervals. Light traveling through the crystal interacts with it at an atomic level.

In the seven-step process, the Cube is the basic volumetric form out of which other crystals emerge. The progression moves to Tetragonal, Orthorhombic, Monoclinic, Triclinic, Rhombohedral, and Hexagonal. As a crystal grows, its atoms and molecules lock in such a way as to manifest in various geometric configurations. There is a central point in space around which the axes of intersection congregate to form the precise geometric form.

The key information lies in the possible relationships of axes and angles that make the whole of atomic latticework possible. The seven-step process referred to earlier unfolds the relationships between planes and dimensions of intelligence. The principles of life are ordered according to the definition of the divine expression of purpose in manifest creation. Nature's rhythmic architectural designs are rendered in three dimensions.[2]

THE FIVE FORMS AND THE SPHERE

Following is a brief description of the five forms that create the physical world—known as the Platonic solids—plus the Sphere, from which all forms are birthed. The interface of these shapes to gemstones will follow in the next major section, "Revealing Geometry's Messages."

Using these forms, either picturing them through visualization or gazing at their geometric representation, as in a *yantra*, prompts integration of spirit and matter—the physical and subtle bodies of the human energy field. Such activity supports the individual in accessing his or her higher-dimensional self and can facilitate profound transformation physically, mentally, and emotionally.

The Sphere: The Birthing Chamber of Manifest Creation

In mystical traditions, the Sphere is considered to be the first act of creation. The Godhead reaches down into the fertile ground of space. The vacuum state is stirred, extending along a plane and then encircling the plane in a 90-degree rotation to create a solid sphere. **Contained within the Sphere is the field of all possibilities in manifest existence. This is the Matrix or Divine Mother.**

As the fundamental form of creation, the Sphere establishes the boundaries for all three-dimensional physical manifestation. From the central point of the Sphere, pure spirit motions as a spiral that constantly changes axes around an infinite center. The originating Sphere weaves the master matrix of life, manifesting the monadic principle of equality in all directions.

Inherent in the Sphere is a twelvefold spiritual energy system, developed by twentieth-century French esoteric researchers Leon Chaumery and A. de Belizal.[3] In this system, a single central Sphere symbolizes the essence of life within. An originating Sphere may be encircled by twelve spheres of equal size. These Spheres represent the twelve levels of actualization in manifest life. On the three-dimensional plane, this completed formation denotes an entire phase of manifestation. It is also depicted and symbolized by the twelve signs of the zodiac, the twelve disciples, the twelve tribes of Israel, etc.

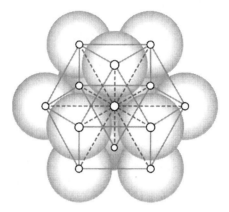

The Twelvefold Energy System of the Sphere

This twelvefold energy system is sourced out of the sun and relates to the center of the Earth. The sun is the One, the home/portal of the Solar Logos/Christ. The center of the Earth is the birthing chamber of the Divine Sophia, the feminine aspect of creation.

The twelvefold system of the Sphere is also displayed in the world of color. As the sunlight angles along the surface of a sphere such as Earth, the full spectrum of color is manifest. From north, represented by the color green, one moves east to blue, indigo, violet, ultraviolet, and white. From negative green at the south there are black, red, orange, and yellow, leading back to north in a full circle.

The Sphere is expressed in the human energy body as a dynamic, circulating energy, moving from above the head, or crown chakra, to the base of the spine, or root chakra, along a column of energy called the *shushumna*, which follows the spine. (*Shushumna* is the Sanskrit term for the vessel that channels kundalini, or spiritual energy, through the multiple levels of human conductivity.) This circulating energy moves simultaneously from the base of the spine upward to the crown chakra, creating a toroidal energy vortex that animates the human form.

The Cube (Hexahedron): The Holy Sanctum of Essence

The Cube is the most solid and complete form in our physical dimension, the spatial container for the earth element. It is composed of the numbers 6, 8, and 12, as follows:

- Vertices (points): 8
- Edges (lines): 12
- Faces (planes): 6

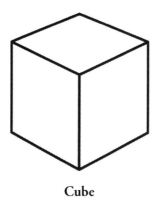

Cube

In the language of alchemy, the Cube is the ultimate symbol for the soul and is considered to be the final stage of a seven-stage process of evolution. The Cube amplifies the focus of one's attention so that it resonates with the central core point of one's being. It solidifies, anchors, builds, and stabilizes energy. It is also used for psychic and spiritual protection.

In the Mayan tradition of light language, the Cube is known for its capacity to stabilize the physical and spiritual planes. The energies of the Earth and Spirit are held in the structure of the Cube. It is the most stable of the shapes, and its function is to contain and confine energies. The value in this form is that the Cube holds and protects the Holy Space within, so that nothing can cause a disruption. **The Cube contains the inner sanctum of energies and focuses their power at its center, thus maintaining the essence of what is within.**

The Cube represents the physical body that has been purified of all its imperfections and can therefore function as a temple for the soul. On the physical level, the Cube is related to the Earth and the root chakra and supports the skeletal structure and dense tissue.

The Cube symbolizes the diamond consciousness of light. In the ancient traditions, it is said to induce the production of soma, considered to be the immortal nectar of life or the "glue" of the universe. The Cube creates the sacred space for spirit to descend into the center of the brain, where the pineal gland sits. This center in the brain is referred to as the "cave of Christos" by esoteric Christianity and "cave of Brahman" in the Vedic tradition.

One of the shadow aspects of the influence of the Cube is that, as a consequence of its natural influence to streamline and focus, it can create too great a hardening, or contraction, of energies. However, when placed correctly during internal visualization and use or when externally utilized, the Cube increases the energetic efficiency of the body/mind without restricting or limiting the flow of life force. The internal activation of the image of the Cube also facilitates the removal of fears and creates a sense of safe space, inwardly and outwardly. The Cube supports a sense of security and logical abstract thought.

The Cube contains the center of the universe as it is defined in space. In the Hebraic tradition, the Cube represents the holiest of holies, or G-d. In ancient Hebrew texts, the Cube is described as a divine construction that manifests as the twenty-two letters of the Hebrew alphabet. The revelatory significance of the Cube lies in its capacity to reveal a map of past, present, and future of the collective consciousness of humanity.

There are three dimensions of the Cube; they correspond to the sounds of creation, the seven planets, and the twelve constellations of the zodiac.

A prime example of the use of the power of the Cube in architecture is the temple of King Solomon, which had a perfect Cube as the center point of the inner sanctum.[4] Another architectural example is the large black Cube at the heart or center of Mecca, which on Islamic holy days is circumambulated seven times by religious pilgrims. This is symbolic of the fusion of spirit (Circle or Sphere) with matter (Cube). The circle, the spiritual dimension out of which the Mother Matrix births the physical, is encoded in the Cube.

The Tetrahedron: Emergence of Spirit in the Trinity

The Tetrahedron is represented by the fire element, the first initiating spark of life, direct from Spirit. It is the fire of the I Am Presence. It carries the dynamic force for creation to manifest out of the unmanifest state. The fire is the inspiration of the God force. It is both creative and transformative, giving rise to the ability to change one form into another. This is seen, for example, in cell division in the process of mitosis.

The Tetrahedron is the minimal system required to enclose space. It is the first form to manifest into three-dimensional reality out of two-dimensional reality, but unlike the Sphere, which supports creation but has no definition, the Tetrahedron defines space. The numbers that compose the structure of the Tetrahedron are as follows:

- Vertices (points): 4
- Edges (lines): 6
- Faces (planes): 4

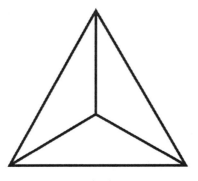

Tetrahedron

The Tetrahedron is the only form that has the property that enables it to rest face down on a table and have a vertex (point)—not a face—on top.

The Tetrahedron is related to the form of four spheres. The three base spheres form the Trinity of the Godhead upon which the One, the source of all creation, firmly centers in a state of dynamic rest.

One Tetrahedron configuration is the *merkaba*, the spirit/light body. The merkaba functions as a time/space vehicle enabling the soul to travel between dimensions and directly access the God force. This geometric configuration appears around the human energy body as two Tetrahedrons. One Tetrahedron is structured within the human energy field in a feminine (Shakti) downward direction and the other in an upward (Shiva) direction. This depicts the eight-pointed star known as Metatron, or the Star of David. This star pattern contains the information for the development of the dual forces of creation in our dimension, the Shakti, lunar (feminine) and Shiva, solar (masculine) principles.

In the ancient Mayan light-language tradition, the Tetrahedron is a transmutative structure that has both destructive and constructive capabilities. Due to its potentially destructive powers, it is rarely used and is considered best left to the Masters of sacred geometry. It carries immense creative forces.[5]

Researcher and healer Theo Gimbel dedicated his life to the understanding of the healing powers of sacred forms, vibrations, and color. His body of research and work, which is referred to as Hygeia Studios, supported the concept of the Tetrahedron as a means of enhancing self-awareness and energizing the rhythms of the body.

Through his comprehensive methods of spiritual research, Gimbel identified the capacity of the Tetrahedron to activate the third eye chakra and the pituitary gland. He recognized that this fostered a penetrating depth of subtle vision.

According to Gimbel, the Tetrahedron creates and maintains the organizational functions of the body. It relates to the color red, which gives warmth as well as the ability to self-generate warmth.[6]

The Octahedron: The Messenger ("As Above, So Below")

The Octahedron is the messaging conduit for the God force and the higher orders of the spirit world. In it is contained the simple mystery school code "As above, so below." This aphorism implies that what is inscribed in the higher dimensions of reality finds its counterparts in the frequencies or harmonic resonance forms of the third dimension.

The Octahedron represents the air element, a principle conductor of information. As both a conduit and conductor, the Octahedron refines the information process so that it can be readily assimilated.

The Octahedron acts as an inverted script for life to flow from the invisible realms of spirit to the manifest. It is a creative imaging system that functions to amplify and translate spiritual energies into utilizable information. The Octahedron can be considered the universal respiratory system for this dimension. It allows the breath of life to enter this domain and infuses light particles with the necessary lively intelligence to order life in the image of God. The pure undifferentiated energies of the spirit world are transduced from the spiritual worlds into the earth plane through the geometry of the Octahedron.

The Octahedron has eight faces, each of which is an equilateral triangle. The numbers that **compose** the structure of the Octahedron consist of the following:

- Vertices (points): 6
- Edges (lines): 12
- Faces (planes): 8

Octahedron

In the Mayan tradition of light language, the Octahedron's function is to facilitate the mastery of discernment. It acts as a filter for unnecessary and insufficient psycho-emotional thought forms, either from the internal or external environment. The Octahedron facilitates an integrative co-creation process for manifestation. It balances the process that infuses spirit to matter.[7]

In Gimbel's system of Hygeia Studios, the Octahedron facilitates a sense of detachment while simultaneously retaining a sense of direction. It assists in developing a state of timeless expansion.

The Octahedron is associated with the power to heal on a physical level. This involves the ability to shapeshift or change the molecular state of matter to facilitate regeneration. The Octahedron relates to the throat chakra (the thyroid gland and larynx), the sense of sound and hearing, and the breath and the respiratory system. The color frequency is yellow.[8]

The Icosahedron: The Life-Force Regenerator

The Icosahedron expresses the principle of the water element and is interconnected with the etheric world. Water acts as a magnetic reservoir for life-force energy, the primordial form of the divine energy that animates living beings.

The Icosahedron joins five triangles together at every vertex. The edges are divided according to the Golden Mean ratio (1.618). These Golden Mean vertices have a powerful effect on regenerating the human body.

One face of the Icosahedron has five triangular portions. Each of these sections has a bio-resonant affinity to a five-pointed star. The head is the pinnacle point of the star of consciousness. The two arms represent the horizontal plane of life and the two legs the vertical anchor to the earth plane; all meet in the central point of the heart.

The Icosahedron has twenty faces, each being an equilateral triangle. The numbers that compose the Icosahedron are as follows:

- Vertices (points): 12
- Edges (lines): 30
- Faces (planes): 20

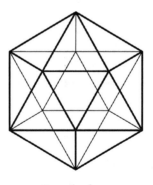

Icosahedron

In the Mayan tradition of light language, the fundamental energetic functioning of the Icosahedron is to multiply, increase, enhance, optimize, and mobilize. The shape is like a sphere with triangular faces that pull away from the center of the sphere. The Mayans understood this gesture to be representative of the state of coming gently to the point. The five triangular points converge into a singular midpoint.

In the art and science of light language, the Icosahedron creates choices, builds energy, enlarges focus, and extends options. **The Icosahedron is related to the water element; it is thus a container for the reservoir of life.**

In the system of sacred geometry described in the Hygeia Studios, the Icosahedron has psychological effects that give rise to multilevel perception. It facilitates the removal of obsessive behavior and thinking patterns, creating a motion or flow of energy that releases stuck patterns and dissolves tension in the body/mind. The physical effects are intended to dissolve structure and soften tissue.

The Icosahedron is related to the adrenal glands and the reproductive system. It is connected to the ability to see images and the added ability to retain and imprint the image in memory. The Icosahedron is connected to all fluid substances in the environment. The primary color association is blue.[10]

The Dodecahedron: Transdimensional Holographic Shapeshifter

The Dodecahedron is a twelve-sided Platonic solid with each side as a pentagon. In the Greek translation of the word, *do* = 2, *deca* = 10, and *hedron* = shape. Therefore, *Dodecahedron* means "the shape of 2 + 10 = 12 sides." Thus, the Dodecahedron carries the mystical number 12.

The number 12 within the Dodecahedron is the perfect division of a sphere. To completely encircle a sphere, 12 equal-size spheres are needed. Other expressions of the number 12 include the 12 constellations/signs of the zodiac, the 12 calendar months, the 12 Knights of the Round Table, and the 12 apostles of Christ.

The Dodecahedron manifests the principle elemental energy of the Ether. Contained within the sacred space of the Ether element live all other elements. All the powers of the elements are present in the Dodecahedron. It was considered by the ancient Greek mystery schools to be so powerful that only advanced Masters of the Net (the matrix of creation) utilized its forces of purpose. In the path of the 12, the Dodeca carries the first vibration through which the One Spirit begins the process of manifestation; it encompasses all that is.

The Dodeca manifests the etheric space for the creative force of the originating sound vibration to communicate the divine impulse of the

Godhead. The Dodeca sources the Will of force. This sacred geometric principle is fundamental to the creation, transformation, transfiguration, and destruction of living matter. Due to the inherently potent nature of the magical properties of the Dodeca, the ancient masters considered that it could be used alchemically only by the highest of spiritual initiates.

The numbers that compose the Dodecahedron are as follows:

- Vertices (points): 20
- Edges (lines): 30
- Faces (planes): 12

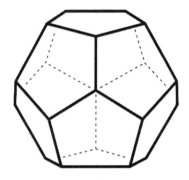

Dodecahedron

In the Mayan light language, use of the Dodecahedron raises one above the seven chakras. It is considered to go beyond the orbital fields and dimensions of the individuated soul. On more practical levels, the Dodeca gives the ability to make choices, providing a range of new perceptions. It helps one pinpoint the center of reality and truth and shifts consciousness and matter.[11]

The magic in the Dodeca lies in its ability to be a shifter, to literally transfigure material reality towards a more primordial expression of the pure origin of matter. It prescribes a life that is moving towards a final and complete rarefied state, graced with the power and force of creation, destruction, and the light of evolution.

In the Hygeia Studios system of healing by Gimbel, the Dodeca is seen to enliven and harmonize inner and outer life. It balances depressive states and raises self-respect. The Dodeca deepens one's personal sense of dignity and influences the etheric energy system, helping to synchronize all internal body rhythms. The Crown chakra interfaces with the Dodeca and is in harmonic resonance with the pineal gland. This geometric field opens the portals to the "multiverse." The primary color is violet.[12]

REVEALING GEOMETRY'S MESSAGES WITHIN GEMS

The inherent value and intention of the radiant consciousness of every gem lies within its celestial geometric structures. The following sections describe the messages revealed by the geometry within each gem.

Revealing Geometry's Message in Rubies/Sapphires

Rubies and Sapphires are in the Corundum family of minerals. Rubies have the most pronounced distinctions from the other Sapphires. Their beauty is revealed through the color value. What gives the Ruby its color is the ferric iron spectrum and traces of chrome.

Ruby has its crystalline structure in the Trigonal System. The crystal shape will vary in different varieties and locations. The most highly revered Burma Ruby often takes the shape of a hexagonal prism terminated at both ends with rhombohedral faces.

The geometry of Ruby breaks up a light beam into two rays. This causes the rays to absorb light differently and thus process information in a variety of ways. The dual-terminated structure allows for the radiant solar power of the Ruby to have a bi-directional flow of light energy. The Ruby's conductivity and strength harness and ground the diversity of life, integrating the principles of manifestation at the core of being. **In legend, the Ruby is thought to be the gem of the soul.**

Ruby embodies wholeness, totality, omnipresence, and the supreme principle of the Father solar force exhibited in the relationship of the Trinity, or three-in-one.

Through the configuration of a rhomboidal twist that can occur in a Ruby, higher dimensions are embedded in lower dimensional structures. What this means is that a crystal structure will morph when the space/time ratios for a family group of crystals are inherently programmed by celestial forces to shift. Dimensions of intelligence are thus uncoiled to accommodate alternate planes of reality. The plane is like a field, or transducer, for specific energetic intelligence to redefine in form and meaning.

The Corundum family of Sapphires is expressed in red, blue, green, orange, yellow, purple, clear, and black. The color will impart specific spectral bands of information central to the theme of Sapphires (see below for blue, yellow, and white—the Sapphires included in the planetary gem elixirs).

When stones are grouped into families, the variation of color indicates the qualities of energy being expressed. These characteristics revolve around shared core energetic principles relative to Sapphires. The various colors and forms of Sapphires correlate to energetic chakra zones, as well as the body's systems.

Sapphires often manifest in the form of hexagonal bipyramids of twelve triangular faces, six above and six below. Blue Sapphire establishes the foundation for the ultimate manifestation of one's spiritual powers and life destiny. Its configuration energetically supports the soul in realizing its destined potential. It opens the sanctuary of inner-dimensional space to pierce the veils of perception.

Yellow Sapphire heightens realization that unfolds the power of the God force. The cosmic force of this gem catalyzes the individual to experience direct cognition of the implicate order of divine creation. One accesses the wisdom to direct the flow of life inherent in the perfection of cognitive and creative intelligence.

White Sapphire, visibly devoid of color, is able to receive the pure white light of stellar consciousness, embracing and reflecting the diversity of the spectrum of celestial vibration. The fullness of the clear light upholds the element of grace as it manifests in all of creation. It cultivates an appreciation for the beauty and love of the divine works of God.

Revealing Geometry's Message in Pearl

Pearl is a gemstone that is organic in nature, created by shellfish called pearl mollusks, or oysters. When a parasite enters the mollusk, it becomes surrounded with a secreted substance called nacre or mother-of-pearl. Mother-of-pearl is approximately 84 to 92 percent calcium carbonate and 4 to 13 percent conchiolin, which acts like a glue to bind the organic elements together.

Pearl is created by stress and functions to alleviate the irritation within and the threat to the life of the host mollusk. It retains this power of protection for the wearer or user.

The natural gemstone Pearl is referred to throughout the world as mother-of-pearl. **From deep within the primordial roots of the psyche, the spherical Pearl elicits the imaginative visionary forces that give rise to the liquid essence of creation.**

Within the sphere of the Pearl is the all-encompassing presence of the Divine Mother that creates, sustains, and supports the changing reality of form. The Mother Matrix embodied within the Pearl has the capacity to balance the fluctuating experience of emotion that is exhibited in the ebb and flow of human nature.

The spherical Pearl embodies the egalitarian armor of compassion that fills the heart with divine love for all creation. One learns to identify all creation as the all-embracing Self. As creation spirals out of the central point into multiple forms of life, each form is interconnected to the original point in the center of the great sphere. The healing impulses of the Mother Pearl facilitate the psyche to move to deeper levels of divine nature, attuning the user to the divine impulses of the Mother.

Pearl leads one to travel to the center point of one's own being, revealing a unified, singular point of intense self-recognition. This state, at once highly focused and multi-dimensionally diffuse, allows one to perceive the holographic unity of creation. One awakens to a compassionate omnipresence, held in the comforting and forgiving arms of the Divine Mother Principle.

Revealing Geometry's Message in Red Coral

Red Coral is one of the organic gems; its color is due to the presence of iron oxide within it. Red Coral is part of the crystal system known as Hexagonal (i.e., multiple crystal structures scaffolding upon one another). This is understood as an "aggregate" system, tiny crystals fused together.

Coral is made up of deposits of calcium and secretions from the invertebrate coral polyp. A polyp develops out of a fertilized egg that attaches to previous coral growth or other underwater surfaces; the new coral is formed from the base of the polyp. Calcium carbonate is secreted at the point of attachment and a new coral colony is formed.[13]

The coral polyp is a primitive type of plantlike animal. Reproduction may be sexual or by budding. Colonies may be male, female, or bisexual, containing both. The solid Coral, which often branches into treelike forms, is the colony in which these tiny animals live. Having a plant/animal, fire/water, and male/female nature, Coral balances the polarities in one's character.

The aggregate formation of the coral colony imprints its design characteristics in the user of the gem or elixir to help form and center his or her core strength towards creative action. It transfers the information needed to organize and center one's own ideas for creative growth and the ability to actualize in the world.

Revealing Geometry's Message in Hessonite Garnet

Hessonite Garnet is in the Cubic system and is a member of the calcium-aluminum group of garnets. These geometric structures are the formative consciousness behind the powerful energies of transformation and constructive imagination inherent in the gem.

Hessonite instills objectivity, nonattachment, and knowledge of the causal regions that govern higher-dimensional worlds. This can be very useful when a person enters higher states of creative cognition, because the ego can run powerful interference patterns that mirror subconscious areas of desire and self-deception. To safely operate in these higher realms, one must master the personal world of desire.

Hessonite habitually takes the form of the twelve-faced rhombic-dodecahedron and the twenty-four-faced icositetrahedron and combinations of these two forms.[14] Hessonite, in the form of the rhombic-dodecahedron, elicits a strong force that is capable of shifting dimensional awareness.

Hessonite resonates with the North Node of the Moon (Rahu), which reaches deep into the subconscious realms, creating a celestial influence that impels transformation. The initiatic course of the Hessonite leads one into the self-reflective path of clarification, purification, and spiritual protection.

The celestial geometry inherent in this stone cleanses the lens of perception and promotes selfless surrender. Pure awareness gains the freedom to create from the sanctum of the causal level of creation. A person may find that he or she is able to access direct perception of past, present, and future from the mind and heart of God.

Revealing Geometry's Message in Emerald

Emerald is a variety of a mineral known as beryl. The beryl is a silicate mineral deriving its green color from the trace mineral chromium. Emerald crystal belongs to the Hexagonal crystal system, a six-sided prism. The atomic structure is formed in independent groups of six-fold rings formed by tetrahedral groups linking through oxygen atoms.

The ancients believed Emerald to be the symbol of immortality and faith. Emerald contains in its architecture the divine spark of God as the first emanation and the breath of life. Emerald energetically embodies the Divine Mother and her powers of renewal, regeneration, and abundance. It creates a heartfelt connection with and a deep appreciation for Nature and the abundance she lavishes upon us. Emerald is also a powerful regenerator for the physiology, accelerating the healing process.

Revealing Geometry's Message in Rose Quartz

Quartz is the most common mineral on earth and is found in a wide variety of geological environments. The Quartz crystal is silicon dioxide, and more than forty types of minerals have been found within Quartz.

The Quartz crystal most commonly manifests in Hexagonal form. However, some modifications of Quartz crystals appear in the Trigonal and Cubic forms, caused by the transmutation of the minerals at various temperatures. The rose color is mostly derived from titanium oxide and manganese.

When Quartz crystallizes in the Trigonal (Rhombohedral) system, it often appears as a double-terminated crystal that consists of a hexagonal prism capped at each end. This is typified in a hexagonal pyramid. In the Rhombohedral style, these crystals have twelve triangular-shaped faces that are mirror counterparts to one another.

Quartz has a unique power to create what is called a piezoelectric effect. Under certain heat conditions, Quartz exhibits an electrical charge. Due to its capacity to maintain and broadcast electrical stimulation, the Quartz crystal has been used in radio, television, and other types of media; sonar (underwater broadcast technology); and in the development of highly sensitive timepieces.

As previously noted in Chapter 4, the Rose Quartz is a universal heart harmonizer, balances the emotional body and soothes deep-seated scars and traumas, assists the heart chakra to open to the universal flow of giving and receiving love, resolves issues of anger, facilitates clarity and integration on all levels, and teaches the highest form of Love.

Revealing Geometry's Message in Diamond

Diamond crystal belongs to the Cubic system. The perfected form of the diamond appears as an Octahedron, which is composed of two equilateral four-sided pyramids fused base to base. The additional forms that the diamond crystal assumes are Cubic and Dodecahedral, which have six square- and twelve rhomb-shaped faces.

The "fire" quality of a diamond refers to its ability to disperse the white light entering it into the spectrum of color. The other criterion used to evaluate the potency of the diamond is its absorption capabilities. This attribute describes the distinct ability of a gem to absorb the many varieties of color inherent within it.

Optical properties that empower the diamond are grand. The refracted index is the term used to measure the ability of the diamond to return a ray of light. Diamonds have a different refractive index for each colored ray. The varied color spectrum is due to differences in the chemical composition of the stone. A high-refracted index indicates that the rays are totally reflected from the surfaces of the rear facets and returned through the front of the diamond. This constitutes maximum refractive and projective powers and can be understood as a metaphor for the power inherent in the soul.

Revealing Geometry's Message in Cat's Eye

Cat's Eye, or Chrysoberyl, is an Orthorhombic shape; the chromatic-chemical composition is a double oxide of beryllium and aluminum. Chrysoberyl is a Rhombic crystal that displays a double refraction that is biaxial—there are two directions of single refraction and three major optical directions.

The three optical directions of biaxial stones often show a different selective absorption to light and are therefore differently colored.[15] This structural characteristic inherent in the stone lends it the ability to absorb light/information and to induce a marked surge in perception.

Cat's Eye has a powerful capacity for absorption and penetration; its mode of conduct is to turn light back on itself. **Cat's Eye functions in much the same way as the pineal gland: it absorbs light, allowing it to penetrate the inner core of the psyche.** The characteristic of the rhombic crystal shape of the Chrysoberyl creates a vibrational shift in dimensional awareness when introduced into the human aura.

Revealing Geometry's Message in Amethyst

Amethyst is a deep violet Quartz crystal whose color is derived from traces of iron. Its structures are organized primarily in the Trigonal crystalline system. However, they often appear in cluster with Rhombohedral tops and in certain cases retain Cubic aspects.

Amethyst strengthens the subtle bodies to develop a deepening sense of ease and surrender to "what is," culturing loyalty and honesty and fostering a contemplative nature. It supports the nervous system towards calmness, tranquility, and peace. Amethyst also expands and slows down the experience of time, giving rise to a transcendent view of reality. It enhances intuitive psychic perception and meditative states, helping one to gain objective insight into life.

6

THE TWELVE ZODIACAL ARCHETYPES
Nature's Blueprint of Our Holographic Psyche

Man is a microcosm, or a little world,
because he is an extract from all the stars
and plants of the whole firmament, from
the earth and the elements; and so he is
their quintessence.

—Paracelsus

Throughout the world, spiritual and religious traditions have adopted the template of the astrological zodiac as an archetypal system. Each zodiacal archetype is subject to a prescribed role in the cosmological expression of life. The fate of the individual in the context of the zodiac is often a clearly defined state of archetypal identification.

However, in gifting us with flowers, gems, botanicals, color, and light, Nature has given us a way to break free of over-identification with our primary archetype and astrological characteristics, to access the cosmic spiritual power inherent within each archetype: the holographic psyche.

As individuals, we are defined at the moment of conception. At the moment of birth, a cosmological archetypal imprinting occurs that shapes the psycho-soul on every level of humanness. Our physical bodies, emotions, mental processes, behaviors, social dispositions, and psychic/spiritual imprints are expressed from the astrological energies that are in play at the moment of birth.

Astrology is a living form of geometry. The angles, vortices, and energetic lay lines, or paths, between celestial objects and human locations in time and space have a direct mathematical influence on the life of the individual. The precise mathematical calculation of our blueprints—in terms of the placement of ascending signs, sun signs, and all other planetary positions and relationships at the moment of birth—take on a DNA-like role that defines our heritage as cosmic-functioning human beings. This blueprint also affects our relationship with all apparent "others," as well as with the grand scheme of evolving life.

In this chapter, we will examine the twelve archetypes of the zodiac and the specific planetary gem elixirs and flower essences most capable of providing therapeutic value for each. These natural remedies assist in elevating the archetype to its spiritual maturity and clarification, thus facilitating the evolution of the human to function as a holistic being.

THE HOLOGRAPHY OF THE ARCHETYPES

The astrological archetypes are metaphors that speak to the holographic persona like a system of personal navigation, illuminating the meaning and function of life's rich experiences. The individual traveling through the sequences delineated by the astrological map finds himself navigating through the holographic regions of the psyche where these universal themes emerge.

The human psyche is a cosmological matrix system that is in resonant communication with the organizing power of the universe. The orchestration of the forces of Nature, in harmonic attunement with Divine design, come together to form reality as we know it. The individual psyche is a cloak for the immortal soul, which in its infinite wisdom and unfathomable compassion creates the primary themes useful for self-realization and enlightened action.

The holographic archetypes, in communion with gem elixirs, flowers, and botanicals, are able to take the psyche to uncharted regions of soul realization. The gem elixirs operate at the causal level of awareness. Here, identity and soul are interlaced, reaching into the fabric of being and offering transformational insights that might otherwise be obscured by the illusions of the personality. The gem elixirs can also lead to a state of heightened awareness. Through this process, one can begin to experience a spiritual perspective of detached witnessing and innocence, out of which can spring forth an enhanced vision of internal truth.

Flower essences provide the psycho-spiritual springboard to propel the persona out of the orbit of the personal and into the transpersonal ground state of being. Botanicals provide the nutritional intelligence necessary for the physiology to support these quantum shifts in the mind/body/consciousness of the individual.

Each holographic archetype provides an overlay of energetic information that has the capacity to catalyze the individual toward his or her awakening. The archetypes are stored in the pool of collective consciousness and thus are universally shared by all human beings. The maturation of the archetypal energies leads to a state of self-mastery.

When the spiritual governing principles of the archetype are able to ripen fully, the individual gains the universal value of his or her cosmic possibility. At this point one is able to function on the level of an integrated wholeness, calling forth the specific archetype's divine blueprint and promoting right action. This spontaneous behavior of natural law supports the individual to become an embodiment of selfless service, opening the door to greater levels of planetary transformation.

In the awakened individual, the full panorama of the holographic psyche becomes visible. He or she is able to bring forth all the wisdom, blessings, and gifts that each of the cosmological archetypes provides. The soul awareness becomes so vivid that the all-knowing radiance of the Divine permeates the individual's life at all times. The beneficent characteristics of each holographic archetype are unified within the enlightened individual, expanding in such a way that time is suspended and knowledge of present, past, and future is available.

To enter the zodiac of unbounded time, the psyche must lose its fixed positions in the relative world. The persona learns to adopt a fluid nature, allowing it to move and shapeshift to accommodate the requirements of its unique path. The resulting heightened states of revelation traverse the dimensions of defined reality.

The holographic psyche is a map that spirals through itself repeatedly, until one achieves dimensional unification and one is able to live life as a multiplicity of form and content. All the signs of the holographic zodiac are equal in value, creating an immeasurable singularity. One is able to view the fluctuation of each archetype as a marker in the sphere of the Now.

ORIGINS OF THE ASTROLOGICAL ARCHETYPES

Both historical and modern applications of the zodiac archetypes act as vehicles that illumine the passageways into the various dimensions of the human psyche. The zodiac is a universal blueprint that can be intimately described through the language of sacred geometry. It is a holographic map that encompasses a twelvefold evolutionary process of the soul's journey through space and time relative to one's present relationship to the earth and heavens.

The realization of the Godhead as the central subject of life requires an integrative perspective that encompasses all points of view. Life requires that we see things from all perspectives in order to understand it and live the totality of our human and divine self. Historical, metaphysical, and metaphorical examples of the twelve-in-one are seen in the twelve apostles of Christ, the twelve calendar months, the twelve primary energy meridians in the human body, and the twelve constellations (signs) and houses of the zodiac.

In order to enclose a single sphere, twelve spheres of equal size are required to encircle it. The biological blueprint found in the helical structure of DNA is based on rotating dodecahedrons, the geometric shape with a characteristic twelve-in-one signature.

A composite methodology of Eastern and Western astrology forms a universal basis for the development of planetary gem elixirs. This composite is founded on the classical astrological archetypes as indicated in the Eastern Vedic, Rosicrucian, and Kabbalistic systems of sidereal astrology and the primary Western system of tropical astrology.

Sidereal astrology is based on the mathematical measurements or placement of the planets within a constellation at the time of birth or at the time of a particular event. It takes into account the procession of the Equinox, bearing in mind that the heavens are in constant motion. In sidereal astrology, the ascendant, or rising sign, is the degree at which the zodiac intersected the eastern horizon at the time and place of birth. Vedic astrology places primary significance on the ascendant as the portal into one's natal chart.

The tropical zodiac correlates to the seasons of the year, not the actual positions in the zodiac. Tropical astrology identifies where the sun was at one's time of birth and places primary significance on this "sun sign" as the key to psycho/spiritual understanding for the individual.

The principle geometric relationship indicators of the zodiac remain the same in both traditions.

The zodiac archetypes can be viewed as metaphorical predictors of the soul's journey upon the human life path. They illustrate a unique futuristic understanding of how human life can evolve to a more advanced spiritual/cognitive level. In both systems, the relationship between human and cosmic processes and the energetic interaction of the planets and constellations with human beings contain archetypal truths that are holographic in nature. The archetypes provide information that gives direction to the course of human development, higher states of consciousness, and the collective psyche.

The Rosicrucian and Kabbalistic systems are examples of Western approaches that also utilize the sidereal system. Because these systems view human evolution as a journey of the immortal soul to higher realms, the esoteric astrologer seeks to link the inquirer to an in-depth questioning of life experience. The aim is to inspire a person to resolve challenges, whether mundane or psycho/spiritual in nature. Astrological gems and flower remedies are tools to augment our capacity to transcend the limitations described in one's astrological chart and awaken the composite knowledge of the soul in its cosmic trajectory.

The Vedic astrological tradition is referred to as Jyotish, which translates as "the study of all facets of the lords of light: sun, moon, planets, stars."[1] It is the science and study of heavenly lights and their effects on human life. The role of Jyotish is to guide the individual to attain the light of life, pure awareness, and the light of the soul (Atma). Billions of people throughout the history of the world have had deep faith in Jyotish as a divine gift to humankind revealed through the sages of India.

MATHEMATICAL BLUEPRINTS

Jyotish/Astrology utilizes precise mathematical calculations to determine the position of the heavenly bodies, past, present, and future. These mathematical relationships indicate the flow of consciousness between personal and cosmic frequencies; an alignment is established between the macrocosmic universe and the circumstances of the microcosmic individual.

In the Vedic astrological tradition, the ascendant governs the personality taken on by the soul. The ascendant is viewed as a gateway that allows the soul and personality to communicate between dimensions. The individual's true knowledge and potential are revealed through this interdimensional dialogue. When obstacles arise, they are seen to shape and define the play of life, rather than denying the soul permanent access to its spiritual destination.

The influence of the ascendant encourages the individual to know himself or herself through the refinement of the senses. The individual learns to process information from both the physical and subtle environments.

Through personal experience, knowledge, and spiritual belief derived through the cultivation of trans-temporal information (cosmic information that is not bound by space and time), the soul masters the complexities of celestial information that awaken a highly illumined sensibility. The soul enters the portal of the ascendant with the opportunity to master the archetypal tools to govern one's space/time trajectories on this earth plane.

The ascendant, also referred to as the rising sign, governs the expression of the soul in its present space/time reality. Each position of the ascendant functions as a prismatic window into the delicate fabric of cognition. **Through the prism of the persona, the soul touches, shapes, and colors the manifest plane.**

The ascendant, which marks the starting point for the positions of the planets in one's chart, is imprinted with profound practical and transcendental meaning, myth, and symbolism inherent in that specific constellation or sign of the zodiac. The embodiment of the universal archetypal truths leads one to see life in the light of mythical and mystical realities. The integration of the twelve holographic archetypes, as seen through Eastern astrology, awakens the transcendental identity that is key to the knowledge of personal empowerment inherent within each sign.

The panoramic layout of the human cosmology is displayed through the constellations of the zodiac. Extending beyond the superficial development of the ego or persona, the ascendant speaks to the inner realms of self-mastery and spiritual realization. Although the persona is a lens for the calibration of the soul's journey on earth, it is easily distorted by the genealogical patterns that are introduced through the ancestral lineage.

The soul is not always able to overcome these impure reflections. Therefore, in its search for spiritual nourishment, it looks towards the realms of color, vibration and sacred geometry as primary vehicles for its sustenance.

Gems, planetary gem elixirs, or other remedial measures are indicated based on the ascendant as the primary astrological indicator. The ruling planet of the ascendant generally indicates the corresponding gemstone that would function as a constitutional remedy. For example, when Gemini is indicated as the rising sign or ascendant, then Mercury is its ruler. This could indicate Emerald for rectifying or empowering the chosen path of the soul's expression in the world. However, according to astrology, there are numerous indicators for identifying the appropriate gemstones to be used for a specific purpose and for a specific length of time. This is but one methodology for gem therapy.

CHARTING COSMIC BIRTHMARKS

The natal chart is the individuated blueprint that reveals the pathways the soul can take to actualize its creative intelligence and potential. The chart defines mathematical relationships between the different planets, the constellations, and their positions in the cosmos to the individual. These geometrical foundations may be seen as personal cosmic lay lines that guide one in the path of self-mastery.

The moment of birth is a cosmic marker, an original coronation in time and space that can never be duplicated. The heavenly bodies create an energetic imprint that is infused into each individual at the time of his or her birth. At this moment the subtle bodies are infused with different spectral aspects of meaning that cause each individual to function as a birthmark or statement of recognition by Universal Intelligence.

These energies are reflected in our whole response to physical and psychological reality. When we enter life, the soul holds the destiny codes, or mathematical calculations, for a specific psychophysical territory that we will chart during the different phases of our existence. Like a boatman who must navigate his journey in reference to the patterns of the stars, the human being plots the course of life through a deep, finely woven interaction with the cosmos. Thus, our course is seen and unseen, deterministic, and at the same time, flavored with the power of self-will.

The highest purpose of astrological understanding is to guide the individual to awaken and realize his or her fullest contribution to the evolution of humanity. In this context, astrology is a form of ministry that inspires and catalyzes the individual to use the blueprint of his or her chart as a means to translate the interplay between cosmic intelligence and the soul's inner guidance.

Using the gifts of Gaia presented in this book, a unifying, seamless current of communication between the persona and the soul is established, and one learns to access soul intelligence directly. This allows the element of grace to propel one into surrender to the directorship of the higher Self. One steps off the platform of personal identity and enters the synchronous rhythm of infinite time. Here one accesses the secrets of spiritual truth and self-mastery.

Grace then extends its influence to produce a state in which one is able to live simultaneously in many dimensions of awareness. **We are complex beings, capable of working within a multi-tiered fabric of vibrational information.** The astrological chart indicates where portals of higher dimensional consciousness will be most likely to emerge.

The codes that are structured into the fundamental blueprint of the soul speak to one's personal time keys or soul rhythms. As the soul awakens to its true cosmic nature, these codes are activated, delineating the precise cycles that the soul will follow to reach the fullest expression of spiritual knowledge. The codes are interwoven with the personal event choices that an individual makes. The spiritual journey toward points of destiny develops purity of heart, intensity of focus, clarity of vision, and dedication to divine truth.

The awakening of this "inner astrologer" decodes the information that allows one's life to unfold through synchronicity that is deeply meaningful and aligned with evolutionary momentum on a personal and collective level.

THE COSMOS AND THE BODY OF LIGHT: A MARRIAGE MADE IN HEAVEN

The forces of nature on earth are upheld through the world of light, color, and sound. The infinite cosmic geometry of the universe is reflected proportionately in the boundaries of finite space. The forces that create and sustain living form have their basis in mathematical representations called fractals, which are inlaid repetitive geometric patterns.[2]

Any interplay of planes, lines, and points (see Chapter 5) creates an archetypal space that is the birth hatch for the geometric patterns of nature. The macrocosmic ethereal seed is the model for the microcosmic bodies. The universal creative intelligence draws light out of the unmanifest as it sends its forces through space. All growth consists of life being pushed out from the inside.[3]

Celestial bodies communicate by light/sound wave frequencies that further define themselves as color and elemental forces. The celestial bodies radiate wave patterns of light/sound/color that interface with the human physiology and psyche. These patterns enter the receptor sites of the skin and the neuronal pathways leading from the eyes to the brain. The interface between these wave patterns and one's brain waves sets up resonant pathways for communication between cosmic intelligence and individual DNA.[4]

Oscillating photonic light and sound frequencies of the celestial bodies create sequences of color and harmonic vibration that are metabolized at the subatomic level of the human being. Atomic structures convert information originating from the heavenly bodies into biochemical messengers that the mind/body complex can then utilize intelligently. When we peel back the veils of fixed conditioning and perception, new biochemical information is able to enter at the forefront of our awareness. This process underlies the field mechanics that create the scaffolding of reality on the level of the human physiology.

One of the most commonly known Western astrological reference points for understanding the nature of a person is the sun sign, which governs the expression of our unique essence or eternal soul. The sun is our vital force as pure existence. The placement of the moon in one's chart governs one's psycho-emotional nature.

Human beings derive their primary psycho-spiritual identity from a unique blend of the influence of the sun, moon, and soul-propagated characteristics, as well as those inherited from one's biological lineage. The sun represents not only the energies inherited from the human father, but also the alignment that the soul has created between itself and the cosmic father blueprint. The same holds true for the moon or maternal blueprint.

At birth, the cosmic matrix of one's life chart differentiates it from the mother/father's. Birth signals the first right of passage. In this singular moment along the time continuum, the individual is infused with the array of the heavenly bodies. The wholeness coalesces, birthing a new human star upon the earth. The heavenly marriage gives rise to the all-possible human. The astrological birth chart is a metaphorical reality. For these reasons, astrology is an effective vehicle for self-inquiry, mastery, and cosmic awakening.

The astrological chart identifies cycles in one's life in which core issues are seen as pivotal for transformation. Growth points may be subjectively experienced as obstacles or challenges, but in reality, they are the soul's opportunity to reconnect us to the cosmic source. Vibrational remedies such as flower essences and gem elixirs are essential to the balance and transformation of energetic patterns that are no longer resonant with the frequencies of the soul.

The astrological archetypes are mythological and mathematical examples that offer profound metaphors to the persona. **Like a system of personal navigation, the archetypes illuminate the meaning and function of life's rich experiences.** The individual traveling through the sequences delineated by his or her astrological map finds himself or herself navigating through the holographic regions of the psyche, where these universal themes emerge.

The concept of destiny, which ancient civilizations often viewed as fixed or unchangeable, can, in the light of modern physics and psychological understanding, be viewed as a process that is at once deterministic and synchronous with the deep knowledge of the cosmic Self. We live in accord with the expansion into all possibility, which breaks the boundaries of perceived destiny.

The astrologer with refined perception can cast the chart of an individual as if that person were a newborn infant with all the possibilities of evolution vibrantly alive. The astrologer, acting as an elder or mentor, has the capability of charging the individual with the immortal knowledge that will help him or her become a fearless Sun of the Divine.

When a vibrational elixir is introduced into the auric field, the bio-resonant frequencies attune the psyche to the celestial sounds and rhythms of the universe. Vibrational elixirs communicate directly with the soul through light/sound impulses that are electro-magnetic in nature. An elixir functions as a translator for the language of Mother Earth. The soul digests the messages of the Mother. The living planet Earth is in a continual feedback loop with all other celestial bodies. The Earth is both transmitting and receiving cosmic information from the solar and galactic systems. Based on the celestial information received, the Earth adapts by modulating the energetic fluctuations that regulate the flow of life.

A vibrational elixir is an alchemical preparation created from a precious gem, flower, or noble metal. The elixir embodies the energetic signature of the original material. The signature varies in reference to the shape of the oscillating wave frequencies inherent in the identity of the gem or plant. The elixir, when offered with a clear spiritual intent, is infused with the power to awaken new vistas of insight. The spirit of the elixir escorts the flow of consciousness back to its originating impulse. **Gracefully and with precise mathematical articulation, the blessing power of the elixir weaves the light of awareness into the shadowy regions of the psyche.**

THE ASCENDANT: FIRST KEY TO SELF-MASTERY

The ascendant in a person's chart refers to the sign of the zodiac that appears on the eastern horizon at the moment of birth. The ascendant denotes the first point in the natal chart where meaning and definition begin to formulate the individual. Each ascendant creates a unique energetic matrix that propagates the substructures of reality.

On the path of self-mastery, each being must locate the essence and exalted powers of the twelve archetypes within his or her own inner structures of the psyche. The soul committed to awakening identifies the secret keys to personal power inherent in each archetype. As an individual integrates the twelve holographic archetypes, he or she gains greater access to the soul, which in Vedic astrology is referred to as the Atman.

Each person's unique astrological blueprint delivers the instructions for self-development. These instructions are similar to the software codes used in computer science, except that the codes of the soul are more luminescent, filled with feeling, color, geometry, and tone. The fulfillment of one's divine gifts and attributes is reflected in the ongoing downloading of this living blueprint. The light intelligence inherent within one's chart governs the flowering of the individual and his or her role in the collective consciousness.

The astrological chart also outlines the obstacles and assets that the individual will have to meet to fulfill the course of his or her life. As individuals move out of the egoic level, bridging the personal and cosmic mind, they gain access to their soul's knowledge and gifts. They shift out of identification with a singular personal archetype to a higher vibrational expression of that archetype that is truly transpersonal, or cosmic, in nature. Once the illuminative light of the soul shatters the boundaries of the individual personality, there is recognition of a universal "I Am" presence that permeates all of the strata of life.

THE TWELVE ARCHETYPES

The Aries Archetype

Ruled by Mars

Fire Element

Cardinal (Directive Energy)

Key Words: Cardinal, fiery, primordial, creative, initiating, sight-oriented, passionate, impulsive, risk-taking, impatient, action-oriented, initiating, vital, pioneering, courageous, associated with the head and eyes

The first sign in the zodiac is Aries, ruled by the planet Mars and governed by the element fire. The nature of the fire element is dynamic, transmuting, and light; the direction of movement is upwards. When well guided, the nature of fire is to aspire, uplift, and create change that illuminates life's issues. The fire spirit ushers in new transformational opportunities for the fulfillment of goals and desires. One of the higher expressions of the passionate Aries archetype is to actualize the true power of light inherent in the fire element.

Aries is characterized by a strong and passionate will. The power of Aries lies in its ability to break through difficult challenges and see clearly and effectively. As light is directed inward through the inner eye, attention floods the persona with awareness, revealing clarity of purpose. This allows Aries to manage goal setting and the location, rhythm, and timing of life's events and circumstances. As the Aries matures, he or she gains the ability to see even more objectively, from both a personal and holistic perspective.

The Aries archetype sees himself or herself in the ultimate cardinal position: ruler over others and projects. The Aries is dynamically forthcoming in the world and possesses natural leadership abilities. This archetype seeks to instill a sense of honor and patriotic feeling on the part of those with whom it comes in contact. It wants to know how a thing will be done, and it wants to get things done quickly and efficiently; it can sometimes act brusquely.

The Aries relies on the strength of the mind combined with a fierce reaching into the depths of the heart. Aries can be passionate and kind to those with whom it is in agreement but can sometimes be without much mercy for those who get in its way. Obstinate, genuine, fiery, quick to anger, and often quick to forgive, Aries can be a good opponent and a great friend or trusted advisor or protector. The ideals of the impulsive young Aries when subjected to its feverish passions and irrational temperament can cause short-sightedness and a loss of control in relation to the goal. The young Aries is ahead of the times, striding forth with headstrong views and effective action.

Spiritual maturity for the Aries archetype involves realization of the universal within the personal Self. The tendency of the young Aries is to passionately exert its force of influence with all its might and right. The mastery of the Aries archetype involves its potential to fully mature into its true spiritual power, a synthesis of the creative force sparked by Divine Will. The gate of initiation is through the surrender of the forceful aspect of the personal will to the purifying fire of non-reactivity. This imparts a clear expression of action that is sparked by the higher Self.

Mars inspires Aries to rise to the full measure of vitality, creativity, and initiatory energies. Mars energy carries the life force and impulse for the breath of life. It provides the vitality, enthusiasm, and endurance necessary for the Aries to be effectively engaged in its own dynamic projects, goals, and visions. The planetary bio-resonant energies of Mars infuse the Aries with physical strength and authoritative powers.

Balancing the primordial, fiery energies of the Aries nature requires extraordinary kinesthetic sensitivity and the spiritual sight known as witnessing. Mastery of the internal fires of Aries relies on overcoming impatience and impulsiveness. One then arrives at a state of spontaneous mind, capable of right action. The surmounting of over-expanded desires, short-sightedness, and explosive passion leads to highly creative impulses.

A high degree of intelligence and successful initiatory conduct and follow-through will bring about the actualization of these creative impulses. The Aries is then able to bring his or her life to fruition through increased fore-sightedness and focused attention.

The higher-frequency Aries archetype exemplifies the passionate expression of rhythmic grace.

PLANETARY GEM/ELIXIR FOR THE ARIES ARCHETYPE

RED CORAL (MARS)

Red Coral balances the passions and focuses the creative power of the pioneering spirit of Aries. The Aries archetype looks out into the world and quickly takes the lead. He initiates swift and decisive action toward goals, desires, and self-oriented needs. Red Coral emits the frequencies to assist the psyche and body to balance, stabilize, and ground these initiating and creative impulses. It supports the Aries archetype to kinesthetically recognize its dynamic rhythm in activity, rather than act on impulse that lacks foresight. It sharpens the mind and clears vision.

Red Coral assists with the development of patience, timing, and the bodily sense of flow, movement, and rhythm. This gem supports the Aries in managing his power, strength, and aggressiveness, while maintaining the passion and determination to follow through with intention. Red Coral initiates a vital process for the Aries to mature into a true leader—one who is able to see the full range of potential and enjoy a new state of freedom that overcomes the tendency towards impulsive action.

FLOWER ESSENCES FOR THE ARIES ARCHETYPE

INDIAN PAINTBRUSH (*CASTILLEJA MINIATA*)

Indian Paintbrush radiates the brilliance of the fiery red ray. This plant spirit guides the Aries's initiatory impulses and inspirational ideas toward a focused and steady stream of action. The teachings of Indian Paintbrush catalyze Aries to bring about concrete earthly materialization of the creative principles. Through the use of this essence, the physical body of the Aries is empowered by a new vitality that inspires the individual to achieve dynamic greatness in the material world. **Indian Paintbrush assists the soul to source the energy within one's nature towards the fulfillment of the soul's desires.**

IMPATIENS (*IMPATIENS GLANDULIFERA*)

Throughout history, sages and adepts have cultured patience as a singular state of self-mastery. The bio-spiritual resonance of Impatiens flower essence raises the vibrational frequencies of the mental and emotional bodies, cultivating a state of patience. Impatiens illuminates the characteristics of the soul—wisdom, foresight, witnessing, and non-attachment. Patience gives rise to eternal grace by creating a present, mind-free state.

The Taurus Archetype

Ruled by Venus

Earth Element

Fixed (Stabilizing Energy)

Key Words: Fixed, slow to change, stubborn, earthy, throat chakra, grounded, manifesting, beauty, appreciation, devotion, creative architect, abundance, attachment, generative and regenerative processes, lush, nurturing, and nourishing

The second sign in the zodiac is Taurus, governed by the earth element. The power of the earth element cultivates a stable, concrete, rooted character that gives rise to manifest form. The earth element of a Taurian archetype is of a fixed nature. This gives the individual the tendency to accumulate and build in the world. The Taurian character is slow, methodical, and often unyielding to change. There is a tendency toward density that can manifest as comforts and luxuries in the physical reality.

The Taurian archetype is related to the field of gravity, which provides a natural law of attraction. Gravity is the principle of earthly existence that fixes us to material reality. Taurus, under the domain and laws of the earth, exhibits fixed or stationary phenomenology. It attracts people, places, objects, wealth, and opportunities.

The force fields of the earth influence the Taurian towards tangible, kinesthetic modes of expression. The Taurian is naturally attracted to architecture, structures, systems, land development, environmental issues, and an artistic form of expressing beauty. In all Taurians an underlying element of aesthetic beauty informs the expression of manifestation.

The mastery of the Taurian persona lies in the arena of balancing the force fields of attraction and attachment. Taurians find themselves in the noble position of being the anchoring principle responsible for stabilizing and solidifying earthly reality.

The other element that is paradoxically present in the Taurian energy field is *akasha*, the space element. Taurus rules the throat and neck area of the body. The throat chakra is home to the akashic element, central to the Taurian psycho-physiology. The space element supports the interplay of all other elements in the creative manifestation process. The voice is prominent for the Taurian archetype. Form follows through the organization of sound vibrations expressed as meaning. Matter follows energy. Mastery and the right use of voice and sound vibration are especially imperative for the Taurian native (sun sign) or ascendant.

The exalted path of the Taurian honors purity of heart and the beauty in all that is. The quest for these virtues becomes a lifelong spiritual process. Taurians may find themselves dedicated to a life of devotion and worship of the creative principles of the Divine Mother. They may aspire to the noblest of human virtues and stewardship of nature.

A charismatic translucent light often emanates from the masterful Taurian native due to the influence of Venus. The Venusian light ray infuses the Taurian with an integrative power of appreciation for the full spectrum of life. It cultures the soul towards a deep love and devotion to the highest values of order, clarity, and appreciation of beauty. In so doing, the element of grace and manifestation flow through the Taurian being. On the other hand, if the Venusian's energies stagnate and attach in the first or second chakra, the qualities of devotion and beauty can degenerate to possessiveness, attachment, and overindulgence.

The green emanation exhibited by Mother Earth is influential to the Taurian, as it embodies the forces of nature and accents the values of the Venusian energies.

PLANETARY GEMS/ELIXIRS FOR THE TAURUS ARCHETYPE

DIAMOND AND WHITE SAPPHIRE (VENUS)

The primary precious gemstone indicated for Venus is Diamond; White Sapphire is a secondary option. When an astrological prescription-quality Diamond cannot be acquired, White Sapphire is the gem indicated for planetary empowerment, balance, and remediation.

Diamond and White Sapphire guide the Taurian psyche to deepen its connection with the beauty, grace, and splendor of Mother Earth and the infinite abundance that is visible and invisible. These precious gems align the heart and throat to elevate the power of manifestation expressed through the highest purity of love, devotion, beauty, and grace.

Diamond and White Sapphire amplify Taurian magnetic attraction and charisma. The gems offset the heavier emotional tendencies of the Taurian and support the heightened creative and artistic expressions of the soul. The gems culture the element of gracefulness. One develops greater mind/body dexterity. The physical and spiritual gesture of graceful movement flows in one's life. A balanced and enhanced connectedness between the two hemispheres of the brain fosters fluidity between the body, emotions, mind, and spirit.

Diamond and White Sapphire soften the feeling body to receive a direct and deep awakening to the intrinsic value of life's beauty. The Diamond mind carries the knowingness that emerges when the senses become finely attuned. One becomes attracted to the subtler levels of creation as experienced through color, light, sound, smell, touch, and taste. These gemstones culture the subtle senses to gain awareness of the light within objects.

FLOWER ESSENCES FOR THE TAURUS ARCHETYPE

WILD ROSE (*ROSA CANINA*)

Roses are one of the greatest mystic healers in the botanical kingdom. The Wild Rose flower essence performs one of the most profound alchemical transformations found in manifest reality. The five-petal star-matrix pattern of Wild Rose is one of the most primordial self-replicating geometric fractals in all creation. This geometric configuration arises out of the spiral dynamics of the Golden Mean.

Wild Rose anchors spirit to wholeheartedly infuse into earth-based life; it literally fuses spirit with matter. **Wild Rose strengthens the inner chambers of the heart to create a union of spirit and matter that consecrates life.** Wild Rose essence cultivates joy, zest, and the capacity to participate in the expressive aspects of life's journey. Wild Rose fosters buoyancy in the emotional and mental fields through a lighthearted spirit. It opens the heart to the flow of grace.

WALNUT (*JUGLANS REGIA*)

Walnut facilitates the Taurian persona to release attachments to objects, people, and places that no longer serve to inspire a soul-directed life. Walnut is a karmic-link breaker. Walnut essence is a counterbalancing force that creates space for greater freedom and liberation. It affords the capacity to be in the world, yet not of it.

Walnut enables one to transcend fixed behaviors and stubborn conditions held in the structures of the mind and the emotional body. Walnut aids the ego in relinquishing bondage to the object; in so doing, the individual finds he or she can increase the capacity to manifest out of the akashic field. The spacious energetic principles of lightness and detachment are coupled with the practical energetic forces through this essence. Walnut opens the space of the throat chakra, referred to in esoteric philosophies as the Rainbow Bridge and second birth canal.

CAYENNE (*CAPSICUM ANNUUM*)

Cayenne essence is fiery and catalytic. It assists the Taurian nature to adapt to change and initiate positive transformational growth. The Taurian nature often finds itself settled into a complacent comfort zone. This is due to emotional attachment and insecurities that originate in the first and second chakras. The tendencies of the Taurian nature create fixity due to their weighty character, bound to the downward pull of gravity.

These weighty, stuck, stagnating, and resistant patterns are transformed by Cayenne essence. It energetically motivates dynamic and spontaneous action. The capacity of Cayenne to infuse the body, mind, and soul with fiery light ignites energies that sustain momentum for change.

COSMOS (*COSMOS BIPINNATUS*)

Cosmos essence is a delicate blossom with deep, rich, radiating, wave frequencies of magenta colors. Cosmos infuses the auric field with harmonizing vibratory overtones that align the heart and throat chakras. It is a profound essence to help the Taurian native call forth the desires of the heart and ideas of the mind, uniting them as an expression of inspired organization and practical form.

The power of sound gives voice to truth. The soul's capacity to synchronize right action aligns one with the destiny energy needed to actualize one's life. Cosmos awakens the expression of appreciation, devotion, love, and joy in the energy field. It enlivens the feeling tone of the heart and gives rise to creative inspiration and ideas. Cosmos is excellent for all forms of communication—feelings, writing, speaking, ideas, relationships, and all forms of partnership. It serves as a bridge between the heart and the throat chakra.

The Gemini Archetype

Ruled by Mercury

Air Element

Mutable (Changing Energy)

Key Words: Air, mutable, communicative, intellectual, relationships, touch, love, sharing, duality, humor, freedom, unstable, focus, novelty, fun, youthful, inquisitive, restlessness, unpredictability

The Gemini archetype is governed by the air element; it is mutable, constantly undergoing fluctuation and change. This creates a dynamic mind, accentuated by the celestial nature of Mercury. The creative impulse of speech and the innate need to venture into the realm of communication is most charming in the Gemini.

Gemini archetypes thrive on discovering ways to communicate, both conventionally and unconventionally. The innate dual nature of the Gemini archetype is the exact condition for this persona to gain self-mastery. The path of the Gemini persona is to learn an integrative approach to choice. The Gemini psyche utilizes a design process that often involves an interior sparring match. The arena of personal reality provides a dualistic continuum of seemingly opposing forces that guide the Gemini on the path of self-mastery.

The Gemini archetype gains firsthand knowledge through experience. He or she is keenly interested in the simultaneous study of many different areas of existence, including people, places, things, philosophies, and ideas. This study provides a fertile ground for the in-depth cognition that Gemini cultivates. Stability and focus are major themes that course through the life stream of the Gemini native.

The first relationship a Gemini archetype encounters is within its own self. The Gemini archetype often experiences two force fields of reality that play off each other until the grand unification can take place. The extreme tendency of engaging in reality through polarizing opposites is how the Gemini archetype satisfies its need to know. In the mystical dance of life, all opposites coexist—inner and outer, visible and invisible, male and female, young and old, light and dark, good and evil. The Gemini persona will often go to extremes to investigate these opposites.

The mutability of the air element lends buoyancy to the Gemini archetype, enabling it to move freely and swiftly. The Gemini is not one to sit idle. Its youthful, free-spirited, and adventurous nature seeks to directly engage with the full spectrum of life. The Gemini persona has a light-spirited willingness to experiment with almost anything life presents. The Gemini enjoys having fun and sees humor as an eloquent expression of the learning process. Novelty and intrigue keep the Gemini persona from becoming bored with the routine of life. Becoming conscious through choice is a central factor for the Gemini persona to maintain its virtues of youthful innocence and loyalty.

The medium of the air element creates coherent wave patterns that, when vibrated, produce a clear flow of meaning in the articulation of sound. The air element within the Gemini archetype governs the sense of touch, life's most visceral form of communication. The Gemini archetype knows that to touch is to love and be loved. The Gemini air element finds expression through the heart and lungs, which extends to the arms, shoulders, and hands.

The Gemini persona works things out in the mind. This is balanced by the truth of the heart, combined with a keen sense of touch. However, the Gemini mind can become a false master. Convinced that duality can be reconciled by a reasoning mind, Gemini seeks to find truth through a detailed synthesis of understanding. Unfortunately, this often leads to a biased perspective derived from the Gemini's enthusiastic embrace of a perceived solution for what once appeared as conflict.

The mature Gemini archetype begins to see that true understanding can never be derived completely from the level of thought. Instead, it comes to a profound unification of heart, feeling, and mind that produces deep insight into life's challenges and philosophical conundrums.

Since the Gemini is profoundly unconventional by nature, it seeks to step out of any form of perceived limitation. It dislikes rules, conditions, forms, and boundaries, seeking to carve out its own sense of ethics rooted in an altruistic ideal. It naturally experiences its core sense of self through its sense of freedom.

When confronted with commitment, the instinctually free, unbounded, and unlimited nature of the Gemini persona finds itself once again in an internal struggle between limits and mutuality of experience. The remedy lies in the ability of the Gemini archetype to view commitment as a form of individual self-expression, fostered on the basis of inner truth. Then relationship can be viewed as a place of unlimited freedom and a template for divine love.

The Gemini learning curve involves the relinquishing of fixed ideas, even utopian ones, that create conditioned responses and control on the level of the mind. As the ego releases its attachments and identification, the Gemini transcends the activity of the mental field and accesses soul wisdom through direct experience and knowing. Awareness expands into the foreground of consciousness, providing an all-encompassing view of reality that reconciles the duality inherent in the mind. This fluid state of realization, birthed out of the Now, renders mechanistic, prescribed truths of the mind obsolete.

The Gemini archetype contributes to society by being a free, innovative thinker—a designer of multimedia technologies and methodologies that have a revolutionary message. Gemini's ability to see the humor and absurdity of life's eccentricities lends itself to a lighthearted, healing humor. Geminis have a flair for conveying their message in an eccentric or extreme fashion. This is how they best make their point and move across communication barriers.

The development of self-mastery allows the Gemini to compassionately embrace herself and others. As the Gemini matures towards adepthood, a divine union takes place. The Gemini psyche learns to sincerely play the field of lover to all that is. The adept level of the Gemini archetype infinitely weaves duality into a unified whole. This allows the Gemini to be at peace with whatever expression unfolds in a given moment. When the persona has married its opposing forces, the mercurial mind is no longer tossed in the sea of duality. "I don't mind what happens" then becomes the mantra of the Gemini.

PLANETARY GEM/ELIXIR FOR THE GEMINI ARCHETYPE

EMERALD (MERCURY)

Emerald assists the Gemini archetype to become unified in heart and mind. Dualities are resolved, supporting the maintenance of stability from within. Emerald penetrates the heart by soothing and opening the individual to infinite compassion and abundance in life.

Emerald calms and anchors to the earth, centering the wandering Gemini tendency. Its influence is balancing, nurturing, and settling to the quick-changing mind and fluctuating nervous system. It enhances direct connection and communication on a soul level. It creates a positive mental environment free from criticism and judgment.

Emerald resonates with the earthly presence of love felt as Mother Nature. The mercurial Emerald frequency has a dual function of grounding and attunement to the earth.

Emerald aligns the heart and mind, thus elevating a felt awareness that resides in the love of knowledge. The intellect is dynamically satisfied and nourished by the heart/mind that is free to explore and discover the nature of reality.

Emerald cultures a contentment and innocence in the heart of the Gemini. The Emerald green ray opens the channels for the breath of life to flow in and out of the heart, interconnecting with all life. This unifying expression cultures a deep sense of contentment and stability in the mind and heart of the Gemini archetype. Unity is birthed out of an awareness of diversity as infinite aspects within the whole. The heart and mind transcend in unison, revealing the truth in each moment.

FLOWER ESSENCES FOR THE GEMINI ARCHETYPE

WHITE CHESTNUT (*AESCULUS HIPPOCASTANUM*)

White Chestnut essence cultivates a silent and clear mind through a deepening of transcendence. As the mind transcends, it transforms the characteristic loops of Gemini thinking, such as worry. The mind shifts towards a whole-brain mode of operation. The intellect's dualistic function recedes as perception takes on the ability to see in a circular and more encompassing manner. Opposing views and dualistic thinking processes are neutralized through nonreactive observation.

White Chestnut strengthens and stabilizes the light of consciousness to open to the unbounded field of awareness. The reasoning aspect of mind is empowered by the innate wisdom of the higher mind, governed by the soul. White Chestnut essence enhances the functional aspects of mind that create organization and efficiency in learning and cognition.

RABBITBRUSH (*CHRYSOTHAMNUS NAUSEOSUS*)

Rabbitbrush essence enables the Gemini mind to focus on the single point value of a perspective, event, or task while perceiving the wholeness in life's events. The ability to simultaneously hold polarities in one's awareness grounds a direct practical knowledge of the truth. The embrace of polarities is vital for the Gemini archetype to gain peace, stability, and contentment. The holographic psyche transcends duality in the light of seeing the integrative values within singularity. Remote, expanded, and focused views of life's events are upheld simultaneously, coexisting in the mind space of the Gemini archetype.

SCLERANTHUS (*SCLERANTHUS ANNUUS*)

Scleranthus essence infuses the Gemini psyche with clarity, so that it can view the full range of choice. Scleranthus supports the Gemini psyche in establishing an inner balance that synthesizes polarized events and choices.

The mercurial nature of the mind becomes more fluid to perceive life's choices through the lens of singularity. The perceiver views all options with an intuitive, objective power of clarity and knowing. Scleranthus enhances a direct communication link between the mind and the higher, self-aware psyche.

Scleranthus, a green-hued flower, cultivates an unshakeable knowing and a directive force that is aligned with one's soul's purpose. The psyche learns how to distinguish between the tendencies of the mind to waver in its attempts to review all possibilities versus the direct seeing that arises in one's awareness when sourced from the higher Self.

The Cancer Archetype

Ruled by the Moon

Water Element

Cardinal (Directive Energy)

Key Words: Water, cardinal, emotional mind, penetrating, hidden, subconscious, sensitive, creative, at home in self, nurturing, calm, flowing, feminine, attached, detached, sensual, gracious, charming, regenerating, feeling

The archetype of Cancer is governed by the water element, whose energetic quality is cardinal, or initiating. This cardinality implies that water, in its descent into the depths of the psyche, exhibits its primordial nature. The Cancerian archetype localizes its energies in the emotional aspect of the mind. Its watery nature falls under the influence of the ebb and flow of the moon's gravitational pull.

This malleability subjects the Cancerian nature to abrupt changes in mood. The Cancerian archetype can find itself withdrawing from the outer world of information and stimuli and putting on its protective coat of armor. This mechanism serves to protect what the Cancer experiences as its inner sanctuary of life. It has an inherent need to protect the finer feeling levels from the bombardment of the external world.

This insular nature of Cancer is necessary for cultivating a holy sanctuary in which it can retreat to integrate its secret treasures and insights. Here, it is capable of opening its protective but receptive shell and allowing the refined insights of the psyche to penetrate its core emotional nature.

The Cancerian archetype is prone to a loss of balance between its inner and outer flow of expression; it can be subject to hypersensitivity and emotional hyperbole. It then becomes unable to distinguish what is truly authentic (i.e. the pure Self, separate from any external force).

In its more mature stable state, the Cancerian archetype maintains balance on the mental and emotional levels. In such cases, this archetype is highly creative, charming, and sensitive, displaying a lot of purity and deep intuition into the nature of reality. The desire to be loving and nurturing, and to exhibit characteristics of both giving and receiving, is at the foundation of the Cancerian experience. A deep appreciation for a sense of safety and home are essential.

In the Cancerian archetype, there can be a tendency toward clinging or overattachment to people, places, or things. The emotional/mental nature of the Cancer can then become confused between the self-empowerment of independence and the illusionary power of dependence.

Cancerian people tend to be subject to psychosomatic illness, which they tend to identify as the source of their problems. Due to their ability to feel so strongly on the level of the body, they mirror their deepest emotions on the physical level, having a difficult time distinguishing between what is actually on the mental/emotional level and what is truly organic. This empathic resonance can be a great talent when cultured through yogic practice, but it can be a liability when the Cancer has not learned to psychically navigate the inner feeling realms of life.

Cancer governs the breasts, which are connected to the watery, lymphatic, cleansing, and nurturing element of life. The water element contains the regenerative aspect of life, which is associated with the pranic life force and the reservoir of one's vitality. This reservoir holds the psychic, regenerative, creative, and procreative energies. It finds its home in the sacral well chakra.

The water element's penetrating power also builds and sustains the life force energy through the subtle bodies. It simultaneously amplifies the senses while refining them, bringing about the capacity to utilize the finest levels of sensory information. Mastery of the Cancerian attributes cultivates heightened creativity, emotional freedom, spiritual cognition, and illumination.

The Cancerian archetype can often obsess over home and comfort. Cancerians will often feel the need to wander from place to place, looking for that perfect sense of home and security. This can make the usual homebody Cancer yearn to be a world traveler, which can bring about experiences that challenge his or her sense of personal safety. Cancerian archetypes are always seeking to feel at home wherever they are, even if the search is misplaced: the Cancerian archetype's deepest quest is to find peace, home, tranquility, and familiarity deep within the Self, thus allowing a sense of home base to be truly established.

PLANETARY GEMS/ELIXIRS FOR THE CANCER ARCHETYPE

PEARL AND MOONSTONE

The Pearl and the Moonstone are symbolic abodes for the lunar forces of nature. They resonate and embody the felt psychic powers of the collective consciousness. These gems bring to the surface the hidden aspects of emotional/mental operating systems in one's psyche. They purify the Cancerian aspect of the psyche that tends toward attachment and nostalgia.

Pearl and Moonstone elixirs graciously reveal barren thought-forms void of truth and reality. They magnify awareness to sort out the real from the imagined distortions of mind and emotion, attuning the individual to the lunar light of insight, wisdom, and creative intuition.

Pearl and Moonstone ultimately calm, nurture, and anchor the Cancerian aspect of the psyche into the depth of Self, where one finds true home. Here, the foundation of peace infuses the emotional ground of one's being. These gems activate the ground of fertility, heightening our sensitivity, sensibility, creativity, and procreative impulses. **They guide one into the primordial realms of being, so often hidden from plain view.** Like the oyster shell that opens to reveal the birth hatch of the pearl, the pearl opens the heart of the Cancerian psyche so that it can settle into the expansive abode of the soul.

FLOWER ESSENCES FOR THE CANCER ARCHETYPE

MUGWORT (*ARTEMESIA DOUGLASIANA*)

Mugwort is a key essence for the Cancerian archetype. Governed by the lunar forces of nature, it is a power plant that opens the psyche to the primordial realm of dreamtime, communicating directly to the soul through dreams and psychic images that impart information and insight into one's life and the nature of reality. Mugwort cultivates lucidity in both the solar daytime and lunar nighttime dream worlds, eliciting insights that create a balancing and harmonizing influence that stabilizes the mind and emotions.

Perception of the mechanics of dreamtime leads to the practical ability to gain command of how one creates personal reality. Mugwort lifts the veils between the inner and outer worlds, between the conscious and subconscious realms. A simultaneous awareness of the ebb and flow of the inner reflecting into the perception of the outer gradually reveals the soul's holographic landscape.

MARIPOSA LILY (*CALOCHORTUS LEICHTLINII*)

The central theme of the Mariposa Lily essence is to infuse the soul with the feminine principle of the Divine Mother. This essence supports the heart/mind to feel the deep reality of unconditional love for self and other. It assists the soul to develop the compassion that heals personal maternal soul history. As the psyche transmutes the scars from natal maternal imprints, the soul grows in its ability to embrace and transcend the human conditions life presents.

Mariposa Lily heals and opens the emotional body. It cultivates the felt presence of the maternal divine that emanates from within. This feminine divine presence moves the heart and mind toward kindness, caring, warmth, and a loving inclusion for all humanity. Mariposa Lily supports the Cancerian heart/mind to cultivate a deep feeling of belonging. It fortifies the soul to experience its place of home and peace from within. The renewed divine love imprinted in the soul develops an unshakeable capacity to flow with the tides of life.

BLACK-EYED SUSAN (*RUDBECKIA HIRTA*)

Black-Eyed Susan is an essence that activates the light of consciousness. It has a deep penetrating ability that illuminates hidden or buried aspects of the psyche. It assists the psyche to bring into light the shadow aspects of the personality that need to be healed, transformed, and integrated into the light of the soul. The Cancerian archetype has a natural tendency to bury the areas of the psyche where unresolved or traumatic experiences are too uncomfortable, thus creating psychosomatic conditions.

Black-Eyed Susan focuses the light of insight that dispels the darkness and shadow images of the psyche that have been locked in the subconscious. The essence catalyzes the Cancerian psyche to bring to the surface of conscious awareness all aspects of the self that call for healing, resolution, and integration. This process brings the Cancerian to a peaceful place within that is home.

The Leo Archetype

Ruled by the Sun

Fire Element

Fixed (Stabilizing Energy)

Key Words: Fixed, fire, supreme identity, solar power, vitality, strength, fearless action, leader, actualization, authentic, teacher, illumination, courage, spiritual realization, higher Self, self-absorption, recognition, power, success

The Leo archetype is a fixed sign governed by the fire element. The Leonine nature expresses a force that elicits others to revolve around its powerful solar presence. The Leo is radiant and charismatic. The central theme for Leo is the establishment of an illuminating identity that is eternally present and unshakeable. The Leo persona accesses its inner strength and courage to stand independently, so as not to be overshadowed by anyone or anything.

The journey of the Leo archetype is toward self-mastery and supreme identification of the God force within. Leos are led by their own nature to surrender to a centrifugal force that will ultimately bring them to a true spiritual center. The tendency of the Leo toward arrogance must be balanced by humble reflection on the importance of his or her place in the relative world. Equality is unity in spirit.

The fundamental need of the Leo archetype to be at the center of attention will often lead him or her to be the leader in group situations. These life situations might include sports, social circles, theater, music, politics, or other areas where being in the limelight is a key component of success. The Leo archetype leads one to seek out teaching or leadership positions, where the ability to garner support for one's beliefs, philosophy, or religious/social actions is paramount.

The egoic shell of the Leo archetype is shed through recognition of the soul/sun identity, which spawns inner wisdom. Spiritual realization leads the Leo beyond societal recognition and provides ultimate balance for the archetypal need for approval, attention, or recognition.

Leo is the lionhearted, heroic figure who is inspired to become a divine teacher of courageous love in action. The challenge for Leo is to harness the appetite for adventure, sexual exploits, and "living on the edge," with the discretion to know when risk is unnecessary or simply unwise. The Leo makes a great lawyer, politician, or other social advocate who is involved in issues of power. Ultimately, that power must be harnessed for the benefit of humanity.

The Leo has a tendency to be narcissistic or self-absorbed, which the Leo must overcome as he or she matures. This can ripen into an intuitive sense of one's place in the historical context of life, an inspiration to "make one's mark" on the world.

As the Leo archetype matures, he or she cultivates a state of authenticity, which transmits a visceral experience of the "I Am" Presence, unifying the threads of the light of consciousness as a singularity of Truth.

PLANETARY GEM/ELIXIR FOR THE LEO ARCHETYPE

RUBY (SUN)

Ruby vibrates in a sacred and holy space that inspires the Leo aspect of the psyche to surrender its pride. **Ruby elicits an initiative process of swallowing the light of God, which has the capacity to reveal the authentic nature of Self.** The core Self engages with life, impassioned by the momentum of the soul to express its glory and beauty. The innate spiritual powers, regal nature, and humble dignity encouraged by the Ruby are the actualizing forces that direct the inner life of the Leo archetype.

Ruby helps build vital life-force energy. The Leonine archetype is guided in his expressive and dramatic desires to achieve the highest potential in all endeavors. Ruby cultures strength, love, and passionate service. It transmits a solar regenerative energy whose range of influence reaches into the depths of physical and spiritual realms.

Ruby secures an authentic, integrative power that runs deep into the substructure of the Leo archetype. This fixed fire quality creates an unshakable throne that enables the Leo archetype to walk directly into the naked truth. It supports the Leo archetype to extract the inner knowledge and wisdom that is presented through such challenges. Ruby empowers the heart to assimilate life, creating an atmosphere of love, enthusiasm, reverence, and zest.

FLOWER ESSENCES FOR THE LEO ARCHETYPE

SUNFLOWER (*HELIONTHUS ANNUUS*)

Sunflower essence enables one to receive guidance and communication from the higher Self. The Leonine archetype accesses its core energy through the intelligence in light, which Sunflower absorbs throughout the day as it follows the sun. Sunflower attunes the egoic structure to the higher Self and facilitates inner knowledge. It teaches one to focus on the inner light of one's being, nourishing the Leonine archetype.

The solar energy of the Sunflower assists in healing masculine distortions in the psyche associated with fragmented imprinting from the father. Sunflower essence reinforces one's authentic identity by strengthening and balancing the masculine energy principle within. It further enlivens the universal masculine principle referred to as "Father."

Sunflower essence facilitates the radiant solar energy to shine through the persona. The Sunflower's center is created out of the pattern of the Golden Mean spiral, which lies beneath biological art. This sacred geometric pattern is the principle energy force of the Sunflower, which has both an expansive, open-ended effect and a focused, centering influence. The spiral dynamics in the sacred structure of the Sunflower empower the soul to radiate a Higher Self–generated identity. The warmth and depth of eternal being is then able to shine through.

Sunflower supports individual metamorphosis by enhancing the higher harmonics of one's inner golden light. This golden light has been iconically depicted as halos, or auric lights, around the heads of saints, angels, and other celestial beings. **As the higher harmonics of gold permeate the individual persona, one's identification shifts from the personal identity structure to that of the transpersonal "I."** This change in identity is sustained through alignment with the great central core Sun. The soul resonates with the brilliance of Truth. Leonine codes of conduct concerned with self-empowerment, confidence, directedness, honor, and creative leadership are calibrated through the strength of this transpersonal "I."

GOLDENROD (*SOLIDAGO CALIFORNICA*)

Goldenrod assists in the establishment of a positive, self-affirming framework to one's identity structure. It supports the development of an internal vertical axis that creates a strong sense of grounding and integration. When properly developed, this vertical axis gives the individual a strong sense of self, helping to integrate the grounded, practical, and stabilizing energies of earth with the cosmic energies of the higher Self.

The youthful spirit of the Leonine archetype is heightened through this vertical axis. Animated participation in human life is anchored in a psycho-spiritual stance that integrates both vertical and horizontal movement. The lines of force that represent the direct soul-generated impulses are played out in the field of life. Goldenrod supports equilibrium and sustains balance on the inner and outer fields of reality.

MULLEIN (*VERBASCUM THAPSUS*)

Mullein flower essence exemplifies an inherent dignity of spirit that shatters illusion and deception. This essence infuses light into the soul to brighten awareness and raise one's consciousness. Mullein invites one to examine one's motives and values, which are conditions of the personality. One cultivates the capacity to listen and respond to life from a position of inner truth, gained through access to the higher Self.

The capacity to take right action is based on a heightened awareness of a deeper level of meaning. One becomes able to discern the flow of life out of which one's action will be taken. This becomes the basis for the Leo archetype to awaken to deeper levels of inner knowledge.

Mullein facilitates a Self-Realization process that strengthens the Leo's ability to stand in truth and freedom with a high degree of spiritual certainty. The qualities of inner listening, clear choice, and decisive action are fostered through this essence, empowering the Leo archetype to be guided by soul wisdom.

The Virgo Archetype

Ruled by Mercury

Earth Element

Mutable (Changing Energy)

Key Words: Earth, mutable, predictable, detailed, seeks knowledge, healing, abundance, perfectionist, analytical, orderliness, obsession, anxiety, details, intellectual, resolution, relentless, appreciation for Nature, grounded, practical

The Virgo archetype is exemplified by the mutable earth energy. He or she is grounded, patient, practical, and attentive to detail, with an affinity for healing the earth. The Virgo archetype is sensitive to the feeling level in Nature, with the capacity to be a good herbalist, gardener, midwife, or landscaper. He or she can be very self-critical and judgmental.

This archetype is usually highly intelligent, articulate, and creative. However, attention to detail can cause the Virgo to be too great a perfectionist, overly concerned with the minor intricacies of life on physical and mental levels. The life journey of Virgos enables them to experience deeper levels of self-love and self-acceptance, essential for them to expand their compassion and become less critical of themselves and others.

One of the central themes for many of the spirited Virgo archetype is a soul-level mission that renews the earth and its inhabitants. The Virgo individual is often likely to be involved in service positions in which he or she can exercise his or her deep concerns for the inner and outer environment and the process of Self-actualization.

The Virgo is attracted to professions that challenge his or her technical and artistic self-mastery. He or she perceives the environment through an aesthetic field of resonance. Virgos have a deep appreciation for the intricate beauty of inner order that underlies all of creation. Examples of such areas of endeavor are mathematics, alchemy, veterinary medicine, human medicine, chiropractic, psychotherapy, technical writing, graphic arts, and other professions in which proficiency in analytical reasoning and synthesis is essential.

The Virgo archetype is associated with fertility and the harvest of the bounties of the earth. The Virgo must seek to become more lighthearted, playful, and able to create time and space for stillness and rest in the activity of everyday life.

This archetype may need to clarify the confusing and wayward impulses of the mind. By engaging the heart more fully, the Virgo learns to solve internal conflicts. This lessens the tendency toward anxiety and obsession. Unless these mental tendencies are addressed, the Virgo persona is relentless and driven. Such distortions, elicited by the shadow aspect of the Virgo, feed control issues, greed, and jealousy. The cultivation of feelings of gratefulness, appreciation, and generosity release the captured Virgo spirit from the confines of a limited mind.

The mantra of the Virgo archetype is perfection; Virgos seek to be masters of all they do. The Virgo can be highly sensitive and intellectually intuitive. The mind is also one of the Virgo's greatest assets and a source of power. The Virgo possesses a marked ability to excel in intelligence of a mundane nature, as well as in unconventional esoteric knowledge. The Virgo is a great synthesizer of universal truth.

Once humility has been cultivated, this archetype is able to discern the difference between the elegance of divine design and the demands of a recalcitrant ego structure. The quick and sharp nature of the Virgo mind turned inward acts as a refined spiritual instrument that can rid the psyche of outworn mental characteristics. The truth of the heart, witnessed through its own compassionate lens, fosters self-acceptance and recognition of the power of the Earth Mother. As the Virgo archetype matures, he or she is given the spiritual grace of harvesting the sacred fruits of transcendental service.

The Virgo soul has a deep resonance with the green ray of the Earth. The prolific presence of green provides the soul of the Virgo with life-giving support, renewal, and nourishment. As the Virgo archetype cultivates a stable and secure feeling of abundance, the capacity to share with the inhabitants of the Earth grows like leaves upon the tree of humanity.

PLANETARY GEM/ELIXIR FOR THE VIRGO ARCHETYPE

EMERALD (MERCURY)

The Emerald green frequency expands the feeling level of the heart, culturing appreciation, gratefulness, and generosity. The Virgo clings to order, detail, and perfection as a finite state; Emerald cultures a deep sense of appreciation and beauty inherent in the changing states of life.

Through the use of Emerald elixir, the heart grows into a greater experience of compassion. The mind is no longer forced to compulsively perceive imperfections in the relative world. Emerald attunes the mercurial, analytical mind to higher levels of heartfelt discrimination. Through its use, one gains the capacity to synthesize what was previously perceived to be disparate bodies of knowledge. The analytical mind is liberated from its bound state and begins functioning from an integrated, holistic, felt perception that is heart based.

Emerald possesses the power to activate the intuition and attain new levels of creative intelligence. This promotes tolerance through acceptance and diminishes the tendency towards a rigid, hypercritical perspective. The chromatic tone of Emerald green softens the edge of anxiety and calms the driven nervous system. The power to forgive oneself and others matures into a state of compassion and peace. The heart is nourished from a well of gratitude for the natural state of existence.

FLOWER ESSENCES FOR THE VIRGO ARCHETYPE

BEECH (*FAGUS SYLVATICA*)

Beech essence quells the critical attitudes of the Virgo mind. It addresses the wounded and dissociated psyche, which clings to the defensive and blaming character of the ego-mind in its attempt to protect itself from condemnation. This habit of mind develops due to critical and harsh evaluation from early social and parental attitudes. A hard exterior character projects and protects through judgment, self-righteousness, intolerance, and perfectionism. Such a shell arises from the need to separate from the pain of believing oneself to be inferior and inadequate.

Beech essence releases a soft and warming balm from the soul that nourishes the emotional and mental bodies. The essence provides a safe cushion to transform and release one's rigid views of the world, others, and most of all, oneself.

Through the nurturing essence of Beech, the Virgo archetype attains a true strength of character that is forgiving, accepting, patient, kind, and receptive to the differences life presents. In the spacious realms of the psyche and feeling body, the Virgo finds a true inner nature that is loving and deeply attuned to the divine. As Beech supports the Virgo archetype to soften the boundaries of definition, intrinsic goodness in heart and peace of mind radiate into the environment and guide the Virgo's life.

VERVAIN (*VERBENA OFFICINALIS*)

Vervain essence neutralizes the fiery intensity of the Virgo's rigid thinking and beliefs, allowing their innate earthly energies to seek a more natural expression. Vervain essence attunes the Virgo persona to the mind/body connection and enables these two expressions of consciousness to function in unison. This growing unity of mind/body frees the Virgo archetype to cultivate his or her finely intuitive sensing body. This in turn allows the measurement and structures of the mind to divine deep truths that inspire and lead, and to dissolve the doldrums that cloud one's spirited nature. Vervain creates the clarity of distinction that imparts wisdom and strength from the higher Self.

HOUND'S TONGUE (*CYNOGLOSSUM GRANDE*)

Hound's Tongue attunes the mind to a refined level of intuitive holistic thinking. This innate style of intuitive thinking is based on the psychic network that allows awareness to be awake to both the physical and non-physical levels of reality. Often, the analytical and cynical mind of the Virgo is entrapped by the material world and spins a web of thinking around matters. The mind separates from its subtle awareness and denies the experience of spiritual presence.

Modern analytical values, materialism, and survival fears dull the Virgo psyche and take it captive. Hound's Tongue essence elevates the overly earthbound psyche so that it can view life and events with spacious objectivity. The Virgo can then bathe in a deep love for the beauty of Earth and its inhabitants. **Hound's Tongue lightens the mind of matter to allow a**

comprehensive wholeness and reverence for life. This awakens the gift of spiritual cognition.

The Libra Archetype

Ruled by Venus

Air Element

Cardinal (Directive Energy)

Key Words: Air, cardinal, balanced, grace, justice, equality, ultimate truth, purity of knowledge, spiritual illumination, relationship, social interactiveness, equilibrium, honor, loyalty, trust, fairness, seeks approval

The Libran archetype is governed by the air element, with strong tendencies toward connectedness, communication, and evaluation. The Libra persona must find inner balance in every nuance of life. The capacity to see the truth in its multiple forms and weigh each aspect is pivotal to the Libran psyche. A deep sense of truth, honor, fairness, and justice are inherent characteristics of their persona.

Libras seek to reconcile the relative condition of duality with the higher knowledge of Unity. Until they have relinquished their beliefs and mental positions, Libras' high ideals about Truth can potentially lead to conflict in this effort. Libras often find themselves endlessly evaluating and weighing the merits of life's every encounter and situation.

The shadow aspect of the persona of Librans drives them to seek identity outside their own inner context. The emotional mind can become confused through social malleability and the strains of obligation inherent in humanitarian service. This may lead to a loss of center and the adaptation of a cloaking mechanism; the psyche develops elaborate defenses that rob the Libra of his or her true spiritual power.

The Libra archetype struggles to align his or her deep desire to alleviate the sufferings of humanity through an authentic expression of the Self. The synthesis of this and other innate tendencies previously mentioned is gained through deep introspection of the archetypal underworld or subconscious realms of the "pleaser." The integration of altruism and authentic creative action is the hallmark of success in the Libran odyssey.

The challenge of the Libran archetype is to be the master of the scales of life, using discernment and discrimination rather than judgment as a means of restoring a sense of balance and order. Knowledge is ultimately found in the "hall of two truths" (relative and Absolute), where the Libran can comfortably reside. Here, both aspects of reality are true at their own level and the use of analytical judgment is seen to have been an illusion. The **higher-octave Libran archetype is capable of seeing that Divine Truth has no need for judgment of this nature; it sees reality as it is.**

The Libran archetype learns to discern through the feeling/knowing body. This is central to the wholeness and wellness of the mental body. For the Libran archetype, equilibrium is a fundamental condition of reality that must be lived on the highest spiritual level. The Libra persona carries in its psyche the sword of truth that cuts through all levels of reality, gaining entry into the inner chambers of the higher mind. Here, wisdom and higher knowledge rest in the dimensions of the eternal; oneness and harmony exist as a state of balance.

The Libra persona perceives the field of relationship to be the primary arena for learning life's lessons. The Libran archetype has a need to relate to people from all walks of life. This archetype is compelled to reform individuals or groups; it therefore seeks to engage with social/political organizations. Their interpersonal dynamics focus on liberation and any fundamental conditions that limit personal freedom.

The Libran seeks to reach a state of equanimity in which he or she has outgrown the deep internal pressure to weigh and pass judgment on personal and global issues. Libran archetypes learn to utilize their psycho-spiritual insight and compassion, leading to a natural state of equilibrium. The mature Libran gains the capacity to experience peace in spiritual detachment, acceptance, and surrender.

PLANETARY GEMS/ELIXIRS FOR THE LIBRA ARCHETYPE

DIAMOND AND WHITE SAPPHIRE

Diamond and White Sapphire elixirs, which are both used for astrological and Ayurvedic remediation, enhance the ability of the Libra archetype to move through life with clarity, ease, and grace. They culture fullness and contentment of heart, promoting a deep level of acceptance of life and its inexplicable events. Seeing what is, nothing more or less, brings into focus the eternal transformational point of balance that yields stillness.

The scales of life reveal a living, creative, moment-to-moment process of balance without end. Truth is not static. It represents the absolute at the junction point of manifest creation, the still point. It is here that the events of past, present, and future are weighed and measured to sustain the equilibrium of life. Diamond and White Sapphire elixirs balance the brain, supporting whole-brain functioning.

Diamond and White Sapphire gems transmit the clear ray of white light. When viewed from different angles, they generate prismatic effects that reveal multiple colors concealed in the spectrum of wholeness. This example of diversity expressed in the unified singularity is like the mind that seeks understanding of all it sees.

The light of the Diamond contains a composite of the full and focused spectrum as it readies itself to give birth to the colors of diversity. **The light released from the Diamond elixir purifies and illuminates the psyche, facilitating the ability to view life, circumstances, situations, people, and events through a multifaceted perspective that transcends the analysis of the mind.**

The Libran mind attempts to make sense of, evaluate, and judge reality in expectation that the absolute state of truth will be revealed. Diamond and White Sapphire gem elixirs cultivate a unified quality of perception that arises out of acceptance of what is. This is a direct realization of truth and knowledge that transcends the ability of the common mind to analyze the virtues of justice, fairness, balance, and cause and effect. "Knowledge is structured in consciousness," as Maharishi Mahesh Yogi stated.

The Diamond mind of the Libran archetype attains personal self-mastery through a delicate and fluid balance in the art of living. Through Diamond and White Sapphire elixirs, the heart expands to embrace the experience of beauty. Thus, in this process of expansion, the heart begins to infuse the mind with the clarity and ability to adjust inner and outer perceptions.

Diamond and White Sapphire elixirs attune awareness to resonate with the highest order of divine design. This state reaches beyond a fixed intellectual notion of Truth and Beauty, Fairness and Justice. The elixirs enhance the mind to move past the illusion of duality, creating unification of polarized energies. This brings about both physical and mental dexterity. Truth is realized out of a unified space that holds opposite values as a center point of neutral perspective.

The elixirs of Diamond and White Sapphire elevate the psyche to surrender mental analysis and receive Divine Grace. Illumination transmutes the Libran tendency to perpetuate the lower court of the mind. A more celestial perspective on justice emerges that reveals an innate symmetry, fluid balance, and impeccable perfection in all things. One learns to see with the Eye of God.

FLOWER ESSENCES FOR THE LIBRA ARCHETYPE

GOLDENROD (*SOLIDAGO CALIFORNICA*)

Goldenrod essence supports the soul in establishing a deep state of centeredness. It assists the Libran persona to shift its point of reference from an externalized position of social approval to an inner core of strength and authenticity. Goldenrod infuses the social nature of the Libra with a more authentic vision that can shore up the natural tendencies of the Libra towards social justice.

The essence of Goldenrod strengthens the line of vertical energy in the individual. This vertical golden staff creates an anchor into the earth's core that serves as a grounded point of reference. The properly rooted vertical energy clarifies and matures the Libran psyche to function as an autonomous being governed from within a central vertical core, bridging heaven and earth, relative and absolute. The establishment of this vital vertical grounding supports the equanimity that Libra thrives on.

SCLERANTHUS (*SCLERANTHUS ANNUUS*)

Scleranthus flower essence infuses the mind with a crystalline clarity. This enables the Libran archetype to see surrounding points of view, choices, and perspectives with an integrative eye. To see multiple perspectives is the social nature of Libras, yet it is difficult for them to make clear and firm decisions or choices. The confusion arises out of over-identification with "other" and an inability to locate their core identity and central point of reference.

Scleranthus connects one's soul with one's vital core center to create

a grounded and stable force of knowing. As the soul stabilizes its vital energy, the mind follows. Scleranthus aligns the pathways of communication between the soul, higher mind, and heart. As this subtle-body alignment allows for the information exchange to flow freely, the Libran archetype gains self-mastery in making decisions and choices that are empowered with the soul's purpose and passion, and the realization of the Libran's core essence.

CORN (*ZEA MAYS*)

Corn, or Maize, is a sacred native plant of the American Indians. It is used in ceremonial worship as an offering of gratitude to the elements and spirit guardians of the earth. Maize is a primary staple of life and nourishment. Corn essence can serve as a vital force that plays a key role in grounding and centering the Libran archetype. This is especially true in dense social environments where it may be difficult to find one's bearings.

Corn strengthens the life force that enables the Libran to live and thrive in crowded, contained, or small spaces. These social conditions are challenging to the Libra archetype, as it seeks to maintain balance between heaven and earth, spirit and matter. Corn essence integrates the vertical and horizontal axes of life. The Libran's horizontal tendency to overextend socially can inhibit the ability to actualize a rooted interconnectedness with Mother Earth. Corn essence supports the soul in its desire to be fully embodied; a stable nexus is created between the heart's winged horizontal expansion and a vertical grounded trajectory.

CHERRY PLUM (*PRUNUS CERASIFERA*)

Cherry Plum flower essence assists the mind in gaining trust when organic shifts occur in the function of awareness, from the common analytical processes of the brain toward a more direct cognitive and intuitive knowing. Cherry Plum energetically encourages the personality to surrender doubt and fear, thus allowing fertile conditions for the innate qualities of trust and knowingness on a soul level.

For the Libra archetype, this means overcoming the fear of losing control and breaking with the familiar conditions that bind the Libran psyche.

Cherry Plum softens defense mechanisms that create an artificial dominance in action and behavior. Cherry Plum essence energetically adjusts inner and outer reality so that daily events unfold synchronistically in the stream of cosmic timing. This organic order of being allows for a spacious opening for the soul to know an unconditional state of profound surrender and ease.

CALENDULA (*CALENDULA OFFICINALIS*)

Calendula is an important flower essence in training awareness to perceive the power of creation through sound and vibration. It integrates the capacities to both transmit and receive psycho-spiritual information vital to the Libra archetype. Libras are communicators; speaking, listening, and truly hearing the meaning of a message is intrinsic to their ability to establish a harmonious exchange of energy.

Calendula flower essence enhances the receptivity of the sense of hearing, entraining both speaker and listener. This heightened sensitivity cross-references to merge information from acoustic, visual, and kinesthetic levels. This is exemplified by the gift of synesthesia, the capacity to hear the sound value embedded in visual imagery (for example, one looks at a painting and hears tones and sounds associated with the images therein).

Through Calendula, the quality of listening takes on a deep experience of sonic contemplation that is experienced through the subtle energy bodies. Calendula opens these subtle bodies to receive the impulses of information communicated externally and internally. These messages are sent from the language centers of another individual or from a telepathic internal level self-generated in the brain.

Calendula essence opens one's ability to listen at the level of the originating impulse, beyond the intellectual meaning of words. Expanded awareness of the spoken word can create bliss, silence, and healing or the feeling of disharmony in the mind/body. Heightened sensitivity to how sound and vibration are organized creates resonance with the subtle patterns of energy within oneself and others. Self-mastery in the Libra archetype includes this heightened sensitivity of how word and vibration influence oneself and others.

The Scorpio Archetype

Ruled by Mars (Eastern Vedic) and Pluto (Western)

Water Element

Fixed (Stabilizing Energy)

Key Words: Water, fixed, transformation, unknowable, unseen, unfathomable, primordial power, sexual fire and passion, regeneration, renewal, hidden mysteries, transmutation, death, collective unconscious, power

The Scorpio archetype is governed by the fixed quality of the water element. The stationary quality provides the Scorpio psyche with a deep and penetrating focus. The Scorpio psyche seeks to delve into the underworld of reality to find the hidden meaning of life and the processes of creation.

The Scorpio can take a very sharp and aggressive approach to the mysteries of life. Its quest is to enter into the mystical regions of the psyche where most fear to go. In search of new life, Scorpio passion uncovers the dark, lifeless areas of existence. This passion, if ill-guided, may lead the Scorpio persona to wander aimlessly into the perilous covert operations within the collective unconscious.

The Scorpio archetype is seen by many as seductive, mysterious, secretive, hidden, and unknowable. In fact, the Scorpio archetype embodies all these characteristics of nature. The Scorpio has innate tendency to gain knowledge and power through the hidden and esoteric mysteries of life and creation. He or she comes to terms with the creative force of manifestation and power by exploring the art and science of the regenerative forces.

The Scorpio persona will find itself consciously or unconsciously confronting primordial fears and its own subconscious conditioning and thought forms. The most primordial fear that we carry as a species is the fear of death; the Scorpio archetype carries the innate power to enter into death's twilight realms. In each moment of breath, the Scorpio holds the opportunity to step through death's door, gaining profound insight into the meaning of life.

The Scorpio individual can learn to transmute the psyche through discovery of the mystical transpersonal process of resurrection. As an initiate in the mystery schools of life, the individual emerges from the illusion of death as a static, unchanging state. The Scorpio can experience the twilight of death as a gateway to the rebirth of the Spirit.

The Scorpio archetype is deeply involved with the process of transformation. As the persona matures, it assumes a profound willingness to transmute energy to higher octaves. Energy can take the form of mental beliefs, crystallized emotional attitudes and patterns, physical dis-ease, or fixity in what appear to be higher, more obscure psychic and spiritual ideologies.

The path of the Scorpio reveals the invisible dimensions of the collective unconscious. The higher-octave Scorpio often commits to soul contracts that support the collective transmutation of mass consciousness, thereby bringing the human species to the threshold of evolutionary, life-supporting jumps in the collective paradigm.

The Scorpio's fascination with the collective unconscious causes it to be attracted to the purges that occur throughout history. The individual is able to swim in the underbelly of political and social unrest, delineating the faulty structures that uphold personal, social, and political ills. He or she seeks to de-fragment and upturn the karmic and ancestral patterns that bind humanity to the self-created illusions that activate negative mass consciousness shifts. As the Scorpio archetype awakens in its individual purpose, it brings about events that challenge and overturn oppression—such as the 2011 uprising in Egypt. This event exemplifies the collective unconscious becoming activated on a mass level to shift global consciousness and magnetize global awareness to the humanitarian issues of liberation, freedom, and equality—fundamental birthrights of every human being.

The higher-octave soul desire of the Scorpio archetype is to break free from outmoded structures of belief, religion, government, and institutions. In such an archetype, the personal identity structure finds itself consumed by the transpersonal collective meaning and destiny of humanity. It begins to function personally in the light of the transpersonal for the good of all. **The Scorpio psyche has the potential to bring transformational forces and higher intelligence into a direct meeting ground with the unfathomable and mysterious underpinnings of the collective psyche.**

PLANETARY GEMS/ELIXIRS FOR THE SCORPIO ARCHETYPE

RED CORAL (MARS–VEDIC)

Red Coral supports the Scorpio archetype by alchemically merging the fire and water elements. Red Coral functions as a ballast between the deep well of the psycho-emotional and the grounding influence of the physical body. The balance of fire and water keeps the Scorpio psyche from sinking deep into the lower astral plane of mental perception.

In its darker moments, the Scorpio may lack the heartfelt discrimination to know how to implement its revolutionary insight in a constructive manner. Red Coral assists the individual in maintaining clarity, steadiness, courage, and inner stability. It directs the primordial impulses of the Scorpio psyche to bring forth actions that constitute renewal and regeneration.

CAT'S EYE (PLUTO–WESTERN)

Cat's Eye is indicated for the spiritually advanced Scorpio archetype. Having gained mastery over one's temperament, the mature Scorpio is able to keep a check and balance over his or her psychic forces. He or she is then able to open to the inherent knowledge of Cat's Eye while maintaining equilibrium and fearless stability. The razor-sharp clarity of discernment is essential for the Scorpio to distinguish truth from illusion, since the psyche is filled with self-projected distortions that seek to play out in the false ground of the mental field.

Cat's Eye activates a penetrating psychic force intended to reveal the reality of hidden truth within the psyche. In this process, the steadying of fluctuations in the core of the Scorpio's emotional being empowers inner vision with unifying clarity.

Cat's Eye assists the psyche to rectify and outlaw outmoded points of reference. Through its use, an individual surrenders to the death of the egoic shell that binds the personality to habit and conformity.

Cat's Eye activates the Scorpio archetype to spiritual vision and regeneration. The gem distills psychic spiritual energy, condensing it to a densely packed locus of spiritual information able to access the seamless past, present, and future regions of personal and universal consciousness.

FLOWER ESSENCES FOR THE SCORPIO ARCHETYPE

BLACK-EYED SUSAN (*RUDBECKIA HIRTA*)

The essence of Black-Eyed Susan focuses the inner light of awareness upon the shadowy or hidden aspects of the psyche. The activation of this transformative power of illumination helps the soul to see through hidden psycho-emotional boundaries, shedding the conditions, patterns of belief, and lingering fears in the psyche. Through the assistance of Black-Eyed Susan, the individual is no longer bound to worn-out defenses and secretive subjugation of creative power.

The focused light of Black-Eyed Susan has the magical potency to resurrect and release the dying soul from suffering due to denial or disassociation. When these fragmented aspects of the psyche are healed and integrated into the light of consciousness, a great surge of life-force energy becomes available.

QUEEN ANNE'S LACE (*DAUCUS CAROTA*)

Queen Anne's Lace is commonly called wild carrot. It roots itself deeply into the ground while yielding a refined and delicate symmetry woven into the white flower. The essence of the flower supports the subtle feeling-body in establishing a grounded state of being. It assists the Scorpio psyche in opening the higher chakras towards greater extrasensory perception, while stabilizing psycho-emotional tendencies in the personality structure.

Queen Anne's Lace facilitates a balanced and clear opening of visionary insight into the hidden psychic and spiritual realms. This is an essential key for the Scorpio psyche, whose innate characteristic is to integrate the invisible realms of reality. **The mundane levels of life are pierced by the awakened insight of the soul through the use of Queen Anne's Lace essence.** The individual psyche is infused with the delicate but vibrant blueprint of the flower, which opens one into core evolutionary change.

This flower essence attunes the soul to the implicate order that underlies material reality. The Scorpio psyche is blessed with the illumination of collective wisdom, which aids the actualization of human potential.

CANYON DUDLEYA (*DUDLEYA CYMOSA*)

Canyon Dudleya essence supports the psyche in remaining balanced and objective in the expanded state of extrasensory perception. This essence is especially indicated at times when the Scorpio persona is overly involved with dramatizing the psycho-emotional life of inner psychic events.

Overstimulation from the challenge of personal drama can cause the Scorpio psyche to leak valuable energy. In the process of communication, the diminishment of power creates an unconscious need to recover life force through pulling on the strength of another's auric field. Authentic expression is founded on a benign reciprocal movement between energetic fields.

Canyon Dudleya supports the Scorpio psyche to gain a telepathic resonance with the core self and the environment. This leads to divine knowledge of the practices of inner containment and benevolent action in the environment. The desired outcome is a state of inner contentment that is not passive but channels psycho-emotional energy toward productive domains of interaction. Canyon Dudleya shifts the focus of soul attention to access the holographic field of self-nourishment.

The Sagittarian Archetype

Ruled by Jupiter

Fire Element

Mutable (Changing Energy)

Key Words: Fire, mutable, unbounded, inspirational, expansive, light, idealistic, knowledgeable, wisdom aspirant, optimistic, joy, enthusiastic, unrealistic, knowledge synthesizer

The Sagittarian archetype is governed by the mutable fire element. The changing characteristics of the fire element foster spontaneity, which reaches into broad and expansive dimensions. The Sagittarian is inner-directed and driven by a transpersonal dynamism.

The impassioned Sagittarian spirit identifies its direction and goals with a positive, unstoppable momentum. The Sagittarian is swift in action and charismatically capable of impressing others with brilliant, ever radiant potential.

The capacity of the Sagittarian archetype is to see into the opportunities and frameworks available in the higher worlds. *Limitation* is not a word that lives in the Sagittarian psyche. The individual aspires to heights that others would be incapable of envisioning. Where most people would perceive obstacles originating out of mind, emotion, or actuality, the Sagittarian hurdles over any boundary. For the Sagittarian, roadblocks are opportunities to reroute the psyche and engage in a new direction or paradigm.

Sagittarian archetypes have the capacity to bring about a limitless dimension of higher ideologies and potentials. Sagittarian archetypes can be definitive, convincing, and noble in performance. The archetype exhibits an altruistic nature and a tendency to aim for the pinnacle of all that is ideal in life.

The Sagittarian is most comfortable reconfiguring reality to support expansive cosmic views. This may create a tendency to overstep the natural laws of order or the simple life sequences that are the foundation for success. The overly enthusiastic nature of the Sagittarian psyche forges a persona that is apt to forego the necessary prerequisites in the learning curve. The Sagittarian wants to run before learning to walk.

This leads to an exceptional tolerance for risk and dramatic intervention. The Sagittarian will often make a premature entrance onto the stage of life; his or her arrogant confidence can prompt shortcuts that leap over time-treasured measures of spiritual progress. This can lead to an optimistic and free-form articulation of new life endeavors or a "fall-on-one's-face" type of personal dilemma.

The noble Sagittarian archetype has a profound gift to articulate, synthesize, and organize large volumes of knowledge that originate from higher creative planes of reality. The higher mind is engaged in the function of overseeing things from a bigger picture. This takes the Sagittarian on a long journey into the outer realms of the psyche to investigate and probe into the nature of reality and the subtle structures of celestial architecture.

The Sagittarian is a universal artist, blending the forces of creation into a unified wholeness. The Sagittarian archetype excels in his or her ability to dwell in the lofty vibrational frequencies, sometimes forgetting to look back to see that not all of reality is up to speed.

The Sagittarian archetype is a performance artist. On the canvas of time, Sagittarians paint a picture of greatness and potentiality that is irrefutable in its truthful pursuit of the absolute level of ideal existence. The nature of the Sagittarian psyche is to enter the unbounded future of all possibility and potentiality. This often causes the Sagittarian persona to be thrown back to the past in order to recalibrate realities that it failed to consider on a realistic level.

Authenticity on the soul level is of the utmost importance, as the Sagittarian archetype matures towards its destined nobility, especially in the spiritual worlds. This allows for simultaneous levels of truth to be revealed in different strata of consciousness. Thus, the Sagittarian archetype gains the wisdom, mastery, and insight to navigate in and out of the planes of reality that serve its highest destiny.

PLANETARY GEM/ELIXIR FOR THE SAGITTARIAN ARCHETYPE

YELLOW SAPPHIRE (JUPITER)

Yellow Sapphire radiates the planetary influence of Jupiter. The gem infuses the spirit with lightness of being, joy, optimism, and insight into the higher mind. Yellow Sapphire enlivens intelligence. It illuminates awareness and enhances insight into the superconscious aspect of mind. Yellow Sapphire bridges conscious and subconscious awareness. The procurement through Yellow Sapphire of a subtle, heightened knowledge into the depths of spiritual wisdom creates a new order for advanced neuro-processing.

Yellow Sapphire enhances the ability to adhere to the demands of inner life and express this guidance in grounded action. It cultures the Sagittarian psyche to synthesize great volumes of knowledge and expound upon the intricacies of manifest creation. The Sagittarian persona maintains its equilibrium through establishing a platform of higher wisdom that responds gracefully to the demands of everyday life.

Yellow Sapphire incrementally lifts awareness into light-filled realms, where knowledge, wisdom, and truth become matters of destiny. This gives the Sagittarian archetype the capacity to originate ceremonial practices that uplift the human species. The cognition of finer and finer levels of spiritual perception is the basis for spiritual practices that guide others toward their highest potential.

FLOWER ESSENCES FOR THE SAGITTARIAN ARCHETYPE

CALIFORNIA POPPY (*ESCHSCHOLZIA CALIFORNICA*)

California Poppy flower essence embodies an important energy signature for the Sagittarian archetype. It grows prolifically in areas where gold is found; California Poppy holds the promise of wealth in the physical and spiritual realms. However, the caveat that "all that glitters is not gold" holds true here. The shadow pattern of the Sagittarian archetype can cause Sagittarians to be attracted to leaders, organizations, and spiritual practices or substances that can enchant and blind the psyche.

California Poppy strengthens the moral ether that infuses into the individual a willingness to utilize the light to see into the shadow. California Poppy supports the psyche in its ability to gain discrimination and discernment based on clear reflections of the soul. As the soul reflects the light from within, the individual loses the need for repetitive use of alcohol, drugs, or practices that are short-lived and offer only fleeting glimpses of other realities.

California Poppy provides a sense of true security and equanimity for the soul. It attunes the psyche to the higher harmonics of gold that cultivate compassion and soul wisdom. As the Sagittarian psyche plumbs the core of being, the path of contemplation and self-reflection can more easily satisfy the craving for love, totality, and freedom. This level of inspired living opens one to a full union with divine love, as the ever-seeking Sagittarian finds a home in the stable, ecstatic, spiritual Heart.

STAR TULIP (*CALOCHORTUS TOLMIEI*)

Star Tulip flower essence enhances the journey of the Sagittarian archetype into the subtler realms of the human spirit. It gently opens the psyche to higher worlds of intelligence that enable the individual to attune to holographic information and divine inspiration. This essence harmonizes the Sagittarian persona with the guidance of the higher Self.

As deep levels of psyche and soul become integrated, one's range of influence is enhanced. Choices arise in one's awareness from direct communication with the soul. Star Tulip opens the channels of receptivity to inner hearing, thus infusing the psyche with visionary information gained through direct contact with the spiritual forces within one's life.

ANGELICA (*ANGELICA ARCHANGELLICA*)

Angelica flower essence can play an important role in the path to self-inquiry. As a spiritual aspirant such as the Sagittarian archetype moves deeper into the quest for truth, the need to shed the skin of forgetfulness leaves the individual in a delicately open position. This vulnerability is necessary to the enhancement of higher vibratory influences that open the seeker to the presence of the God Light.

The intensity of this experience produces the "burning bush" quality that can deeply imprint the voice of God. It can also create challenges to the equilibrium of the individual. Angelica strengthens the auric field so that it can serve as a protective shield of light.

Angelica also assists the feeling-body in gaining the mortal strength to tolerate direct contact with the angelic realms and beyond. This catalyzes a process that leads to recognition of the Self as Divine. As sensitivity is both heightened and aligned, the individual is able to extend the sense of radiant self-renewal into the environment as a whole.

CLEMATIS (*CLEMATIS VITALBA*)

Clematis flower essence is integral to the Sagittarian archetype. It assists the persona to ground, focus, and maintain Presence. The Sagittarian moves back and forth between time zones in the psyche, retrieving visionary information useful to present action.

Clematis essence has the vine-like quality to travel from the ground to the highest points of sky-based reality. It provides the safety for the Sagittarian psyche to climb to its highest levels of aptitude. Having strengthened connectivity with the body/mind, the Sagittarian can fulfill its life hopes and dreams.

Clematis creates the depth of inner focus that lends divine effectiveness to the eclectic spirit of the Sagittarian psyche. Once the Sagittarian perceives its status as eternal and self-regenerating, it is able to lift itself to the highest realms of productivity without leaving the ground state of Being.

The Capricorn Archetype

Ruled by Saturn

Earth Element

Cardinal (Directive Energy)

Key Words: Earth, cardinal, practical, self-actualization, achievement, organization, timekeeper, enduring, persevering structure, function, forms, systems, grounded, task-driven, boundaries, limitations, obstacles, rigidity, conventional, humorous, instinctual

The Capricorn archetype expresses its essence as the cardinal earth element. Its essential nature identifies and shapes primordial structures that give rise to stability in life. This archetype exerts a gravitational pull that originates deep within one's innate being.

The instinctual urge to master the world of form gives the Capricorn dominion over the world of pure space. The Capricorn initiates through physical form; its world is expressed through concrete structures, systems, institutions, and methodologies that advance earthbound reality. The choice of career or life purpose is grounded in a sense of practicality inspired by the doctrine of Spirit.

This archetype also learns best through the rudimentary principles that give rise to the physical world. Capricorn is sensitive to the fluctuating rhythms of organic process. It strives to define structure without losing creative vitality. The nature of the Capricorn archetype is persevering, steadfast, and resilient at overcoming obstacles. Practicality guides individuals over, around, or under an obstacle, returning them to their goal-oriented path.

The Capricorn archetype is compelled to explore the kinesthetic domain. Acceptance and appreciation of physicality is expressed in the worship of the body as a temple. The individual is lured by the thrill of sexual expression and the possibilities of the infinite variety of tactile sensation. In fact, Capricorn yearns to explore multiple forms of physical and sexual expression. This individual has the potential to become a powerhouse in mastering the primordial impulses of the body.

Capricorn archetypes are at home with the ancestral rhythms of nature that dance life into the human condition. This universal intelligence is both terrestrial and extra-terrestrial in origin. The sacred infrastructures of the celestial world hold the blueprints for physicality. Such archival knowledge of the soul empowers one to live in the timeless tradition of wisdom.

Total acceptance of "what is" allows subtle awareness to identify intrinsic value in matter. From this non-referential vantage point, the Capricorn psyche shifts into a transpersonal experience of unbounded freedom. The individual approaches reality with a non-judgmental, innate clarity that bears direct witness to the state of Is-ness. Life's events are perceived as a comfortable matter-of-fact expression of physical existence. The mature Capricorn loses narcissistic identification with personal consciousness through a finely woven fabric of holographic awareness.

The Capricorn soul exhibits a deep sense of loyalty resulting from invincibility on the level of the heart. Stability in love gives the Capricorn the strength to let go and align with Heaven and Earth. From this holistic vantage point, the Capricorn gains a divinely humorous perspective on the foibles and challenges of human nature. As the embodiment of the Laughing Buddha, the archetype adopts a soul-level knowingness that belies the seriousness of everyday dilemmas. This engages the Capricorn's gut level, its instinctual abilities, leading to a sixth sense that penetrates the barriers of limitation.

Capricorns carry a strong bio-resonant attunement with the planet Saturn. As universal timekeepers, they preserve the old and uphold the architectural and spiritual value of ancient civilizations. The Capricorn thrives in an environmental model committed to the authority of the soul expressed as a fountainhead of wisdom.

PLANETARY GEMS/ELIXIRS FOR THE CAPRICORN ARCHETYPE

BLUE SAPPHIRE AND TANZANITE (SATURN)

Blue Sapphire and Tanzanite strengthen and stabilize the nervous system. These gem elixirs have the capacity to reach deep inside the substructure of the nervous system and reveal areas that have been blocked due to emotional or physical constriction or trauma. Both Blue Sapphire and Tanzanite have the capacity to subtly relax the Capricorn psyche; painful events from the past and the mental constructs associated with them begin to soften, losing their shape and form as they rise to the surface for healing and dissolution.

These gem elixirs clear thought-forms and beliefs that have been brought forward from the depths of the subconscious. Blue Sapphire and Tanzanite carry the magical property of creating a time bridge that synchronizes the present with the All-Present. In this transcendental state, fragments of the psyche that have been left behind in other frameworks of being can be re-integrated. Third-dimensional time codes are broken, and the individual is able to move forward into a freer and more elevated state, in tune with the originating rhythms of the soul.

As this state takes on a more stable form in the Capricorn archetype, the individual finds that the timing of life's events is more supportive of personal success and spiritual advancement. The soul path is made clear through the blue light of truth that both eliminates illusion and brings forth a depth of faith. From this standpoint, courage to overcome the challenges of life's circumstances becomes available.

The strengthening of the spiritual aura through Blue Sapphire and Tanzanite gives the Capricorn a feeling of profound invincibility. He or she feels in touch with the divine organizing power inherent in all creation. These gem elixirs purify the Saturnian aspects of doubt, pessimism, and grief, which rob the soul of joy and resilience. Surrender to a divine source becomes easier, and perseverance on the life path becomes more vigorous.

These gemstones give stability to the Capricorn's soul path by enabling him or her to sense the innate rhythms of life. Synchronicity is enhanced and personal reality is rendered more meaningful. Perseverance translates into an unshakeable faith and dedication to the divine organizing force behind creation.

FLOWER ESSENCES FOR THE CAPRICORN ARCHETYPE

SAGE (*SALVIA OFFICINALIS*)

The Capricorn psyche has the potential to access the depth of wisdom inherent in the collective consciousness. Sage essence offers the archetype the opportunity to access this wisdom by releasing the elements that have locked the psyche into positions antithetical to transpersonal growth. Major soul themes such as acceptance, compassion, and non-judgment can then enter into the field of awareness of the sage Capricorn, creating a reality of non-duality and grace. Life events are then viewed as a spiritual/emotional union that can aid the adventurous side of Capricorn to unite with the fully practical. The growth of acceptance as a sage gives the Capricorn the ability to see from all perspectives, creating knowledge of the sacred significance in all of life's myriad expressions.

SAGUARO (*CEREUS GIGANTEUS*)

Saguaro cactus flower essence plays a key role in the ability of the Capricorn archetype to digest ancient and future expressions of time. Linear time and random hyper-dimensional aspects of time are synchronized. The soul information carried by the individual in the light corridors of the DNA is given expression and stability through Saguaro.

The individual soul is a complex being formatted in many time expressions, cultures, inter-linguistic formations, and locations in other parts of the universal geography. Saguaro essence has the wisdom to tie all of these seemingly disparate parts of the psyche together. This allows the individual to be released from limiting biological influences while borrowing strength from ancestral knowledge. The time traveler can then become a truly authentic pioneer in the quest for the development of consciousness.

In the Capricorn psyche, a conflict naturally exists between linear time reality (where there is never enough time) and a visceral sense of the infinite all-present. Saguaro helps the individual to adapt a fluid state of being that supports both expressions of experience simultaneously.

Saguaro gives rise to the strength and power of Truth at a core level of being. This supports the peaceful state of acceptance that the Capricorn psyche needs for its stability. Thus it is able to break the psychic lock that has been imposed on the soul by false external authorities, such as governing bodies, teachers, and parental figures.

A holographic landscape can then emerge that increases the individual's capacity to live as an independent identity not bound by time. The external time values necessary for being grounded in this dimension can be honored while at the same time giving the soul room to stretch into its own expansive possibilities. **In the incubator of the Saguaro cactus, the ancient and futuristic knowledge of the soul can flower into a language that gives voice to the spiritual Heart.**

JOSHUA TREE (*YUCCA BREVIFOLIA SSP.*)

Joshua Tree flower essence symbolizes the aspect of the Capricorn psyche based in deep time-honored tapestries of knowledge. Joshua Tree is a plant that lives to be many hundreds of years old and thus holds the imprint for multiple psycho-spiritual evolutionary possibilities. Knowledge of the soul's ancestry becomes a flavor of feeling that sensitizes the psyche to its authentic spiritual parentage. Joshua Tree inspires the Capricorn to exhibit its most self-originating characteristics.

Joshua flower essence modulates one's internal timelines and movements toward one's personal destiny. It opens the individual psyche to view the compelling choices that are available in a myriad of parallel realities. It then helps the individual to align with the deep ancient truths of his or her soul's reality.

The Capricorn psyche learns to hold a trans-temporal memory that is outside the confines of material and emotional conditioning. This memory is released like a time capsule that activates transitory shifts in awareness. Joshua Tree catalyzes the ancestral codes—timeless and universal—held within the Capricorn archetype, thus allowing awareness to leap into its future counterparts, assisting one in retrieving knowledge of the future to benefit the present.

The Aquarian Archetype

Ruled by Saturn (Vedic), Uranus (Western)

Air Element

Fixed (Stationary Energy)

Key Words: Air, fixed, truth seeker, lightning insight, intuition, change, unconventional, innovative, quick, unpredictable, inspirational, imaginative, ideas, visionary, futuristic, creative intelligence, receptive to light, divine guidance, spacey, false pride, aloof, rationalization, purposeful, socially minded, humanitarian

The Aquarian archetype is governed by the fixed air element. It exhibits a dynamic yet consistent style of intelligence, acting as a conduit for universal intelligence to anchor into the Earth realm. The Aquarian visionary psyche functions as a cosmic receiver and transmitter of divine inspiration. It has the capacity to organize inspiration into creative ideas and new constructive thought-forms. For this reason, the Aquarian persona is highly skilled and impassioned, bringing in new, innovative concepts, systems, technologies, and other formative structures that have an evolutionary, transforming value for the planet.

The Aquarian individual's heightened mental faculties can operate as a psychic antenna to bring forward new paradigms that serve humanitarian causes and uplift collective consciousness. Aquarians are visionaries, capable of seeing into the future and infusing the present with inspired ideas, concepts, creative solutions, and technologies, of both a physical and non-physical nature. Their futuristic intelligence conveys a cool passion for the welfare of planet Earth and its human habitat, as well as our place in the cosmos.

Aquarian archetypes often have a very sharp and swift-moving mind that can grasp large volumes of information, creating order and symmetry for new lifestyles. The Aquarian persona is known for its tendency to break through rules, forms, and standards—even those the individual might have personally established. They are transformers by nature, independent and free-spirited.

In the immature stage, the Aquarian can exhibit self-centered, self-absorbed, and narcissistic attitudes. But as the Aquarian archetype matures, it accelerates at lightning speed, going beyond the limitations of the small self to become a clear receptacle for purpose to manifest in an extraordinary, magical fashion.

The Aquarian archetype is a truth seeker of the highest order. The archetype has a detached element to the persona that allows the individual to act with certainty, yet be free from attachment. The Aquarian is aware that all things change and that conditioning is a frozen state of mind. The lightning intuition of the Aquarian psyche melts conditions of mind and breaks with stagnant conformity. The ever-youthful and wise Aquarian sage breathes life into unseen territory and breaks the boundaries of religious, cultural, and scientific points of view.

Through attunement with the forces of nature, the Aquarian psyche thrives on the adventures of life. The individual manifests an internal energy of enthusiasm that infuses the persona with magnetic, charismatic qualities. The Aquarian persona is ushered along a novel and unique path of actualizing all that is imaginable. However, his or her unguided, immature imagination can cause the Aquarian persona to be spacey, creating convenient lapses of memory and actions that others view as inconsiderate.

A pivotal growth point for the Aquarian archetype is to maintain constant surveillance of his or her perceptions and emotions, so as not to intellectualize emotion or develop premature convictions. The Aquarian persona must self-censor in order to transmute the tendency towards false pride and self-importance.

The Aquarian will often exhibit a uniqueness that empowers the characteristic need to turn things inside out. But due to its revolutionary nature, the Aquarian psyche can often provoke a stunned or shocked response from his or her environment. For the Aquarian archetype, purpose and destiny are not fixed ideas, but rather an ever-present, evolving reality. The Aquarian is able to create order out of chaos and chaos out of order.

The lightning ray of intuition for the Aquarian is instantaneous, infusing energy and inspiration into humanity and the Earth. New realms of vision, insight, and future possibility are organized for manifest expression. The flash of ideas and the imagined scope of new forms of reality present themselves in the foreground of awareness. Aquarian archetypes propel planetary awareness into the future like the birth of a new star.

PLANETARY GEMS/ELIXIRS FOR THE AQUARIAN ARCHETYPE

BLUE SAPPHIRE AND TANZANITE (SATURN–VEDIC)

Blue Sapphire and Tanzanite bring the Aquarian psyche to a profound center of stability while maintaining momentum in the midst of transformational change. These gems pacify the irritability of the nervous system when the Aquarian is attempting to adapt to the fluctuations and input of the higher mind. When the nervous system is functioning smoothly, it infuses the Aquarian archetype with penetrating and truthful insight. **Blue Sapphire and Tanzanite, through their transcendental influence, increase the Aquarian mind's capacity to absorb lightning flashes of information and insight from a relaxed, nonattached perspective.**

HESSONITE GARNET (URANUS–WESTERN)

Hessonite Garnet stabilizes the Aquarian psyche within its creative reservoir of energies. This gem activates the innate talents and powers of the Aquarian archetype. It has a positive influence that manifests as a guiding force.

Hessonite imparts a realistic perspective to the Aquarian archetype. The individual is better able to accept change, be in the present, and see into the many layers of meaning in life's events. The gem assists with the development of discernment, especially between the inner truth and the superficial appearance of outer reality.

Hessonite builds a protective aura that assists in maintaining stability when the Aquarian becomes overshadowed due to irrational or heightened psychic energies. The Aquarian psyche then learns to function out of a position of strength, surrendering to the over-lighting guidance of the soul.

FLOWER ESSENCES FOR THE AQUARIAN ARCHETYPE

LARKSPUR (*DELPHINIUM NATTALLIANUM*)

Larkspur flower essence harmonizes the higher mind and visionary ideals with the soul's passion to inspire and move individuals toward transformational change. In this way Larkspur supports the innate leadership qualities of the forward-thinking Aquarian. As the Aquarian psyche matures, the Aquarian individual gains the capacity to function in leadership roles while simultaneously empowering other individuals to become their own leader and actualize the highest potential in any given circumstance.

QUAKING GRASS (*BRIZA MAXIMA*)

Quaking Grass flower essence embodies the Aquarian ideal. Quaking Grass essence synthesizes and harmonizes a group consciousness field matrix. It supports core individual consciousness in the context of collective group processes of life. It helps one's individual awareness to objectively maintain its center and expand outwardly to see oneself in the wholeness of life, thus identifying one's personal role, purpose, or gift to the world.

Quaking Grass softens the ego's membrane and opens the psyche's doors to the transpersonal life of the Aquarian archetype, so that we can live collectively as single cells on planet Earth within an even larger body of life.

ROSEMARY (*ROSMARINUS OFFICINALIS*)

Rosemary is a powerful grounding force that links the higher mind with the body. This is key for the Aquarian archetype, who tends to live in the lofty realms of the higher mind. This flower essence supports individual consciousness in establishing a secure place in the world, allowing Aquarian psyches to voyage to the outer regions of their souls' capacity and transform their visions and insight into practical knowledge. As Rosemary cultivates a grounded presence, the Aquarian psyche can grow in its authentic soul force, which can inspire the growth of humanitarian ideals.

STAR TULIP (*CALOCHORTUS TOLMIEI*)

Star Tulip flower essence enhances the pathways of the senses, allowing the user to travel deep into the subtle structures of creation. Through the use of this essence, awareness becomes receptive to the pulse of life that originates from Source. Star Tulip also opens the channels of perception to receive information from the higher worlds of light beings.

Star Tulip helps the Aquarian archetype navigate through earthly life with grace; the soul is able to maintain a deep life-force stream of light-packed information that serves to guide the psyche in daily life.

The Piscean Archetype

Ruled by Jupiter (Vedic), Neptune (Western)

Water Element

Mutable (Changing Energy)

Key Words: Water, mutable, truth, authenticity, faith, surrender, allow, transformation, wisdom, vision, imagination, dreams, creativity, entranced, illusion, ideal, spiritual

The Pisces archetype is escorted into the eternal moments of Truth through the mutable expression of water. The nature of water is to flow and change with the unpredictable forces of nature. The power of mutable water creates a vortex in the Piscean psyche that draws it deep into the mystical realms of reality and Truth.

At this depth, the individual requires the light of the soul to vigilantly monitor the Piscean persona. The Piscean archetype is called to master discernment and discrimination at every ebb, turn, and pull, as the seduction of water in "e-motion" may cause "seeing sickness"—an inability to know real from unreal as seen from the objective view of the higher self.

Piscean archetypes can be challenged by impressionability and vulnerability to the energies and thoughts of others. This can cause the individual to seek approval, try to please others, and create emotional dependencies based on past conditioning. On the other hand, the Piscean possesses the power to imprint others with its presence and enthusiasm. The choice becomes to face the authentic inner self or act as the mirror player to what others require and expect.

The Piscean eternally stands at the gate of transformation, prepared to leave behind the old world and its ways. The Piscean is perpetually completing and starting anew, gaining life knowledge and lessons to purify the psyche and release karmas of the past.

Pisceans require a constant link to the personal and universal level of their psychic-spiritual being. Piscean archetypes must learn when to surrender wholeheartedly to the ebb and flow between personal and universal evolution. Pisceans feel that it is deeply important for their actions to be wholly authentic, pure, and in service to the transformational light of evolution.

Piscean archetypes are on an eternal quest to link with the soul's deepest purpose and desire to be one with the universe, to surrender in totality and merge into the absolute wholeness of life. Once such soul-level communication is established, the persona feels safe to enter into the unfathomable depths of being. The soul lovingly leads the persona into the dance of surrender.

The psychic force stirs the watery nature of the Pisces, inviting the soul to swim in the unbounded ocean of life. This graceful movement within the Piscean archetype spontaneously opens the individual to a quality of letting go that travels outside the domain of the mind and into the infinity of the heart. This call to Oneness and surrender for the Pisces archetype is experiential, not intellectual.

As outdated thought-forms, beliefs, and habitual actions are released, freeing the static mind, the Piscean psyche dips into the realms of spiritual death in order to cast off the hidden vestigial parts no longer needed for its primordial awakening. Out of the darkest depths of the internal void, the archetype is able to escape the jaws of death and make life new.

The Pisces archetype is a born mystic and will go to great extremes to know the highest Truth. However, the Piscean persona has a tendency toward superstition and unexamined habit. The decision-making process for the Pisces can either favor the transformational process or lead to vehicles that weaken the persona and protect habituated unconscious motives.

The Piscean encounters the contrast between the expansive aloneness that offers submergence into the Light and the fear of emptiness associated with feeling alone. The empty feeling of aloneness is a signal that summons the Pisces archetype to pause and reflect. A little time goes a long way for the Pisces.

The life of the Piscean is marked by a ring-pass-not of fear that can only be overcome by diving headlong into the inner landscapes of the psyche and surfacing in moments of clear perception. The inner light of the spiritual process guides the Pisces to overcome both the spiritual and physical fear of death. Crashing into the barrier of loneliness and separation, the archetype can come to a point of direct unification with Divine Love.

As the Piscean matures, he or she is inspired to perform selfless acts of service as a celebration of the One. The intensity of self-consciousness is dissolved in a transpersonal state of ecstatic union.

The Piscean psyche loves to love with all its heart. It can be enchanted by the illusion of perfection and thus lose sight of Truth. The mature Piscean takes a step back from the romantic fantasy of Oneness and learns to carry the message of pure love into the complexities of the real world.

Although the Piscean is a dreamer, the mature archetype views imagination as a practical doorway to the creative process. **More than any other archetype of the holographic psyche, the Pisces is able to shape reality out of the fabric of dreams and imagination.**

PLANETARY GEMS/ELIXIRS FOR THE PISCEAN ARCHETYPE

YELLOW SAPPHIRE (JUPITER–VEDIC, NEPTUNE–WESTERN)

Yellow Sapphire provides a clarifying influence for the Pisces archetype. The gem elixir uplifts the psyche by creating positive, optimistic thoughts and a joyful disposition in life. The yellow ray of illumination pierces the veil of the persona, authenticating the true nature of the soul and initiating rites of passage through purification, transformation, and integration. At this point, vision can be empowered with knowingness. The divine impulse of grace allows one to surrender and serve the God-force of life.

Yellow Sapphire infuses the mind with clarity and discrimination. It increases visual acuity and activates higher functions of intelligence that create foundations for order and practical wisdom. Yellow Sapphire uplifts the Piscean spirit when the waters of the psyche become heavy. It strengthens character and protects from the many incoming influences that bend the spine of the Piscean archetype. The objectivity that Yellow Sapphire cultivates provides an emotional balance and stability to the Piscean persona. Yellow Sapphire empowers the Piscean archetype to live in the light of the true authentic Self.

PEARL AND MOONSTONE

Pearl and Moonstone balance and stabilize the emotional nature of the Piscean archetype. They provide inner, self-directed nourishment to the Pisces persona. Both gem elixirs cultivate emotional contentment and reduce the Piscean's sentimental, self-centered need for attention and recognition from the outside world. This frees the Piscean persona from the tendency for self-pity.

Pearl and Moonstone impart a knowing experience, giving rise to emotional fulfillment from the depths of the inner world of silence.

FLOWER ESSENCES FOR THE PISCEAN ARCHETYPE

ROCK ROSE (*HELIANTHEMUM NUMMULARIUM*)

Rock Rose flower essence provides an anchoring in the core Self. It cultivates a strengthening and grounding element to the Piscean archetype at times when the psyche is challenged to surrender the protective mechanisms and identification with egoic structures. When the psyche is challenged and feels the reality of a personal death, physically or psycho-spiritually, Rock Rose infuses the soul with transcendental courage to overcome fear and to realize the presence of Self. As the awareness of the presence of Self grows, the watery "e-motion" of separation and annihilation dissolves in the clear, still pool of the psyche, as it reflects the light of the soul.

CHAPARRAL (*LARREA TRIDENTATE*)

Chaparral flower essence is a powerful psychic cleanser. The Piscean archetype is especially impressionable both to externally and internally generated information, images, thought-forms, emotional conditions, and subconscious programs. The challenge of the Piscean psyche is to develop clear censoring membranes and filters that prevent negative and destructive information patterns from entering the mind/body complex.

Once the mind/body complex receives and assimilates distorted information, the subconscious translates the material into the creation of personal reality. It is vital, in both the conscious and subconscious realms, for the Piscean archetype to gain mastery of this internal censoring process, which determines what dreams become living reality for the Piscean.

Chaparral essence assists the psyche in navigating the transpersonal realms of life, without identifying or losing the Self in the astral distortions that appear in the many mirrors of the psyche.

ANGEL'S TRUMPET (*DATURA CANDIDA*)

Angel's Trumpet flower essence is a powerful guardian for the soul, as the persona surrenders its identity, memories, and attachments to its common life roles. Angel's Trumpet heralds the signature of soul as it enters into and awakens to the pure existence of life in the transpersonal worlds. The ultimate expression of the Piscean archetype is to experience unification and an unconditional merger with the all-pervading presence of non-personal love. As the Piscean archetype matures, Angel's Trumpet facilitates the acceptance and surrendering of what is. **Death and birth are equal participants in the seamless wholeness of pure existence. Here is the virtual space that houses the holographic psyche within each being.**

7

THE SEVEN CHAKRAS

Dimensional Bridges

*And, in the end, the chakra system in our
bodies is how we find our way back to the
most ancient mystery of all—God, the
Oneness, the Omniscient.*
                        —Rosalyn L. Bruyere

Spiritual awakening requires us to bridge the physical and nonphysical levels of reality. This bridge is created and functions within the *chakra system*, an energy matrix that governs the essential process of evolution on all levels—physical, mental, emotional, psychic, and spiritual.

The chakras organize the whole mind/body complex; they are the medium of connection between spirit and matter, body and consciousness, and time and space, functioning through omni-dimensions simultaneously. The full integration of the chakra system within itself and with the cosmos leads to the unfoldment of human actualization and unity consciousness.

The traditional major chakra system consists of seven centers, often referred to as "wheels of light." The chakras—open, vital receivers and transmitters of life-force information—are located along the central axis of the spine within the etheric energy body and extend into the subtle bodies. The location and qualities ascribed to each of the seven chakras are as follows:

- Chakra 1: Base of the spine—survival and the experience of grounding in this plane of awareness
- Chakra 2: Sacral/genital area—sex and the creative force

- Chakra 3: Solar plexus—power and the right use of Will
- Chakra 4: Heart—love and the process of Divine Communion
- Chakra 5: Throat—communication and the expression of Purpose
- Chakra 6: Third eye—accessing subtle and visionary perception
- Chakra 7: Crown—illumination and celestial wisdom

In the East Indian yogic tradition, the chakras are seen as pathways, or gates, of initiation. The consciousness interplay that is elicited through the articulation of the chakra system brings the full promise of Self-Realization. **The evolutionary cosmic forces that open, clarify, and refine the human chakra system lead to the systematic stripping away of ego identification with the mind/body complex, bringing one into the intimate experience of the Self.**

The fact that there are seven major chakras is not surprising. In the ancient traditions that articulate the science of spirit, there are seven primary levels of life. The base-seven paradigm is a fundamental model for the world's religions and healing systems. Theosophists describe creation in terms of seven cosmic rays, with seven evolutionary races. In Christianity there are seven days of creation and seven seals. The Jewish Kabbalistic tree of life is composed of seven horizontal levels.

Secular Western culture operates out of a base-seven system of frequencies that can be viewed in the seven colors of the rainbow, the seven days of the week, and the seven notes in the major scale. In both Western and Vedic astrology, seven inner planets furnish archetypal information about the psyche.

In this chapter, we will explore the chakra system as the holographic field for human experience. We'll delve deeply into the purpose and function of each chakra and offer a description of the flower essences and gem elixirs that support mastery of each chakra.

THE COSMIC COMMUNICATIONS NETWORK

Human experience—generated through emotions, thinking, senses, and subtle psychic perception—is processed through the chakra system, providing powerful holographic learning that infuses the soul with knowledge and wisdom. As the soul enters physical reality, it begins to lose memory of its origin, but the blueprints generated at the source of one's being hold the inherent destiny for spiritual realization. **Layers of compressed information stored in the chakras contain data pools that the soul utilizes to realize and establish higher organized states of consciousness.** As the soul grows in presence, these layers are peeled back, opening the Self to its omnipresent relationship with God.

Each chakra organizes itself through a geometric shape that defines the space in which it manifests and through which it functions. It also vibrates in a specific frequency and color (light). For example, the heart chakra is seen as two overlapping triangles, one pointed upward, the other downward. Its sound frequency is 528 Hz (the "love signal"), and its color frequency is that of the green spectrum, one of the most abundant colors of the earth: sustaining, nourishing, revitalizing, and oxygen related. These organizing principles allow the soul to conduct the flow of intelligence between the human and cosmic experience.

Each chakra is an energy vortex, functioning within its defined field. The nerve ganglia and endocrine glands of the physical body form a network of transceivers and transducers that send information back and forth through the portals of the chakras. When the chakra centers are interconnected and communicating superfluidly, omni-dimensionality is integrated; our mortal self is connected to our divine potential within.[1] The data generated through this communication network creates a bridge between the visible and invisible worlds.

THE PROCESS OF INVOLUTION AND EVOLUTION THROUGH THE CHAKRAS

The chakra system is arranged as an energetic step-down series in the involutionary process of spirit descending into matter. The spirit enters the fontanel, or crown chakra, carrying the pranic breath of life that infuses the cerebral-spinal system and the upper brain. These are the chief centers of consciousness in the body, where the first impulses of involution begin to move from unmanifest to manifest. The spiritual energy current then descends to the third eye (the threshold of wisdom and divine sight), throat, heart, solar plexus, sacral area, and root center.

The creative spiritual energies travel through the *shushumna*, a subtle column that runs from the fontanel along the length of the spinal cord down to its base. As it descends, the undifferentiated energy current splits at the third eye, differentiating itself into positive and negative electromagnetic currents, which move through the subtle bodies in a serpentine fashion, defining and infusing the chakra centers along the spine.

As the two energetically woven currents—one feminine, one masculine—move through the chakras, they unify the dualistic energies of creation within us. The male principle in the Vedic tradition is called *Shiva*, the formless being, or pure consciousness. *Shakti*, the female principle, is the expression of divine consciousness and the life giver of creation. These currents are also referred to as the *Ida* (moon) and *Pingala* (sun) channels.

At each location where the two currents cross in their descent, the energy becomes neutral, opening up the portal for the manifestation of the specific chakra at the location where this occurs. Each of the five lower chakras, from the base to the throat, houses a corresponding, or bioresonant, element—ether (throat), air (heart), fire (solar plexus), water (sacral), and earth (root).

The five elemental forces, "rivers of life," coalesce within the soul's light information system—the chakras—formatting the physical body. This light intelligence organizes itself as organs, tissues, and glands within the mind/body complex. The heightened and quickened frequencies emanate from the crown, and the lower and slower frequencies resonate at the base of the spine.

The caduceus, the universal symbol for medicine, is a pictorial representation of this crossover and step-down process of energy transformation. The caduceus emerged out of a system of medicine that, like the Vedic tradition, was built upon the natural laws of the spiritual world. It originated with the worship of the Egyptian god Thoth as the god of knowledge. The Greeks acknowledged this manifestation process as the Greek god Hermes, who represented scientific and occult knowledge.

Caduceus

The harmonious interplay and union of these two principle energy currents through the chakras moves one toward a state of Self-Realization in a natural, evolutionary process. As the chakra system clears and develops through spiritual practices and quantum energy technologies—such as meditation, chanting, yoga, breath work, flower essences, and gem elixirs—the psyche gains a holographic nature.

The subtle physiology responds in powerful and immediate ways to these practices and technologies. Yogic practice, for example, circulates energy through the nervous system and spinal column, moving the living spiritual power of the *shakti kundalini* toward the crown chakra, to be united with the Shiva energy principle there. In this evolutionary ascent, the two currents unify in the center of the brain, behind the third eye, also known as the "cave of Brahman." This supports a superfluid state of physical, emotional, and mental functioning.

Thus, the evolutionary process becomes a lifelong journey to Self-Realization. Rather than try to escape life's dichotomies—light and dark, good and bad, love and hate, jealousy and acceptance—awareness scans them in their totality, ultimately synthesizing them so that they can embody the fullest expression of human potential. Thus, hate becomes love, fear becomes courage, and the wholeness of the brain is given full jurisdiction.

COMBINING GEM ELIXIRS AND FLOWER ESSENCES TO CREATE CHAKRA FORMULAS: AN INTEGRATIVE APPROACH

Gem elixirs and flower essences have been grouped in this chapter according to specific themes central to the transformation and developmental process within each chakra, as well as their relationship to the transgenerational clearing process previously described in this book. The elixirs and essences lead to inquiry of one's personal and, at the same time, collective evolutionary processes.

This chakra classification of the gems and flowers addresses universal themes collectively shared on a soul level. Plant/mineral intelligence interfaces with human intelligence, catapulting one's awareness into the next incremental level of development. Information from the essences and gems facilitates the electromagnetic flow of consciousness into the human nervous system, utilizing visual, auditory, and intuitive modes of communication.

The chakras are the arena for healing to occur between the physical and subtle bodies. The first four chakras—root, sacral, solar plexus, and heart—govern the functioning and transformation of the physical body. The upper three chakras bridge matter and spirit. The balance and mastery of energy through these chakras brings one further into the inner sanctum of the highest manifest destiny of one's soul. Through opening and integrating the full spectrum of the chakras, unification of body and spirit is enhanced.

The chakra-classified plant and gems seek to accentuate the information matrices of the basic principles of creation. Each formula is designed to assist individuals in moving through their personal initiatic gates into the transpersonal realms of their greater being. The chakra system formulas can be used as vibrational learning tools to transform the personality to function as a vehicle for the transpersonal Self.

The goal of this system is to address psycho-emotional and mental conditions and patterns, thus allowing the higher Self to emerge as a primary governing field of consciousness. As an individual grows into deeper levels of the core Self, the healing power of grace flows into the physical, emotional, and mental bodies. **The chakra formulas assist in shifting the "I" identity to the universal "I Am."** A self-referral loop in consciousness is created, which feeds back awareness to its essence, or true Self.

The chakra formulas are intended to bring one to a deeper realization of our humanness through the invocation of advanced states of awareness. The role of flower essences and gem elixirs is to awaken consciousness and assist in setting the foundation for the development of the human light body. The biological form we inhabit is undergoing great strides in its ability to function at levels previously thought to be superhuman, including the experiences of telepathy, empathic knowing, and subtle body travel in consciousness.

This advancement of the human species is occurring through the bio-resonant exchange between the heart and activation of the DNA, thus increasing the ability of our blueprint to access previously dormant human intelligence stored within the DNA. As the human being moves toward an exalted state of the heart, compassion unfolds as a golden spiral of love.

The chakra healing system of flower essences and gem elixirs is a trans-dimensional model. Plants and gems bridge the gap in personal human awareness and activate the "aha" moment of unity and instant knowing. At these intersections of vibrational interface, the formulas unlock key notes in the ascension of consciousness, directing the personality to function as a lens for pure awareness. The shift of the "I" identity to the universal Self, or "I Am," occurs through the subtle, resonant imprinting of creative intelligence.

The electromagnetic impulses of flowers and gem elixirs feed the nervous system through the central portal of the heart chakra. Flower essences specifically serve as a thread weaving the fabric of consciousness into Unity. Each essence acts as a sutra or vibrational code in consciousness that funnels awareness to deeper levels of insight and realization. Gems particularly strengthen the celestial geometric structure of the human light body. As Maharishi Mahesh Yogi says, "Knowledge is structured in consciousness." **Flowers and gems expand awareness, allowing one to begin to cognize knowledge, information, and insight directly from multiple holistic fields of life.**

The bio-resonant geometric structures inherent in gem elixirs and flower essences activate a self-referral loop in which the individual's consciousness returns awareness back onto the "I Am," or the Self. The personality tendency is to focus on the physical, emotional, and mental levels. However, the soul's innate healing power shifts the personality toward states of transpersonal expression. From this vantage point, the individual can see and act as a universal or galactic human being in the larger order of life. The development of human potential and collective consciousness becomes the forefront of one's soulful living.

The transgenerational clearing formula for the chakra system addresses what is known as planetary *miasms*, which have been stored in the collective repository of cellular memory and collective unconscious. A miasm is a distortion that manifests in the energetic blueprints of the individual and further projects into the physical levels of life. An individual miasm is inherent in the cellular memory that is carried collectively through our lineage. A planetary miasm is a distortion in the blueprint of the species that is shared collectively.

Flower essences, gem elixirs, and other vibrational types of remedies taken frequently can accelerate the timeline of the psycho/spiritual healing of these miasms. Living systems of healing integrate fragments of time into the Eternal Now. The all-encompassing past, present, and future in the non-localized point of the Now opens a channel of the soul that bonds with the collective destiny and higher potential of life upon planet Earth.

Quantum physics reminds us that knower, known, and object of knowing are one. We cannot separate or objectify the process of medicine making from the medicine person or from the medicine itself. Bio-resonant geometric flower essences and gem elixirs are prayerfully empowered with clarity of intent. Intent is a wordless prayer imprinted upon the waves of silence emitting through the sacred bio-geometric matrices of the heart. Each formula is activated in Love. Love flowing out of the heart center of the medicine maker imprints the medicine.

A synergistic chakra formula of flower essences and gem elixirs heals through the coherent synergy of tonal frequencies, which the individual human energy body uptakes as a symphony of light, sound, and geometric intelligence.

Each individual formula is a doorway into energy education, revealing intimate personal knowledge and universal themes layered in the field of human consciousness. The first four chakra fields address the principle areas of life related to the physical, emotional, and mental levels. The first two chakras are a unified team of influence; the issues of survival and *dharmic* creative force are inherently woven together as life-stream issues of great importance for the stability and meaning of every human being.

The three "upper" chakras open the vortex to Source that allows all other levels to unfold in their principal manifestation. The fifth chakra is the bridge through which all light-coded information for manifestation and illumination flows.

Each chakra formula assists the individual to energetically ascend the steps of life's lessons into his or her divinity. This ascension process through the chakra system builds a platform of consciousness that is at once solid, interdependent, life altering, and radiant. The chakra formulas act as bridges. As the individual transitions from the third-dimensional material world consciousness toward subtler realms of inner life, the quickening of life energy requires greater responsibility and capacity to manage and navigate. The chakra formulas support practical and spiritual issues and challenges that the soul faces in daily living, year after year.

The flower essences and gem elixirs indicated for each chakra can serve as a whole formula, can be taken individually, or can be combined in any combination. Regardless of which chakra you wish to focus on, every essence or elixir supports and strengthens the electrical-magnetic anatomy of the heart. **To use an analogy, the heart chakra is like a wormhole, a space/time passageway into the infinite, unimaginable dimensions of life.** It is recognized as the central processing unit of life on every level, unlimited in its range of time, space, and dimensionality.

Each flower essence and gem elixir is chosen to infuse its pure signature of consciousness into the formula in such a way as to reinforce the inner stability and constructive power of the sacred geometric blueprint within every form.

Let's now look at which formulas will most significantly influence transformation through mastery of each chakra.

THE ROOT CHAKRA

The first chakra, the *Muladhara* (foundation chakra in Sanskrit), is located at the base of the spine in the coccyx area; it houses the earth element. The *kundalini shakti*, the primordial life-force energy, is stored as a kinetic energy coil in the base of the spine. Kundalini creates a dynamic flow of subtle energy that refines the articulation between the chakras and creates a deep level of energetic and psycho-spiritual expansion and integration.

On a physiological level, the earth element in the first chakra governs the formation of our physical structure, shape, and size, as well as the condition of our bones and the channels of elimination. **An openly integrated, vital, and balanced root chakra lends strength, stability, and groundedness to the body and psyche.**

The earth element, housed in the root chakra, embodies the densest and most crystallized form of energy in the subtle field. A primary function of the root chakra is to engage the primordial instinct to survive. This mirrors the ancestral processes necessary for human beings to exist in situations that elicit the "fight, flight, or freeze" response. This is especially relevant in life-threatening situations, such as war, poverty, and epidemics, as well as acts of God, such as earthquakes, famine, hurricanes, and tsunamis, all of which present a significant challenge to survival.

In modern society, social discord and competitiveness at the expense of human consideration have become common. Today, war, terrorism, and environmental challenges demand our individual and collective attention. To address these issues, we need to engage the global healing of the root chakra.

Mastery of the root chakra involves the integration of the archetypal warrior energy and the harmonizing power of wisdom, compassion, and knowledge inherent in the divine feminine. This, combined with knowledge of the development of the kundalini as a scientifically validated force, will lead to a new awakening of our human potential.

The root chakra contains frequencies of information that impart knowledge connecting us to all life, allowing us to feel that we are part of one spiritual community. The psycho-spiritual characteristics expressed in a vital, stable, and open root chakra include honor, loyalty, stability, security, justice, a sense of belonging, and the desire for the well-being of all of humanity.

Imprinting from one's family of origin can have a profound soul-level impact on one's sense of rootedness and belonging. The inherent integrity within one's family of origin has the capacity to create a solid spiritual foundation. However, this is often missing in our modern-day life. Through the use of nature's gifts, such as flower essences and gem elixirs, it is possible to heal and balance the root chakra, thereby supporting a deep connection with Mother Earth.

A deep sense of faith is sustained by the earth-based frequencies stored in the root chakra. One gains a sense of belonging, feeling fed, supported, and protected by the presence of the Divine Mother. Any irrational fears imbedded in this chakra can be transmuted through a deeper cognitive sense of the earth's intelligence.

The root chakra, when open to the transformative frequencies of the new consciousness of Gaia, will usher us into the collective journey that is meant for the well-being of all people. The challenge of the contemporary human is to be grounded in the shift of personal reality as he or she awakens to new space/time dimensions. **The galactic human must learn to be in right relationship with all sentient life.**

Bio-Resonant Remedies for Mastering the Root Chakra

Planetary Gem/Elixir—Ruby (Sun)

Flower Essences—Star Thistle, Star of Bethlehem, Shooting Star, Yellow Star Tulip, Trillium, Hound's Tongue, Manzanita, and Corn

This group of flower essences and gem elixirs cultivates a stable, superfluid state that simultaneously opens perception to the physical world and provides in-depth insight into the spiritual dimension. The purpose of these remedies is to ground the root chakra securely and safely in the physical plane. As this process occurs, attachments to the material plane are lifted, freeing the spirit. The soul regains its spiritual authority and makes room for more purposeful expansion.

These remedies address the thought-forms, emotional conditions, and soul imprinting associated with survival fears, anxiety, and insecurity. Through their use, the ego gradually learns to let go of its concern with the acquisition of material goods, and the individual, freed from the myths and social conditioning imposed by fear-based living, begins to perceive the world as a supportive place.

As the root chakra develops and broadens its base, one learns that abundance is not a physical commodity. It is immeasurable and can only be experienced through a state of gratitude for sufficiency. One consciously affirms to soulfully receive and attract people, places, money, or material goods that are in support of personal and global evolution. As the psyche embraces the universal truth of abundance as the nature of life, the ego surrenders its need to perpetuate survival-level beliefs and behaviors, which condition the mind/body toward limitation and contraction.

Embracing the laws of abundance creates unbounded potential and balance. The soul builds faith that resources will appear in perfect divine timing. Personal needs and desires are aligned with universal laws and possibilities that support a state of ease. Competitive instincts of the ego dissolve, and the soul is able to cooperate with the organizing principles of life. One's identification with the body and physical plane shifts to a finer state of witnessing, being in the world yet not of it.

Personal reality is limited through one's investment in outdated beliefs and concepts. As the root chakra consciousness matures, these impediments are dismantled, revealing the source of one's true spiritual identity. This leads to an invincible experience of faith, continuity of knowing, and commitment to right action. The intelligence of the flower essences and gem elixirs has the capacity to align the persona with the soul.

A superfluid state within the root chakra assists the individual in opening to unconditional love. This mysterious, omnipresent love transcends the mind, the emotions, and even the imagination. The heart is able to fall into a vibrational resonance with the root chakra, which develops a firm foundation for holographic awareness. The state of time is stretched, resting on the infinite. The mind and heart know the nature of an infinite and abundant universe.

PLANETARY GEM/ELIXIR FOR THE ROOT CHAKRA

RUBY (SUN)

Ruby radiates the stellar frequencies of the sun, the giver of life. It has an affinity for the root chakra, the solar plexus, and the heart. Through the synergistic interplay of these chakras, the individual gains a stronger foothold in the material world while maintaining his or her dominion in the spiritual. Growth of *bala* (the unconquerable strength of body, mind, soul, and spirit) becomes an active process of realization through the essence of Ruby.

The root chakra holds the foundation for life to manifest. It is the focal grounding point for the earth element of the physiology. Ruby supports and strengthens the body in mastering the physical and psycho-emotional functions of resilience, agility, flexibility, and inner strength.

Ruby transmits the red ray of vitality and positivism that regenerates and sustains life. It strengthens the pathways between the causal level of reality and the physical body. It energizes and activates key portal points in the etheric blueprint, enlivening the communication between the physical body and its etheric envelope.

Through the physical body, Ruby increases the core vitality of the individual. It strengthens the physical heart, which circulates oxygen and pranic life force to the cells, organs, and tissues of the body. Through increased oxygenation and nourishment, the cells are able to hold the higher frequencies of energy and light that support illumination.

Ruby also has an important influence on the adrenal glands, which are responsible for how we respond to the world. It can liberate us from conditioned responses and fears, known and unknown to us. When we experience fear, any threat to the survival of our ego and/or our physicality, the adrenals react through preprogrammed conditioned responses, such as the fight, flight, or freeze response. The empowering quality of Ruby transforms this fear-based conditioning, supporting the adrenal glands toward a state of ease, strength, and stamina.

Ruby assists in the ability to transmute ancestral, biological, genetic programs, reducing the habituated, unnecessary reactiveness of the adrenals. This transformation leads to acceptance of what is, rather than fear of what will be, thus reducing adrenal exhaustion and extinguishing the personality's tendency towards anxiety and paranoia.

Ruby is the gem of empowerment that resonates deep within the root chakra to align the core identity structure with the personality. It acts as a grounding force that integrates dissociated aspects of the personality with the core self. The gem elixir establishes the clear, benevolent authority of the inner teacher.

Ruby is one of the most powerful of the gems in light of its ability to establish soul-level authentication. It permeates the human auric field, illuminating the sense of Self and supporting the soul to direct life. It assists in shifting the personal self into a transpersonal state of reality that can better serve the destiny of the soul. One learns to function as the Knower, becoming unshakable and deeply rooted in the core of one's Being.

Ruby's gifts unite the mind and heart in the sun/soul central identity, supporting the alignment of the mental and spiritual bodies. The feeling level of the heart becomes so lively that Higher Intelligence, beyond the level of the mind, gains supreme authority over the intellect.

Ruby is the teacher of divine passion in action, directing creative intelligence to govern from the heart of compassion. The gem elixir inspires the power of divine authority to seat itself in the sacred heart. It opens the emotional body to receive love and nourishment. It teaches us that divine passion, though at first founded on the infantile need for touch, can ultimately offer a blend of personal affection and transpersonal awareness.

Happiness and the state of bliss can exist independently of any particular love object. Through access to the cosmic mind, the personal self draws further and further to the Divine Father intelligence that allows one to know love at any moment. Although personal relationship may remain, the soul identity becomes more fluid in its expression. It draws on the infinite capacity of this all-embracing love, despite personal obstacles or constraints.

Ruby touches subterranean portions of the psyche that have remained in shadow, particularly the areas that have been weakened due to a diminishment of the solar force. Ruby activates the inner fire element, and use of Ruby in the initial stages can illuminate the shadow aspects of the lower self. Drenched in the fires of transformation, the lower self has the opportunity to surrender its false identity into the fullness of spiritual realization. The heart, alive with the fire of spiritual commitment, is transformed into a bearer of pure light. The individual can then take the raw, uncharted experiences that life brings and transmute them into the finer expressions of truth and beauty.

One of the most significant afflictions of the human being is the anger/resentment/fear loop. When one uses Ruby elixir, the initial stages of the activation of the fire element can begin to clear through anger, resentment, or fear. As Ruby shines the light of awareness, users become aware of how they have compromised their inner core identity or authenticity, enabling them to reclaim lost portions of themselves.

Ruby supports the mental body to gain clarity of mind and confidence in action. Inferior thought-forms dissolve, clearing the pathway to greater confidence, self-esteem, leadership abilities, and inspired thought and action.

Ruby assists the personality in surrendering its false sense of will and authority. It activates a simultaneous surrendering and dissolution process, assisting in the building and reconstructing of the Father principle.

Ruby supports the intensity and focus necessary for fulfilling spiritual practice, as well as the quest for divine intimacy. Ruby's powers of clarification bring the solar plexus issues of will and authority into a broader, more transpersonal reality. Through this awakening, one gains trust in the natural ability to view the inner Father principle as the embodiment of solidity and self-empowerment. The psycho-spiritual shields established by the inner Father/teacher allow one to lead life with courage and increased personal effectiveness.

Ruby governs the catalytic conversion of our personal self into cosmic being. It alerts the individual, sense-oriented lower mind to the existence of cosmic order. As the attention becomes centered on the cosmic level, the personal self becomes a functional expression of nature. The power of God the Father within begins to be expressed in the true meaning of "thy will be done."

Contrary to the instinctive, more primitive emotions of fight, flight, or freeze, Ruby initiates spiritual accountability. We become more responsible for our words, deeds, and visions because they are more grounded in sacred knowing.

In this transpersonal reality, the personal self is permeated by a spontaneous love that creates the foundation for right action. The reactive tendencies of the personality that were born out of fear or isolation no longer determine the person's actions. The orientation shifts to the level of the heart, where trust in God and unyielding faith can lead to freedom from suffering. The heart chakra functions as a generator and receiver of love. Ruby engenders a new state of psycho-spiritual Presence that brings strength of attention to the higher mind.

FLOWER ESSENCES FOR THE ROOT CHAKRA

STAR THISTLE (*CENTAUREA SOLSTITIALIS*)

Star Thistle resonates with the soul to cultivate feelings of abundance and generosity. Feelings of lack—even poverty—are not simply based on an external state, but often arise out of feelings of self-doubt, unworthiness, or discomfort in the physiology due to ancestral conditions of isolation, loneliness, and fear. This flower essence enables one to deepen his or her sense of rootedness in the world, releasing dependence on the external as a means of security.

Star Thistle realigns our sense of connectedness and the ability to bond with others, thereby creating a sense of stability, fullness, and belonging in the psyche—contributing to the balance and health of the root chakra. With this sense of relationship, one can experience a more fluid perception of divine intelligence and merge with its infinite nature. As this energetic fusion occurs, a sense of wealth, well-being, and creative presence grows. One learns to live from the state of abundance, creating new opportunities out of the infinite present.

STAR OF BETHLEHEM (*ORNITHOGALUM UMBELLATUM*)

Star of Bethlehem cultures inner peace and comfort in the physical and subtle bodies. It releases trauma associated with survival-level conditions from the past and allows for the future to emerge out of the stillness of peace. Star of Bethlehem cultivates a transcendent state in the subtle bodies that washes through the nervous system, clearing genetic and acquired memories that bind and obstruct the energetic fields. It locates awareness of peace in the heart chakra and anchors it in the root chakra. The clarity that this stillness brings transcends the pains and imprints of karmic forces left on the battlefields of mind, body, and soul.

SHOOTING STAR (*DODECATHEON HENDERSONII*)

Shooting Star cultures a feeling of belonging and at-homeness on the Earth. It creates a grounded feeling of centeredness during temporal shifts or experiences of unfamiliar territory in space and time. Shooting Star opens the heart to the feeling level of life in all things, extending the psychic awareness into the field of matter. It unifies the heart with one's origin of life and its present physical manifestation. It supports the nervous system to create a calm and centered feeling that permeates the whole body.

YELLOW STAR TULIP (*CALOCHORTUS MONOPHYLLUS*)

Yellow Star Tulip increases one's heartfelt capacity to receive. It allows a greater exchange of energy between oneself and the environment, illuminating a pathway from the heart to the solar plexus into the root chakra. This pathway expands the radiant field of the heart and fills the mind and whole body.

The flow of perception moves from within oneself toward the environment and from the environment toward oneself. This self-referencing perception creates a new relationship to one's personal environment that dissolves the boundaries of false definition and a feeling of separation from the world. The world is our feedback loop of literal and metaphorical truth. **To see with the eye of spirit is the essential gift that cultures the ability to unlock the holographic psyche.** This process is greatly enhanced through the use of Yellow Star Tulip.

TRILLIUM (*TRILLIUM CHLOROPETALUM*)

Trillium assists us in grounding and balancing our energies in the base chakra. The ego perceives that the material plane is necessary for survival, but Trillium assists the personality to shift to a soul-level awareness that produces a more fluid interchange between the material and spiritual realms. Once this connection is made, action takes on a more profound character of spiritual knowing, supporting greater actualization of the soul's purpose and increased clarity of service to humanity.

HOUND'S TONGUE (*CYNOGLOSSUM GRANDE*)

Hound's Tongue expands the mind to be sensitive to heightened perception, leading to spiritual insight about the events and forms of the relative world. Hound's Tongue opens the flow of awareness between the physical and subtle, visible and invisible worlds of reality. Consciousness is unified through a level of perception gained out of the direct sense of knowing that Other is a reflection of Self. Hound's Tongue activates the creative cognitive mind in such a way as to illumine the perceiver. This instills deep meaning in thinking, being, and acting in the world, while not being of it—an attribute of higher octaves of the root chakra.

MANZANITA (*ARCTOSTAPHYLOS VISCIDA*)

Manzanita flower essence serves to anchor the soul forces into the physical domain, the body. This essence enlivens the body consciousness to deeply realize and embrace the sacredness of the physical vehicle as the temple of the soul. The channels in the physical body are given support to center consciousness as a receiver and giver of nourishment. Manzanita cultures the psyche to embrace the soul's individuated expression of divine intelligence in physical form.

CORN (*ZEA MAYS*)

Corn flower essence is vital in facilitating a synthesis between the electromagnetic energy field of the individual and that of the earth. It also assists in bridging earth and cosmic energies. The galactic human being must be able to maintain rootedness in the midst of shifting time/space values. Corn supports consciousness to create superfluidity in relationship to natural changes in both internal and environmental cycles of expansion and contraction.

THE SACRAL CHAKRA

The second, or sacral, chakra is located in the genital/pelvic region. It houses the water element and is called the *Svadhisthana*, "dwelling place of the Self," in Sanskrit. **The psychic, primordial, and creative principles that govern life reside in the second chakra.**

The sacral chakra is associated with our basic emotional and primal nature, as well as our experience of nurturing and nourishment. It is infinitely correlated with the physical and etheric reproductive systems in both the male and female. A healthy second chakra governs our ability to unify opposites, thus functioning as an integrated center from which the creative process flows. The higher octaves of the second chakra strengthen one's sense of personal and transpersonal identity, increasing one's ability to manifest and succeed in the external world.

The powerful magnetic and gravitational weight of the water element housed in the second chakra stores and maintains *prana*, the vital force that sustains life. The water element is governed by the force of gravity, which precipitates a natural downward movement of energy within the body. However, this energy can become stuck, like a pool of stagnant water, when we become identified with or attached to our psycho-emotional beliefs and identities. This can stir up emotional states of fear, restlessness, possessiveness, attachments, confusion, or uncertainty related to eating, sleeping, or sexuality.

The second chakra is the arena where the higher instincts for ecstatic union are integrated with the primordial energies of sexual/emotional expression. The creative impulse of the second chakra toward unification of the *shakti/shiva* requires individuals to clarify their personal desires in terms of the transpersonal. The higher development of the second chakra promotes detachment, while sustaining the capability to attract the people, places, experiences, and objects necessary to nourish one's spiritual evolution.

A healthy sacral chakra creates a feeling of abundance and security that gives one the confidence to create financial prosperity, ecstatic fulfillment, and personal power. Integration of this chakra provides a deep sense of self-sufficiency. Once mastered, the creative principles of the second chakra promote joy and deep satisfaction, permeating the entire consciousness and elevating one to divine grace and appreciation.

The sacral chakra also houses the primordial energies of the collective consciousness to support the procreative process. This is important because growth of the planetary population has brought a need for creative solutions to the health, preservation, and evolution of humanity. We are facing a turning point in our individual and collective evolution that requires the exploration and actualization of individual creative powers. Physical and spiritual discoveries pertaining to DNA have the potential to bring forth new advanced blueprints for the human species.

Self-sufficiency is a key component to the advancement of human potential. This requires that our inner and outer functioning be directly sourced from creative intelligence itself. The life-force power within the sacral chakra holds the key to the transformation codes of life. The reconfiguration of the human molecular structure will create forms of life built from previous blueprints of the human species.[2]

Once we stabilize our energy system at higher frequencies, new information systems will be established. These will be more super-fluid and infinitely creative in nature. As the primitive need for biological preservation of the species diminishes, the flow of human evolution will be directed toward higher orders of being, regeneration, and longevity. **The sacral chakra is the portal that will define the future human.**

Bio-Resonant Remedies for Mastering the Sacral Chakra

Planetary Gems/Elixirs—Pearl, Red Coral, and Hessonite

Flower Essences—Hibiscus, Sticky Monkeyflower, Pink Monkeyflower, Easter Lily, Crab Apple, Calla Lily, Basil, and Pomegranate

This group of bio-resonant gem elixirs and flower essences cultivates the sacred sexual spirit. This can be experienced as a self-regenerating birthing process that is initially activated through the second chakra, whether expressed through union with a beloved in physical form or union with the Divine Beloved through pathways such as spiritual practices and disciplines, encounters with nature, etc.

The sacred sexual spirit assists the soul in embodying ecstatic states of divine love. The ecstatic path of this mystical love unites the piercing power of passion with the mystical chalice of receptivity. In the sacred sexual spirit of ecstatic love, *kriyas*—ancient yogic body movements and hand positions—may spontaneously arise from the intensity of energy being generated. Such ecstatic worship opens the gates to the transpersonal realms of the holographic psyche. Here lies the arena of personal, social, and spiritual transformation our human species has the possibility to undertake.

The life-force energy of the two united principles of masculine and feminine flows inwardly and upwardly with a momentum that brings forth the illumination of consciousness. As one opens to the primordial impulses of divinity in creation through the use of flower essences and gem elixirs, an initiatic rite of passage referred to as the "purificatory fires" becomes activated. This creative energy resides deep within the subtle etheric bodies.

The heart and sacral centers are synchronized in the field of divine love. In this field, the mind/body is elevated in its ability to receive, generate, and express Love and devotion. The intensity of chi (life-force energy) saturates all cells, tissues, organs, and glands. There is an increase in the soul's capacity to transform lower vibrational memories; *samskaras* (karmic scars) are transmuted into light, dissolving the negative imprints of the nervous system. The opening of the sacral well allows for the flow of love-force energy to infuse the cerebral spinal fluid, thus bathing the higher centers and uniting the upper and lower quadrants of the physical/energetic bodies.[3]

As awareness expands through the use of the prescribed flowers and gems, the veils of illusion that separate one from divine union are pierced, and the psyche accesses direct pathways of cognition. The integration of the mind/body unit sets up a state of spiritual equilibrium that frees the personality from conditions and attachments that have limited its creative independence.

The tendency of the common mind is to set up a conceptual structure that rigidly seeks to armor itself. It then translates, defines, and pins down its defense structure so as to keep in place a limited, localized character identity. Flowers and gems counteract these inherent fears and preconditions. The potential of the holographic psyche lies in its ability to support the expansion of awareness that produces self-acceptance, clarity, and confidence born of the integration of intelligence as a whole-brain/field function.

The sacred sexual spirit inspires the surrender of egoic boundaries to the infinite. The deeper levels of vulnerability, reverence, and honesty that characterize this spirit warm the heart and fill the body with radiance. The fear of losing one's self is gradually subdued by the unifying presence of the God force. Cultivating the sacred sexual spirit has the capacity to bring psycho-emotional partnership to the level of mystical, transcendent union. **The soul learns to experience love as a force within itself, free from the notion that lover or loved must have a reason or cause.** One learns that the archetype of the Beloved is a state born from within.

PLANETARY GEMS/ELIXIRS FOR THE SACRAL CHAKRA

PEARL (MOON)

Pearl is attuned with the moon cycle and the second chakra. It resonates with the subtle energies of the moon, which governs the mind and has an affinity with the emotional body, our watery nature, and bodily fluids. The electromagnetic resonance patterns of Pearl amplify the divine feminine. Pearl can enhance a sense of nurturing and sensuality that evokes a yielding, flowing, and gracious expression of being.

Pearl has an ability to harmonize the ebb and flow of the tides within the psycho-emotional body affected by the gravitational pull of the moon. The gem transmits to the emotional body knowledge of how to adapt to physiological and external change. It supports the emotional body to respond in a resilient and flexible manner to the challenges of everyday life.

Pearl helps one maintain a reservoir of spiritual energy that enables the psycho-emotional to be self-contained and emotionally centered. This creates a delicate but powerful balance that generates the radiant quality of peace in mind and heart.

Pearl creates a harmonious and nurturing influence. The spherical construction of the Pearl brings a universal calming, sensitizing, and balancing quality to the emotions. It has the ability to gently awaken a virtuous nature, cultivating faith, charity, purity, and spiritual knowledge. When emotions become raw or out of balance, this elixir soothes and balances the emotions by expanding the heart.

Pearl also has the capacity to stimulate creativity and intuition. It can illuminate the impulses from deep within the hidden recesses of the psyche, bringing to the surface the deeply rooted impressions lodged in the unconscious. Pearl cleanses the shadowy content of the psyche and thus cultures a refined and balanced disposition. The ebb and flow is between a greater level of emotional detachment and the heightened sensitivity gained through increased vulnerability.

Pearl enhances subtle perception, including precognition. This elixir also activates the dream state, giving rise to vivid imagery of an archetypal nature that is beneficial in self-examination.

In addition to its association with the sacral chakra, Pearl has a gentle influence on the solar plexus and heart chakras. It has a stabilizing effect on the emotional creative energies generated in the second chakra and a transformative influence on the emotions associated with will and power, which are psycho-emotional themes of the third chakra. It also facilitates a deep witnessing value. The vibratory frequencies of limiting emotions are neutralized and brought to a finer feeling level, thus becoming integrated with the heart center.

For a watery-natured person, Pearl can produce an increase of the water element, creating edema, swelling, tendencies toward weight gain, and excessive psychic/emotional turbulence. On the other hand, the elixir has a healing influence on the stomach and the ability to neutralize negative emotions. It aids in the capacity to assimilate nutrition.

The strong electromagnetic force field of Pearl can create an excess of greed, attachments, sentimentality, and over-involvement with familial and social responsibilities. However, Pearl can also generate positive feelings of mothering and nurturing and tap into the archetypal energies of the Great Mother.

In China, Pearl is considered a love potion. It can also be used for longevity, as well as to treat skin disorders. It has traditionally been used to reduce heat in the body, calm anxiety, and settle the nervous system. It has also been used to enhance fertility, conception, and growth.

RED CORAL (MARS)

Coral is an organic material composed of calcified skeletons of coral polyps. Red Coral resonates with the planet Mars. The auspicious power of the Red Coral increases riches and removes the obstacles and dangers of the Mars energies.

Coral grows in the depths of the oceans, yet it has a fiery quality. The elixir acts as an amalgamating force for the alchemical union of the opposing elements of fire and water. Red Coral's virtues balance the intensity of the fire element through the soothing influence of the water element, thus calming a fiery temperament. It harmonizes the vital passion and warrior strength of Mars energies with the grace and creative powers of the primordial waters of life, which reside in the second chakra.

Red Coral brings into balance the unification of opposites. The elixir inspires clear-sighted, dynamic, creative, and pioneering actions. Out of the fertile, creative power within the second chakra, Red Coral supports an experience of self-nurturance and empowerment. The harmonizing influence of Red Coral imparts an understanding of how to work with the egoic self to stabilize a state of focused presence.

The guiding influence of Red Coral anchors the fiery Mars energies in centeredness, as opposed to self-centeredness. The emotional body learns to transmute anger, impatience, judgment, indecisiveness, and selfishness through the positive alchemical influences of Red Coral.

People needing Red Coral may have tendencies toward melancholy, depression, mental worry patterns, or inability to focus and take action. Edgar Cayce stated that Coral quiets emotions and attunes one to nature and the creative forces.

In worldwide traditions Coral is worn to stimulate fertility. Red Coral enhances attunement to the natural world of instinct and creative forces. It fortifies the vital body energy, catalyzing action, building strength, and cultivating courage. Red Coral is associated with the heart, circulatory system, and blood, and it has an ability to stimulate the metabolism. Coral's organic nature has a strengthening influence on the whole skeletal structure and can be useful in strengthening the spine and regenerating tissues and capillaries. Individuals with excess water element do very well with Red Coral.

Red Coral is also associated with the third, solar plexus, chakra. See "Solar Plexus Chakra" in this chapter for more information regarding this aspect of Red Coral.

HESSONITE (MOON'S NORTH NODE–RAHU)

The Hessonite gem resonates with the forces of the moon and has a powerful influence on the subconscious and creative forces housed in the sacral chakra. It is specifically attuned with the north node of the Moon, referred to as Rahu in Eastern Vedic astrology.

When one is in a main astrological Rahu cycle or sub-cycle, the energetic patterns he or she encounters may be extreme from both positive and negative perspectives. Depending on the placement in one's chart and one's spiritual maturity, this astrological influence can create great instability, chaos, unpredictable change, frustration, anxiety, fears, and setbacks. Rahu can activate old habits of a destructive, aggressive nature. It may cause a person to grasp at delusions created out of desire and to never feel a sense of satisfaction. This can lead to perpetuating more desires that never meet with fulfillment, causing feelings of lack, aloneness, abandonment, and disconnection from Source.

However, the Rahu period is also known to attract great personal and social power. It can magnetize wealth and other material gains, fame, spiritual discrimination, success, and the ability to attract.

The potential for transformation during the Rahu cycle is great and lies in one's ability to illuminate the subconscious creative powers of the second chakra. Such a transformational process transmutes delusions, desires, and tendencies into ingenious imagination. Inherent in this rite of purification is the springboard to creative endeavors, inspiration, originality, insight, and authenticity.

Hessonite supports the transformational potential within the second chakra by breaking the bondage of mental conditioning and rectifying negative energies in one's field. **Hessonite brings one into the present and supports transformational awakening toward living in the now, accepting what is, and learning that change is a form of stability.**

The vibratory intelligence of Hessonite can guide one through the enchanted realms and subtle dimensions involved in the spiritual journey. Hessonite can protect one from getting caught in the fantasies and seductive motives of the imagination, which are energetically locked in the second chakra. It promotes insight, self-examination, and self-inquiry into one's true nature and being.

Hessonite also helps to harness the primordial creative powers and pure imagination that arise through the portal of the second chakra. It increases one's ability to discern the difference between exaggerated fantasy and unconventional possibilities. Hessonite creates a magical air that carves pathways into manifest reality. This produces outcomes that are unusual, original, and ingenious, leaving the rational behind when no longer necessary.

Hessonite helps balance the sacral chakra and activates the creative, untapped energies from deep within one's emerging consciousness. It clarifies the subterranean mind fields, reducing confusion and removing the veils of illusion, so that clear vision permeates awareness. Hessonite strengthens the psyche in such a way that it gains immunity to temptation. It can assist in dismantling addictive, obsessive, compulsive, and neurotic patterns and habits.

Hessonite deepens inner sight, allowing one to travel safely into uncharted landscapes of the psyche. The protective power of Hessonite guards the gates of the underworld. One is able to gain entry into the shadow world of self while remaining centered, independent, and balanced. The gem ameliorates unfulfilled desire and lust that feed the control mechanisms of the psyche, robbing one of the objectivity needed for heightened spiritual awareness.

Used at the appropriate time, Hessonite ushers one's soul power to the foreground, directly guiding one to a profound state of inner freedom. In this emerging state, a person is able to maintain a clarity and discernment that sees through temptation, seduction, and desires that arise out of the delusions of the psyche. These subconscious issues hold the key to unlocking the primordial energies of the second chakra. Hessonite assists the psyche in clearing the debris of the past from this and other lifetimes.

Rahu is a blessing in the evolutionary pantheon. The influence of Divine Grace ameliorates the shadow effect of Rahu and points to the fact that Rahu is a gift from God. As the shadow self is brought into the purifying realm of self-inquiry, one is able to witness areas of the psyche that have been shrouded by denial or self-deception. The illusionary aspects of the unconscious are brought to light, leading to the realization that by letting go of what had previously been held sacred or inviolable, one aligns with Truth. Hessonite assists in releasing the sacred well of knowledge, held in the second chakra and brought to the forefront through the powers of Rahu.

FLOWER ESSENCES FOR THE SACRAL CHAKRA

HIBISCUS (*HIBISCUS ROSA-SINENSIS*)

Hibiscus facilitates an energetic opening and unification of the sacral and heart chakras, allowing divine, ecstatic energy to flow through the physical and subtle bodies. It opens the pathways of receptivity for the healing and transformative powers of creativity and love. A harmonic resonance between the heart, soul, and body is thus established, allowing nourishment of all kinds (nutrients, emotional, mental, and spiritual) to be fully received. As this process unfolds, these pathways of receptivity deepen into the touch of the divine ecstatic state.

In the Ayurvedic system of evolution and healing, Hibiscus is overseen by Ganesh, the deity that removes obstacles. This flower essence dissolves the patterns that cause obstacles on the energetic levels of the sacred, sexual, and creative expression in one's life. With the infusion of Hibiscus essence, these forces are able to ground more fully, as one begins to feel more at home and natural with one's instinctual, sexual nature. Thought-forms that prevent the individual from entering into ecstatic states of intimacy begin to dissolve.

Hibiscus concentrates one's attention into the fluid, conductive energy of the "now," facilitating the release of transcendental wave-forms of bliss. It is these infinite waves that carry the regenerative power for life expression, creativity, and love.

STICKY MONKEYFLOWER (*MIMULUS AURANTIACUS*)

Sticky Monkeyflower opens the channels of communication between the soul and second chakra. As the soul's impulses release into the sacral chakra, setting up a resonance field with the heart, a growing exchange of intimacy is developed with Self and other. This art of communion becomes a present, living reality.

Sticky Monkeyflower assists the soul in releasing fears held in the heart and sacral chakras. Through the dissolution of fears, receptivity to deep penetrating truths concerning relationships, love, and sexuality illumines the psyche.

This essence teaches the soul how to safely bond through the mystical and unexplainable realms of intimacy and sacred sexual love. Sticky Monkeyflower guides the psyche to embrace partnership as a higher shared purpose, unifying the two souls in the art of sacred communion with each other.

PINK MONKEYFLOWER (*MIMULUS LEWISII*)

Fear is the most primal emotion within the sacral chakra. All of the Monkeyflower essences address the interface between fear and intimacy from different psychic vantage points. As an individual enters unbounded states of union, an instinctual fear of death arises. This death is an egoic passing away, a psychological death that has the capacity to leave one free from conditioned referencing and identity. Pink Monkeyflower lifts the weight of fear that occurs as the personal identity and ancestral cellular memories dissolve. The mental and emotional fields are imprinted with the soul qualities of receptivity, courage, and bravery.

Pink Monkeyflower penetrates directly into the heart chakra, opening one to the inner regions of one's primal space. This accentuates the awareness of inner heart space to disclose the vulnerable aspects of the psyche that previously have been used to defend one's ego or identity.

Pink Monkeyflower also facilitates a personal and transpersonal state of trust in the giving and receiving of human and divine love. This allows the emotional body to gain confidence to access deeper levels of love. Feelings of rejection, guilt, or shame are transmuted into self-acceptance, love, and compassion.

EASTER LILY (*LILIUM LONGIFLORUM*)

Easter Lily opens the pathways for the soul to touch deep into the primordial field of the sexual spirit. This flower essence guides the psyche out of the psychological duality of the mind, which polarizes and divides sexual from spiritual expression, integrating these two seemingly diverse energies.

Easter Lily calls forth the elements of elegance and grace from within the soul. It assists the psyche in gaining awareness of the physical and spiritual nature forces that are divinely seductive. In this process, the transpersonal field expands and the gap between personal and divine dissolves. Personal identification is surrendered in the presence of the beloved Self.

Easter Lily symbolizes the pinnacle of Christic light, which lives as the passion of creative power from within.

CRAB APPLE (*MALUS SYLVESTRIS*)

Crab Apple essence supports the deep transformation and unlocking of the psychic, creative shakti coiled within the sacral chakra. Crab Apple dissolves and washes away the thought-forms hidden in the crevices of one's personal Pandora's box. The washing away of the ancient beliefs of sin gradually occurs through the realization that the body is the temple of the soul.

Crab Apple clears the psyche and body of thought-forms imprinted in the mind and cellular memories. It addresses the mistaken understanding of one's sexual nature as imperfect, unworthy, tainted, or repugnant, which has created impressions in the mind/body field that weaken the core energetic expression of the soul.

Crab Apple energetically cleanses the emotional and mental bodies, revealing the eternal witness of white light within in its pristine state of origin. It washes away toxic emotional and mental imprints that have been taken on psychically from others or in self-judgment.

Crab Apple enhances the dissolution process of egoic structures that are no longer useful to one's present reality. As toxic psycho-emotional conditions are cleared out of the mind of the sacral chakra, whole-body awareness is led to the holy land of the soul. The body turns its attention toward the sacred and bathes in the radiant purity of the white light.

CALLA LILY (*ZANTEDESCHIA AETHIOPICA*)

Calla Lily facilitates the feminine and masculine forces within the psyche to function in harmonic resonance, inspiring the power of the soul to help it release the boundaries of social definition related to gender. The psyche can then truly begin to explore new levels of creative power and authentic expression of the sexual spirit.

One experiences freedom in the realization of oneself as a whole, sacred, sexual being. Shakti and Shiva unify at the base of the spine and rise through the chakra system. As each chakra establishes unification, the polarities integrate, opening consciousness to the timelessness of the soul and creating life out of the realms of visionary manifestation.

Calla Lily brings the soul through the primal and social initiatic gates of self-love, acceptance, and integration, setting up the energetic matrix for the illumination of the holographic psyche.

BASIL (*OCIMUM BASILICUM*)

Basil brings equilibrium to the heart and sacral chakras. It is revered by ancient cultures as one of the most sacred plants. In the Hindu tradition it is regarded as the flower that unfolds the depths of love and devotion in the heart.

The essence of Basil activates an alchemical marriage of spirit and matter. In the fusion of spirit and matter within, the ecstatic state of eternal wholeness is awakened.

Basil creates a steadfast and balanced relationship between the dynamic force of surrender and the autonomous formation of identity. It creates balance in cases where an individual or a couple exhibits imbalances in terms of dominance or submission, bringing harmony and truth to the expression of love and sexuality.

POMEGRANATE (*PUNICA GRANATUM*)

Pomegranate flower essence acts to balance the creative force in both men and women. The essence transcends gender identification and creates a rebirth of soul energy in alignment with one's life purpose and destiny. Such a birth can be internal in terms of psycho-spiritual processes, or it can be external, in the form of physical manifestation such as a new career, a creative endeavor, or the birth of a child.

Pomegranate enhances a person's access to his or her spiritual gifts. With the help of this essence, the individual's perspective is shifted from limitation to abundance and he or she can actualize the fullness of life with greater ease and acceptance.

THE SOLAR PLEXUS CHAKRA

The third chakra, the solar plexus, is called the *Manipura*, "the city of gems" in Sanskrit. It is the largest chakra of the body, expanding around the naval area, and it is the source point for the fount of pre-natal nourishment, out of which all major *nadis* originate.

The solar plexus plays a central role in the transformation of the ego self into the divine Self and the development of the light body. The solar plexus houses the fire element, which governs the sense of sight, intellect, and will. The fire element is a transmuting power that regulates the metabolic processes within the physical and psychic bodies. Its direction is upward; the path that it takes through the physiology is a threefold triune function localized at focal points in the eyes, navel, and thighs corresponding to Aries, Leo, and Sagittarius. It governs one's identity and the process of manifestation that leads to outward recognition.

Within the solar plexus chakra, digestion affects how information is metabolized from the physical and subtle levels. The solar plexus functions as a type of light generator that illumines the infinite space within, generating both an internal and an external light. The qualities generated by this inner light uphold the power of our essence as it is expressed through the soul and into the manifest world.

The eyes, the windows of the soul, focus the light of the solar plexus, giving rise to divinely inspired vision. As intelligence receives the visionary impulse of the soul's eyes, then one can determine direction, goal, and action for manifestation in the world.

The solar portal is a space in which the manifestation of the higher Self can emerge. The will force associated with this chakra, which is the initiating principle of one's vision and purpose when surrendered to the God force, allows the higher Self to become an active guide and witness to one's life. *Dharmic*, or purposeful, action creates a magnetic grid that aligns one with the synchronous order of nature.

Once Spirit is set free, the radiance of the solar Self guides the development of character that actualizes the soul's passion and purpose. As the soul force grows through the inner light, one's sense of knowing and course of action in the world transcends the ego. The attributes of strength, determination, and courage lend meaning to the cosmic "I Am" presence. The transparent spark of divinity radiates into the environment in the same manner as the shining light of the sun. The principle of authority that governs life in action is a transpersonal phenomenon akin to the realization of "I" as the God force.

Bio-Resonant Remedies for Mastering the Solar Plexus Chakra

Planetary Gems/Elixirs—Yellow Sapphire, Red Coral, and Ruby

Flower Essences—Sunflower, Yellow Star Tulip, Fawn Lily, Tiger Lily, California Wild Rose, Wild Oat, Larkspur, Larch, and Echinacea

This group of gems and flower essences cultivates the development of the higher purpose lived through the solar plexus chakra. It expands the influence of personal identity to reflect the infinite reality of the cosmic solar matrix. The soul undertakes a voyage in which there is a gradual, mystical infusion of the higher-dimensional continuum of the Oversoul into the personality structure. The new vibrational frequencies that carry the patterns for an individualized Christic identity merge with the light-filled vortex of the solar plexus.

As the solar plexus chakra matures through grace, spiritual practices, flower essences, and gem elixirs, the individual experiences a shift from an isolated arena based on the narcissistic needs of the personal self to a transpersonal, all-encompassing, cosmic identity. The experience of this new identity is based on direct cognition of an inherent connection to a galactic nexus. Higher-dimensional aspects of the soul are braided into the present mind/body unit. The subconscious mind becomes a permeable reservoir that is illumined by specific flower essences. Prayerful intention can then bring about a permanent and irrevocable unification of the mind/body/spirit.

As we continue to surrender the ego/will to the higher impulses of a transpersonal Divine Will through the use of these vibrational materials, synchronicity forms the backdrop for powerful evolutionary events to occur in our personal reality. This results in the integration of linear thinking and reasoning with instantaneous awareness of right action. This level of realization combines the freedom and power of spiritual alignment with the flow of personal choice. The solar plexus thus becomes the seat of an invincible faith and knowingness that guides and carries the soul through life.

PLANETARY GEMS/ELIXIRS FOR THE SOLAR PLEXUS CHAKRA

YELLOW SAPPHIRE (JUPITER)

Yellow Sapphire has an affinity for the solar plexus, third eye, and crown chakras. The solar plexus, being the largest of the chakras, is naturally attuned to Jupiter, the largest and most expansive of the planets. Yellow Sapphire resonates with the frequencies of Jupiter, activating the Jupiterian qualities of expansiveness, benevolence, kindness, and graciousness in the auric field of the individual.

Yellow Sapphire brightens the field of the mind and opens awareness to the higher Self. The gem provides a gateway to higher learning, facilitating mental clarity by expanding the mind's ability to comprehend in a holistic context. This process unfolds the capacity to research knowledge out of one's own field of consciousness. It sharpens the intellect to function clearly and articulate finer levels of perception and insight.

This inner sight guides one to see/feel into the celestial realms in order to witness the interaction of space and time. Yellow Sapphire assists in cultivating stillness, silence, and peace, and it reveals the intricate order of subtle light that lines the cosmos. To gaze into the center of Yellow Sapphire's pristine array of geometric patterns is to look into the eyes of God.

Through the use of Yellow Sapphire, the solar plexus chakra is cleared of disturbances that obstruct the light of consciousness. A soft cushion of objectivity for seeing within is cultivated. Thus one gains a subtler understanding of life events and their relationship to the formation of both personal and multidimensional reality. **This gem elixir supports the expansion of personal space/time reality, as it stretches into the transpersonal realms of the higher Self.** This permits accelerated synchronization to occur, creating fertile ground for benevolent opportunities and good fortune to grace one's life.

The living intelligence of the planet Jupiter governs the higher orders of spiritual life. The Jupiterian energy radiating through the Yellow Sapphire acts as a divine host; through its majestic design it opens sealed interdimensional portals. As the solar plexus chakra receives Yellow Sapphire's radiant intelligence, the soul is escorted into the once hidden chambers of the ancient wisdom-keepers. The wisdom-keepers are the guardians of Truth and Higher Knowledge—the Ascended Masters, angelic light beings, and teachers on the inner planes. These subtle beings of divine intelligence are the benevolent protectors of the ancient universal systems of initiation.

The golden yellow field of light generated by Yellow Sapphire fills the solar plexus chakra and inspires joy, generosity, kindness, gentleness, and power. It strengthens one's faith, devotion, and inner sense of Self as a divine being whose birthright is to receive great reward and good fortune. As the light of spirit lifts the heart, a presence of love, protection, and guidance from the angelic worlds becomes tangible. Yellow Saphhire elixir expands awareness of the presence of sentient light that is the ordering principle of life on earth and on the celestial planes.

Yellow Sapphire assists with the integration of the solar plexus chakra with the third eye and crown chakras. It imbues the spiritual laws of initiation necessary for entry into sacred mysteries of life and co-creation. Under the guardianship of Yellow Sapphire, one learns to discern between and acquire the ability to use the human attributes of instinct, intuition, cognition, and original and innate intellect. This gem elixir expands one's insight into direct cognitive awareness of the celestial planes, which contain sacred knowledge. As the initiate seer is made ready, the protective veils of intellectual ignorance gradually melt away. This gives space to increase one's learning abilities and retain universal knowledge expressed as practical wisdom.

As a result of this process, the seeker gains divine status and can learn to penetrate the fabric of creation through the focal point of inner vision. The sublime meaning behind the surface of relative life is revealed. One views life as a field of metaphorical teaching that the soul dreams into the external world of matter. Yellow Sapphire, empowered with the Jupiterian essence, brings a harmonious integration between material and spiritual awareness.

Yellow Sapphire has the capacity to uplift and requalify energy through the navel plexus, attracting opportunities and good fortune. The gem elixir attunes the soul to its destiny. Destiny is both absolute and relative to one's state of consciousness. Yellow Sapphire adjusts the cranial field to support the evolution and majesty of one's soul.

Through the use of Yellow Sapphire, the frequencies that form present awareness shift to a higher level of vibration. Karmic patterns are transmuted to reveal the new orders of relationship between self and other. This may take the form of a new career or direction in life that is more fulfilling and serves humanity in a larger, more universal capacity.

RED CORAL (MARS)

Red Coral has an affinity for the solar plexus as well as the sacral chakra, due to its resonance with both the fire and water elements associated with those chakras, respectively. While the sacral chakra is the home of the water element, the solar plexus is the home of the fire element in the human physiology. The harmonic blend of the fiery components of Red Coral, with the balancing influence of the water element, inspires the vision to command one's life through a greater sense of selflessness, compassion, and inclusiveness, releasing personal will and ego.

The solar, or navel, plexus is the largest chakra and is where all the major *nadis* originate. It is the source point for the vital creative energy known as *chi* in the Chinese system. Red Coral creates a resonant attunement with the solar plexus chakra that provides the impetus toward transformation.

The light body, the eternal sanctuary that carries the authentic spiritual vibration of the soul, can be uplifted and sustained by Red Coral aiding in the transformation of the binding influence of the ego. The higher Self becomes the fundamental source of both action and knowing, illuminating the solar plexus in its role as an inner light generator. Red Coral assists in the development of a strong sense of the Atman, or eternal Self, directed by Spirit.

Red Coral entrains the initiate to extol the virtues of selfless service, decisive leadership, and wisdom. When one has mastered the art of surrender, the personal will dissolves into the transpersonal God force. The eyes take on a transparent luminescence that reveals a window to the soul. Thus, the celestial guardianship of Spirit enables one to envision life from the highest levels of awareness.

Coral has been used in many different cultures. Coral inlays and ornaments have been found in Celtic tombs dating from the Iron Age. Coral is one of the "seven treasures" in Buddhist scriptures, and Tibetan lamas use coral rosaries. It has been used through the ages to stop bleeding, protect from evil spirits, and even ward off hurricanes.

In Ayurvedic medicine, Red Coral has historically been used in cases of excess mucus membrane secretion. It acts as an astringent, tonifying the membranes and tissues. It has been used in cases of eye problems, indigestion, fevers, loss of appetite, and obesity. All these physiological conditions are centered in the solar plexus and are governed by the metabolic function of the fire element.

[Note: Ruby can also be used for the solar plexus chakra. See "Planetary Gem/Elixir for the Leo Archetype" and "Planetary Gem/Elixir for the Root Chakra."]

FLOWER ESSENCES FOR THE SOLAR PLEXUS CHAKRA

SUNFLOWER (*HELIANTHUS ANNUUS*)

Sunflower essence has an affinity for the solar plexus chakra. It embodies the radiant solar energy and guiding light that clarifies and distills one's relationship to the Father. Sunflower essence qualifies the imprinting of the biological father with the transpersonal Father principle. The Father archetype represents authority, power, leadership, direction, action, and identity—all issues associated with the third chakra.

Sunflower balances the ego in its journey to unify with the higher Self.[4] The ego's veil of perception is lifted, revealing Truth. Thus, the ego gains the ability to release identification with the small notion of self, and this allows authentic spiritual power to govern one's life—the central theme within the third chakra.

The sun consciousness grows in its radiant capacity to compassionately guide the actions and momentum of life. Sunflower rectifies life events in which solar energies have been either overpowering or have lacked strength. This process brings to balance the right use of power generated from within the solar plexus chakra.

Sunflower cultivates an innate sense of guidance from within. It navigates the psyche towards an awakening into the central core of Self. The God Self is brought forth in its full expression, supporting the mystical inception of Divine Grace.

YELLOW STAR TULIP (*CALOCHORTUS MONOPHYLLUS*)

Yellow Star Tulip cultures the heart toward universal love and compassion. It creates a heartfelt empathic link with the life stream of people, plants, animals, and the environment. This process opens the solar plexus towards empathic action. As a result, a more global persona is cultivated, inviting one toward a deep awareness of caring and participation in the stewardship of the Earth and its inhabitants.

Yellow Star Tulip aligns one's soul energies with collective evolutionary trends. One's receptivity to the subtle impulses and bio-geological event messages of Gaia are directly experienced in the mind/body awareness. **The opening toward feeling-based knowing is cultured deeply in the heart.**

FAWN LILY (*ERYTHRONIUM PURPURASCENS*)

Fawn Lily warms the light-coded matrices of the solar plexus to allow the integration of transpersonal soul knowledge with everyday events. The heartfelt desire to deepen the significance of one's life grows stronger as spiritual gifts open through the use of Fawn Lily. This can lead to a profound commitment to serve the earth in a greater capacity.

Fawn Lily softens the membranes of the subtle bodies, allowing the life-force energies to flow more fully and effectively. The result is a greater recognition of an individual's uniqueness, which allows for the inner light of the navel plexus to radiate out into the world his or her gifts, talents, and skills.

TIGER LILY (*LILIUM HUMBOLDTII*)

Tiger Lily essence opens the energy matrix between the sacral and solar plexus chakras. This opening produces a spiraling energy vortex that houses the regenerative force of creative passion.

Tiger Lily activates the powers of the dynamic feminine energy within the soul and infuses it deep within the chakras, especially the solar plexus chakra. This transformative feminine power transmutes self-centered egoic will toward a transpersonal Divine Will, allowing for a renewed flow of grace that supports the development of synchronicity and coherent actualization.

Tiger Lily strengthens the collective spirit for successful leadership from the soul. Tiger Lily cultivates an integrated maturation process that fosters cooperation, harmony, and co-creative processes among individuals, groups, and organizations. The feminine principle, so vital and often missing in the manifestation process, is necessary for embracing a planetary vision that honors collective health, harmony, and human rights.

CALIFORNIA WILD ROSE (*ROSA CALIFORNICA*)

California Wild Rose assists the individual to embody the power of spirit and the forces of love through the whole body. The power of spirit and force of love create a fusion and communication link between the third and fourth chakras.

California Wild Rose conveys a Venusian quality that is symbolized in this flower's five-petal numerical value. This numerical value has a deep correlation to the human form, which bonds spirit and matter. The destiny of every soul is to fully embody spirit while in the human body. Divine union is invoked through the marriage of spirit and matter.

Through the use of California Wild Rose, a dynamic love force and passion for life are cultivated in one's being. The joy of participating in life takes on a timelessness that lifts matter free from a state of inertia and allows the infusion of spirit. Spirit sets its course to ignite, animate, and give direction to the creative spark in the dynamic expression of life. California Wild Rose flower essence is a carrier wave for spirit to manifest into matter.

WILD OAT (*BROMUS RAMOSUS*)

Wild Oat flower essence aligns the solar plexus chakra with the third eye. Wild Oat attunes one to life purpose and assists in birthing its manifestation. Each individual soul is encoded with subtle pictorial information that identifies its purpose on a personal and collective level.

Wild Oat assists the individual in gaining the discipline and realization necessary to perform purposeful action. **Through the use of this essence, the individual opens to the innate codes in his or her genetic blueprint and translates them, first to the level of enhanced soul sensibility, then to the level of action.**

Wild Oat strengthens the electromagnetic currents, fostering synchronous action in daily life. The Will, directed from the higher Self, infuses the persona with illumination, guidance, and a sense of service and devotion.

Wild Oat enables one's consciousness to root itself in the destiny of the soul. This facilitates the harmonizing of the solar plexus and heart chakras. Wild Oat addresses and clarifies questions of personal identity and the soul's decision to incarnate on the physical level. This essence catalyzes self-realization and accesses the power within to embrace one's true calling, allowing spiritual leadership and self-empowerment to emerge from the essence of one's own nature.

LARKSPUR (*DELPHINIUM NUTTALLIANUM*)

Larkspur flower essence invokes the quality of joy that rises out of the soul when one is purposefully participating in life. Larkspur centers the radiant shakti energy in the heart and solar plexus, igniting inspiration, enthusiasm, and charisma. The quality of being a global participant unfolds out of an eternal state of authentic spiritual empowerment, clarity, and humility.

Larkspur essence catalyzes the skills of true soul leadership. The soul leads with a combination of both intuitive and practical sensibility, which guides projects that serve a greater good for both people and the planet.

LARCH (*LARIX DECIDUA*)

Larch essence creates a path of articulation between the solar plexus and the throat chakra. This alignment creates a deep confidence with which one can express one's fullest being. Larch catalyzes the soul's internal modes of creativity. Creative intelligence sprouts a world-changing self-confidence that can light the flame of the heart and mind and give rise to personal empowerment.

Confidence is the ability to act in integrity with oneself. With rising confidence, the soul's power becomes more expressive, freed from the conditions of fear and failure. A peaceful state of confidence secures one's ability to be in the world as a full participant.

Larch essence dissolves the boundaries of mind that bind and separate. As the transpersonal soul nature emerges, the qualities of leadership dominate the awareness, indicating that the persona now rests at the feet of the soul.

ECHINACEA (*ECHINACEA PURPUREA*)

Echinacea flower essence is one of the most powerful botanicals. It reconstitutes one's origin of light, strengthening the core Self. The fragmented parts of personalized self are reorganized and aligned toward a state of integrated wholeness.

Echinacea cultures the qualities of endurance, strength, and fortitude. These qualities of the soul are essential when one is deep into the transformational process of releasing the identity structures of the ego and learning to navigate reality from a non-referential state.

Echinacea assists the soul in maintaining a steadfast state in one's core structures of being. In this core state of unshakable strength and endurance, the personality that oversees third-dimensional reality can now seamlessly interface with one's multidimensional transpersonal reality. This integration of functioning allows the psyche to safely experience timeless movement, which is an advanced state of the heart that calibrates functioning out of the eternal. The timeless heart holds to nothing and is at the core of Life Alone.

Echinacea energetically elevates the soul to preview life's events as they approach from the horizon of imprinting. It gives one the ability to witness events simultaneously, allowing the rhythmic time/space intervals of the soul to process the information of life's events as they emerge from the event horizon.

Echinacea strengthens the core point of self-referencing within the solar plexus, which feeds one's subtle systems. This core referencing value creates a regenerative and integrative process that originates in an eternal light center. The heart/soul light braids the separated aspects of one's persona into the whole of the holographic Self.

Echinacea flower essence stabilizes the psyche as one establishes the central core of Being. The mind/body unit learns to anchor as an eternal felt referencing of Self. The mind's attempt to cling to a temporal reality is released, and the fragments seamlessly reconfigure in wholeness. The soul is unencumbered and can explore as free form an ever-expanding, non-localized field of awareness.

THE HEART CHAKRA

The fourth chakra, the heart (*Anahata* chakra in Sanskrit), is located in the area of the cardiac plexus or lungs. The heart chakra is the home of the air element. It is associated with the qualities of timelessness, communication, compassion, kindness, and gentleness.

This chakra brings integration between the upper and lower parts of the body, uniting the four directions in the vertical and horizontal axes. The heart creates a vortex of energy that allows awareness to penetrate through multiple levels of reality, culminating in a point of unification at the heart's center.

Within the center of the physical heart is the spiritual heart. It is here that the qualities of purity and innocence, as well as the state of "I am That, thou art That," are cultivated. It is through the heart chakra that the emotional body is purified and transformed, creating the foundation of compassion. The heart chakra transmutes emotional energy into the finest feeling level.

The cultivation of the heart chakra brings one into an intuitive experience and wisdom state. Through the heart, one remains youthful, as awareness transcends false time consciousness.

Purification in the heart chakra dissolves obstacles blocking both the upward and downward flow of transmuted energy from the other centers of the body. Distortions in the heart chakra can give rise to anxiety, indicating that one may be out of rhythm with one's cosmic pulse of life. But integration within the heart promotes an objective witnessing state. Awareness can freely and easily interact with a subject/object while maintaining an inner experience of true Self.

Balance, coherence, and integration of the heart chakra support a self-generating energy of radiant love that feeds the physiology, thus creating happiness and bliss. Within this center, the synchronization and rhythm of the physical heart can be phase locked in resonance with the rhythms of the Earth and cosmos. The experience of past, present, and future is integrated towards an all-time consciousness.

The heart chakra regulates the spiral vortices of love; its governing influence spans the range from the physical to the spiritual realms, functioning as an amplitude regulator. The matrices of love inlaid throughout the physical and subtle bodies create a platform in the mind/body field consciousness to be propelled into the realms of the upper chakras, where awakened consciousness unifies with the God force.

The heart chakra, as the seat of feeling, is the arena of emotional transformation on the personality level; feelings of separation, loneliness, and sadness are transmuted into unity, belonging, and bliss. This process fosters a mastery over the patterns of the breath, instilling conscious control of the heart rate and respiration.

Through mastery of breath, one can consciously direct the pranic life force to any area in the physiology. Circulating prana supports cellular intelligence throughout the whole body. Within the heart chakra, one can enter into a selfless spiritual devotion that serves collective humanity and the divine.

The heart is the center of "spin" in the body. It is where the greatest amount of electrical focus resides, acting as a harmonic wave. Seven discrete layers of the heart are arranged exactly in the spin angles of the tetrahedron. Thus the geometry of the heart contains all of the symmetry of the spins. **The actual physical shape of the heart enables it to weave all electrical waves into one.** Thus, the wave-form of the heart becomes self-replicating, an infinite fractal image of itself.

The resonant frequency of the heart holds a ratio of 1.618, the ratio of the Golden Mean. The shape of the heart literally translates into the Golden Mean spiral. The resonant sound of the heart phase-locks and orders the sound in the liquid ventricles of the brain to function as superconductive pathways for ecstatic experience.[5]

As the heart chakra grows in the coherence of love, it sets up a bio-resonant harmonic feedback loop with the DNA. One becomes a body of love.

Love is the predominant emotion/feeling field behind brainwave coherence. Increasing the capacity to generate and assimilate love precipitates organization of a fluid light body. When the heart chakra is radiating the coherent emotion of love, we awaken higher frequencies of intelligence. Coherence of the individual heart entrains the heart chakra of humanity and Mother Earth. **Each human heart is integral in the cosmic event of planetary enlightenment.**

Bio-Resonant Remedies for Mastering the Heart Chakra

Planetary Gems/Elixirs: Emerald, Rose Quartz, and Diamond

Flower Essences: Holly, Evening Primrose, Baby Blue Eyes, Bleeding Heart, Mariposa Lily, Zinnia, Shooting Star, Mallow, and Fawn Lily

This group of flower essences and gem elixirs for the heart chakra calls forth the indwelling child state of innocence and unconditional being. The focused heart light cultivated by these essences and elixirs transforms and expands the capacity for joy, compassion, kindness, childlike purity, innocence, and unconditional love. This heart light transmutes the limited emotional content held in the mind/body complex, thus cultivating the finest feeling level of love and wholeness.

Through the use of these elixirs, the power of the illuminated heart assists the soul in giving new expression to the ancestral origins of light and consciousness within the core Self. This recapitulation of the original soul light infuses the heart with a transpersonal presence. **The process of healing the fragmented and wounded aspects of the personality brings forward an expanded unification that permits the wisdom and talents of the soul to emerge.**

The color-coded prisms of the soul guide one on a journey to the transpersonal dimensions of the psyche. Through these elixirs and essences, hidden aspects of the soul are now able to become present in this dimension as well as others. The original light of the heart washes through the emotional pain of rejection, alienation, withdrawal, and loneliness, filling the emotional body with the nourishment of love and light.

Early in life, the developing ego becomes identified with internal and external conditioning that can create separation and suffering. As the individuated consciousness grows in its ability to focus light through the heart center, the ego-bound structures become transparent. The power of a focused heart light dismantles inauthentic belief structures and conditions of mind. The transparency of the ego cultures the quality of sacred objectivity.

As these elixirs heal the mind and heart, the gap of separation becomes seamless, and a renewed and balanced state is sustained in the emotional field. The emotional body is free, thus unconditionally supporting a clear lens of perception. This is a direct inspiration from the womb of the originating heart light. At this stage, the ego is a transparent face in which the divine soul of light can shine.

The radiant heart light enables the inner child state to draw on an unlimited reservoir of love and acceptance through the spiritual union of maternal and paternal forces within our own higher nature. The emotional body is sourced from the light of spirit and the joy of our heartfelt Presence.

Presence is the experience of self-love as Love itself. The hardened aspects of the personality gently melt away, revealing the beauty and innocence of the indwelling child state. The heart-light state of the inner child moves fluidly, free from the deliberations of the mind. The soul comes forth in the openheartedness of all life experiences. The heart light radiates as the power of spirit to see beyond human conditions with clarity and compassion for oneself and others.

The soul that radiates as the original heart light is graced with power and authenticity to manifest the desires of the divine for all sentient life. This powerful group of essences and elixirs creates a centrifugal force that magnetizes life-supporting elements out of the divine design. Through the illuminated heart of the soul, the emotional body is cleared to feel freely the creative and cognitive forces of the soul's manifest destiny on earth. The source of joy and contentment is likened to a baby's breath, the eternal now.

PLANETARY GEMS/ELIXIRS FOR THE HEART CHAKRA

EMERALD (MERCURY)

Emerald gemstone vibrates the geo-chromatic frequencies and harmonics of the planet Mercury. Emerald refines all forms of communication—including speech, writing, and inner communication—with higher intelligence. The gem elixir further attunes one to the higher values of the heart center, thus generating love and appreciation for Mother Nature, abundance, prosperity, goodwill, and kindness.

Emerald deepens one's ability to love self and other, opening the portals between the human heart and the heart of Nature. This enables the free flow of energetic exchange that gives rise to heightened appreciation and reverence for all life. The abundance of life becomes lively in the heart, pouring forth the movements of devotion. Emerald renews zest for life and love of the pure essence of existence.

Emerald infuses all the subtle bodies with the vibration of divine love. It opens the heart to the Divine Mother energies of love and receptivity, and it has a calming, soothing, and deeply relaxing influence. It also stabilizes the personality and brings into balance the universal male/female energies. The sacred process of union within takes place in the inner chambers of the heart center, culturing feelings of devotion and gratitude.

Emerald aids in the communication and circulation of information on the inner and outer planes. It radiates the green ray, which has great healing power for regeneration, growth, and renewal of life. The power of the Emerald green ray is essential to the life of all plants, animals, and human beings. It supports the health, integrity, and balance of the physical body.

The light within the Emerald elixir is integral to the mind/body consciousness undergoing the mystical transmutation of our personal realities. **Mastery of the use of words in the act of co-creating holds the key to the kingdom of heaven on earth and other planes.** Ultimately, the gem teaches the divine vibration of love that is the living foundation of truth, wisdom, and creation. It purifies the heart chakra to radiate universal love and establishes the holy ground of peace and contentment.

As one utilizes the Emerald elixir, the mind/body engages in the process of self-regeneration, activating the power to directly metabolize color and light. The geo-chromatic and harmonic frequencies of the Emerald elixir saturate the physical body and radiantly cascade into the subtle bodies.

The abundant green ray found in plants teaches us how to metabolize cosmic light directly from the source. It is the green ray of nature that metabolizes light and releases oxygen into the environment. The green chlorophyll within the infrastructure of plants produces the breath of life for sentient beings on Earth. The green ray inherent in Emerald nourishes the cells that are responsible for metabolic respiration.

The Emerald green ray is the most abundant, sustaining, and focalizing point of balance in the spectrum of light. It harmonizes and acts as a medium of conductivity, as well as a point of convergence of energies. The mystical Emerald ignites the spirit of eternal renewal.

The geo-chromatic resonant frequency of Emerald is attuned to the planet Mercury, which has a direct association with the air element. The air element is the medium that, when vibrated, creates sound. The organization of vibrational patterns traveling in air communicates kinesthetic, felt meaning; the subtle impulses of intelligence conducted along the airwaves establishes the neurological pathways for communication of information, including advanced levels, such as telepathic communication, which pulses through the mind field and registers visually on a soul level and in the brain and nervous system.

As Emerald receives and transmits the cosmic energies of the planet Mercury, it functions as a conduit for higher orders of intelligence. The planet Mercury is referred to in Greek mythology as the messenger of the gods. The celestial mercurial nature is articulate, quick, fluid, adaptive, and brilliant. Its brilliance infuses the field of the intellect.

The mercurial influences govern intelligence, especially as it displays itself in the mind field. Habitual modalities of thinking and perceiving reality gradually give way to the faculty of higher cognition, and direct knowing enters the foreground of consciousness. Cognition is a function of intelligence within the supraconscious mind field. The mercurial mind, having mastered the art and science of communion and communication with the God intelligence, radiates the brilliance of Truth.

The highest capacity of communication associated with Mercury comes from Spirit. Emerald elixir, in its harmonic attunement with the planet Mercury, functions as a conductor of cosmic knowledge—"a messenger of the gods." One gains the capacity to better apply the spiritual wisdom of discernment, discrimination, authenticity, and truth in each moment.

Emerald is capable of transmuting and transmitting multidimensional layers of information. Mercury's innate nature has at its disposal the divine power of the Word or *logos*. The mercurial supraconscious mind grows in self-mastery on the level of communication through entering a state of communion with the God force. This predisposes one to be a sensitive co-creator for the shifting of life on earth and the development of alternative technologies. The fundamental values of Truth can then become a living reality in the fullness of one's life.

The disposition of the mercurial mind is to inquire into the nature of reality, beliefs, fixed perspectives, and judgments. **Mercury governs the radical structures of linguistic architecture, which have the potential to catalyze the mind to change physical reality.** It offers us the ability to swing free of the normal standardization of the mental field and to become a vehicle for the will and functioning of the mind of God.

At auspicious, celestial time intervals, using Emerald elixir will activate the higher mercurial powers of the supraconscious mind. This opens one to the portal into multiple worlds of reality and avenues of communication. The challenges posed by Mercury include confusion, miscommunication, ill use of words, anxiety, weakness in the nervous system, and interrupted flow of pranic breath on the subtle levels. Emerald elixir neutralizes and transmutes these undesirable aspects of mercurial influence.

Emerald elixir can catalyze advanced initiatic spiritual processes. In order to be a messenger of the gods or conveyor of true divine inspiration, one must gain the ability to travel and communicate beyond any space/time measurement. Emerald elixir opens the portals of celestial intelligence that expand the heart. Emerald conducts the subtle celestial values of sound and light in a downward spin through the subtle physiology. It cultivates a superfluidity that alters the matrix of the mind/body to become so flexible as to even impart the capacity to shift shape or form. The mind/body consciousness then begins to learn how to live the immortal life potential inherent in our DNA.

Emerald elixir enhances the metabolism and conductivity of light. Light conducted coherently in the physiology becomes laser-like in nature. This laser phenomenon acts like a universal glue that upholds the unifying value of creation referred to in the Vedic texts as *soma*. Soma is the food of the gods; it creates both infinite coherence and superconductive communication. It is the immortal elixir that can be generated from within and can feed us eternally.

ROSE QUARTZ

Quartz is one of the most abundant minerals on earth. Rose Quartz reveals its significance through its geo-chromatic resonance with the human heart, the most distinguishing characteristic of Earth's inhabitants. The magnitude and power of feeling within the heart is what defines our human species; it is our energetic signature to all other living forms of intelligence.

Rose Quartz elixir opens the emotional field, softening the human heart. It assists one in cultivating a sensitivity that resides in the heart, the holy grail of love. Rose Quartz is a universal harmonizer for the heart, creating balance, equilibrium, and the knowledge that one is interconnected with all other beings and sentient life on the planet and beyond.

Rose Quartz generates, transmits, and amplifies one's divinity through the heart chakra. The human heart is a primary orchestrator, liberator, and communicator in the soul of life on Earth and throughout the galaxies. Rose Quartz assists the heart chakra to radiate the coherent emotion of universal love. The emotional frequency of Love enables one to cross dimensions without the loss of energy; in other words, it allows one to experience the Self as a radiant being that unboundedly travels beyond the galaxies.

Rose Quartz allows the heart to enter a state of surrender, graciousness, and open vulnerability, to feel true reality within self and others. This occurs while simultaneously maintaining a strong center and integration of core Self. One's soul self is never lost in the unbounded movements into the unified experience of Love. It imprints the meaning of unconditional love as an eternal state of peace in acceptance. One experiences the merger of "I Am Thou," "I Am That," "I Am All," and "All Is I." Rose Quartz guides the heart to its all-encompassing pinnacle of Radiance.

DIAMOND (SEE THIRD EYE CHAKRA)

Diamond is ruled by Venus, often seen as the Goddess of Love and Beauty. Diamond illumines the prismatic heart center as it aligns with and is perceived through the third eye. (See Third Eye for a detailed description of this gem.)

FLOWER ESSENCES FOR THE HEART CHAKRA

HOLLY (*ILEX AQUIFOLIUM*)

Holly flower essence unwraps the shields that bind the heart, thus clarifying a pure feeling level of the heart and cultivating the expression of love as it unifies. This essence transmutes and qualifies all expressions of emotion towards a steady state of love, compassion, understanding, and unity.

This steadfast state of the heart facilitates an expansion that breaks free from definition and boundaries imposed by the mind. The energetic momentum gained through freeing the heart creates a vortex that sources the authentic powers inherent in the field of love. Opening to the unified field of love brings one into an eternally spacious state of life that is beyond time-bound reality. Time, like love, is free, shifting its reference points to create a light continuum of fluid momentum. The heart is pivotal in its ability to retrieve the experience of "all-time."

Holly creates a reservoir of radiant heart light, supporting an interconnected state of timeless felt love. This reservoir of heart light is imbued with the capacity to heal traumas, past events, and memories that freeze the mind/body complex. **Holly returns the individual to a place within that is innocent, free, unconditional, and undetermined.** Holly adjusts and integrates the layers of the heart, aligning it with the third eye, or Ajna center, which cultivates the spiritual sight and wisdom necessary to pierce the veils of separation.

Holly secures the base of the heart. As this still point deepens, the psyche is able to safely navigate in non-referential time/space reality. A stable heart is the foundation for the opening of the time-portal gates that allow for consciousness to travel interdimensionally and into higher realms of intelligence and our future selves.[6]

Holly encourages the heart to come into a unifying resonance with creation. The essence cultures the awareness of the heart to feel into the subtle pulses of nature's rhythms. As the heart gains in its capacity to expand its range of amplitude, the refined feeling expressed quiets the mind, which becomes attuned to the whispers of nature. In this process the heart expands in the fullness and regenerative power of universal love.

As transpersonal dimensions deepen, the receptive and transmitting chambers of the heart become balanced. As this balance deepens, gratitude and love emerge. Holly essence cultures a state of gratitude that is beyond object referral. This simple teaching of gratitude is established in the felt presence of Love.

Holly supports the heart chakra in its functioning as the filtering chamber for the communication of filaments of light between worlds. A heart that generates the coherent emotion of love holds the passport that will allow one to breathe into many dimensions. An unconditional heart is the focal point for navigating in a non-referential space/time reality.

EVENING PRIMROSE (*ONENOTHERA HOOKERI*)

Evening Primrose essence assists the soul in infusing love through the subtle and emotional bodies. It reconstitutes maternal feelings of love and belonging. This process traces one's emotional origins back through time to retrieve the defracted light that was emotionally lost due to trauma. Evening Primrose assists one in identifying overlays of conditioning placed by the ego personality cloaking the transpersonal Being of the soul.

Evening Primrose opens the emotional body to a deep acceptance of one's present life stream. As one gains the capacity to respond to life with love, a deeper alignment of the emotional body with the creative life force is cultivated. This transpersonal love generates an impressionable self-love and self-acceptance that infuses the persona with the knowingness of being love.

BABY BLUE EYES (*NEMOPHILA MENZIESII*)

Baby Blue Eyes flower essence reconstitutes the paternal feelings of love and belonging. The paternal love within the soul actualizes from a self-assured, direct knowingness that one is loved and honored. This state grounds the paternal principle of love.

Baby Blue Eyes essence nourishes the emotional body towards a state of innocence, fluidity, and trust, which anchors one in the world. This ground state is formulated directly from the paternal core energies drawn from deep within the soul.

Baby Blue Eyes and Evening Primrose essences are primal for the reconstituting of the two principle forces of creation, the maternal feminine and the paternal masculine. These essences synergistically function to re-parent and heal the traumas that have alienated the inner child. The paternal love frequencies are fortified from an intimate field of love and belonging within one's heart chakra. A feeling of divine presence accompanies, protects, and guides the delicate nature of one's inner child.

BLEEDING HEART (*DICENTRA FORMOSA*)

Bleeding Heart essence reveals the key to unlocking and freeing the heart. This essence assists the heart to pour forth in an unbroken stream the felt truth encoded in the word *love*. It unravels the beliefs and expectations of the mind and dissolves the glue of bound emotions that cause one to cling to the other for love. Bleeding Heart essence lubricates the mind, and in so doing, it frees the heart to learn the difference between conditional and unconditional love.

The heart/mind grows in its capacity to feel into the absolute love frequencies as a living field infinitely looping back on itself. Bleeding Heart supports the growth from personal to transpersonal love. This allows one to rest in the simplicity of recognizing that one ultimately loves for love's sake alone, since love knows no reason and has no conditions. The experience of love expands as a pure felt mind/body/heart reality.

Bleeding Heart cultivates a direct connection to the unifying field of regenerative, self-sustained love. Many of our wants, needs, and expectations—and even our desire to give and receive love—go back to early conditions of lack, separation, and incompleteness. **Bleeding Heart essence opens the heart-light space within to allow Presence of Love as oneself to flow unconditionally in and out as the Holy Breath of Life.**

MARIPOSA LILY (*CALOCHORTUS LEICHTLINII*)

Mariposa Lily radiates the primordial Mother Divine principle.[7] The expression of Mother Divine takes on many forms in nature: cradling, embracing, and all receptive gestures that nurture unconditional love. This flower essence brings forth the powerful birthing and weaning processes that, although forceful in their expression, can be realized as the outgrowth of compassionate action. The emerging creative power of the feminine and the delicacy of feeling emanating from Mariposa Lily give it the divine sanction to heal. Self-realization is developed through the stability and safety inherent in the feminine intuition.

Mariposa Lily connects us to Mother Earth, giving rise to the forces of nature that support the individual in love, nurturance, and abundance. The receptive and balanced flow of energy from the maternal wing of the heart center is enhanced, and this gentle movement opens one to the feminine principle, which encourages one to unite and embrace life's events without being bound. Mariposa Lily supports clear and healthy relationship between mother and child; the adult persona, as it heals its relationship with Mother, enters the archetypal passageway to reunite with the Divine Female archetype.

Mariposa Lily helps release contraction, possessiveness, and emotional neediness, which arise due to feelings of being unloved or abandoned. As the essence connects one with the Divine Mother principle within, an allowing quality sets the rhythms for grace to flow through the heart of life. Grace births strength of heart and forgiveness of those actions, events, and people that have harmed, abandoned, or not adequately expressed love. The power to forgive and heal is the gift of the Mother principle. Her bliss is then felt as a knowing presence that accompanies the eternal child.

ZINNIA (*ZINNIA ELEGANS*)

Zinnia flower essence touches into the aspect of the psyche that houses the playful grounds of innocence. The intelligence of Zinnia essence integrates the originating light of the soul with an invincible strength of youth that knows no end. It lives an eternally manifesting and dynamic holographic reality. This integration process catalyzes an inner-child state that animates the psyche with insightful humor, objectivity, and fluidity, which permeate life's events. One is able to see the humor behind life's circumstances.

Zinnia helps to embellish life with a profound lightness of spirit that grants the personality the capacity to release its attachment to reactions associated with events or conditions. As one's personal story takes on a free-spirited, spacious character, one becomes unbounded, able to live life as an expression of light. Lightness, laughter, and joy are the medicines of Spirit. They lift awareness beyond the boundaries of the mind, the emotions, and the material world. Zinnia ushers in the joy of felt objectivity, dancing and playing in all forms of life and learning to live as fullness.

SHOOTING STAR (*DODECATHEON HENDERSONII*)

Shooting Star flower essence anchors the feeling body to its home within the heart center. The heartfelt experience of being at home and belonging on planet Earth is central to the soul manifesting its full potential. The ability to transcend alienation and live in the world as it is, accepting "what is," is a profound soul-level challenge facing our global population.

Shooting Star supports the soul in maintaining a cosmological interconnectedness between the soul's origins and present-day reality. It guides the soul to know the graceful touch of humanity and helps us embrace our humanness through the heartfelt light of self-acceptance.

Shooting Star opens the channels between the cosmic self and the human fields of emotional resonance within the heart. The human experience of love unites the soul with the soul of earth, allowing for fuller participation and presence in human affairs. One's original light prevails, with love as the bonding force that grounds the feeling of peace within self and humanity. The soul body recognizes its dimensional nature, releasing the conditions of alienation and aloneness. A deeper sense of belonging takes root as the flow of love and belonging moves freely through the feeling dimensions of one's being.

MALLOW (*SIDALCEA GLAUSCENS*)

Mallow flower essence creates a soft, malleable exchange portal deep within the core chamber of the heart, enhancing the heart-light energies involved in the giving and receiving of human love, warmth, and friendliness. This expansion of human warmth allows for a more dynamic, fulfilling, and integrated social life.

As the individual's interconnectedness with society grows, the communication networks deepen within the inner heart and throat chakras, which extend out to lovingly greet others. Mallow guides the heart/soul to participate in the world from a grounded relationship to Self. When the heart radiates warmth and friendliness to others, it is accompanied by a deepening ability to trust in others as a harmonizing source of comradeship.

FAWN LILY (*ERYTHRONIUM PURPURASCENS*)

Fawn Lily calls forth our innate spiritual gifts encoded in the soul destined to be shared with the world. It softens the ego boundaries of the mind, allowing the warmth and compassion of the human heart to emerge as a felt Presence.

The light of Fawn Lily melts the protective shields of the mind. It helps the psyche to recall the beauty of the inner light through all its multiple forms of expression and incarnation. Touching the nature of beauty, one is lifted into seeing with the spiritual eye. Beauty is revealed through the devotional heart that sees the essence behind all forms.

The natural gifts inherent as soul knowledge enter the foreground of awareness unconditioned by the mind, social norms, or culture. Fawn Lily gently softens the sensing, feeling body, creating a clear, heart-light state that is fluid and playful, yet has passion and purpose.

THE THROAT CHAKRA

The throat chakra, *Vishuddha* (pure), is associated with the element of ether (*akasha*) and is the seat of sound in the body. The throat chakra houses the space out of which the vibratory field of sound and language as soulful self-expression evolves. In the vibratory sound of words transmitted from the throat chakra, a direct imprinting of meaning and intention is felt by another that transcends the actual words spoken. **The throat chakra is the canvas upon which data or information may be recorded relative to time, space, and matter.**

The throat chakra is the home of the ether element, the field of space from which all other elements manifest. It is the spiritual birth canal, the point out of which the other four rivers (elements) flow and ascend in one's journey towards Self-realization. The four basic elements—earth, water, fire, and air—are all ultimately refined to their purest state and dissolve into *akasha*, the space principle. The throat center creates the space, the infinite void, to accommodate matter. It is both the source and goal for manifestation and expression.

Ether holds the vibratory hum of the universe. Creative wave-forms of vibration enter into harmonic resonance with one another here, creating greater symmetry and order. The throat center is where creative intelligence can focalize and be imprinted into the nervous system. This sets up a field of harmonious vibration and diminishes discordant influences.

The energetic principle of connectivity and communication resides within the throat center. The throat center organizes, controls, transmits, and receives communication. The coordinating influence for the entire chakra system resides in the throat chakra and is responsible for the individual's sense of free will. The throat center receives information through chemical messengers and specialized hormones that distribute the light of consciousness to human form. From the genetic code of DNA to the bioelectric forces of the nervous system, the light-encoded programming that regulates, distributes, and translates sacred information is housed in the throat center.

The throat chakra is the center of communication on many planes of awareness, facilitated through symbolic language. Information is funneled through the cranial field, fed to the brain and central nervous system, then expressed through the throat chakra. The throat serves as a center for information processing and distribution.

When properly supported by the throat chakra, the brain is able to store large volumes of meta-like information, downloading it into the throat chakra as resonant impulses of intelligence. Data is organized as an ascending array of encoded light that diminishes the boundaries between self and other, inside and out. This facilitates an intimate level of connectivity between the past, present, and future, which governs the formation of personal event scenarios.

The throat chakra formulates spoken communication as well as clairvoyance, telepathy, and other psychic powers. The pure sound manifested out of the unification and articulation of the heart and throat centers affects the listener by changing the conditions of his mind and being.[8] The unification and balance between the heart and throat chakras permits expression that displays the full depth and breadth of feeling in the heart. The spectrum of emotions in the throat chakra ranges from joy and ecstasy to grief and anguish.

The throat center serves to bring the physiology to a blissful state of non-duality—a non-reactive full/empty state. The bliss state is not a self-generated state of eternal happiness but an objective, physiological phenomenon calibrated through a superfluid nervous system. It processes and records events while maintaining a fundamental sense of well-being in a timeless flow of reality.

The bliss state serves as a platform for awareness to access intricate data-forms that describe the mechanics of our evolutionary holographic design. The throat chakra resides in the field of dreamtime; its receptive nature opens the doorway through which intuition and higher knowledge can be acquired.

Bio-Resonant Remedies for Mastering the Throat Chakra

Planetary Gem/Elixir—Blue Sapphire

Flower Essences—Sunflower, Mugwort, Cosmos, Star Tulip, Indian Paintbrush, California Wild Rose, Saguaro, and Calendula

The throat chakra serves as a cosmic gateway for manifestation on this plane of awareness. The throat accommodates the space, or *akashic* element, and is the center for unifying all subtle vibrations of the cosmic physiology. This group of flower essences and gems enhances communication matrices of the chakra system and the primary stellar, or planetary, entities that govern the intimate order of mind, body, and soul. These flower and gem essences induce and ground the elemental and stellar influences, as they are brought through the gateway of the throat center.

A bio-resonant interaction takes place between the flower essences, the energy emissions of the celestial bodies, and the glandular system of the human physiology. These three individually defined modes of intelligence— plant, planet, and human—create a harmonic symphony that expresses unique aspects of unified consciousness.

Each flower essence in this group is a conduit for clarifying and enhancing the beneficent and exalted planetary influences that align the individual's mind/body/soul complex with the cosmic destiny of Earth. These flower essences anchor and radiate the related planetary energies, awakening genetic memories of origin and godliness.

This group of essences/elixirs also opens the throat chakra portal to the interdimensional planes of existence. It synchronizes the expressive capacity of the throat chakra with the deep intuitive knowledge of the heart. They facilitate a holographic awareness that is the basis for communication with advanced levels of intelligence, both visible and invisible. The essences/elixirs act as superfluid conductors for cosmic energies, vitalizing the whole body.

PLANETARY GEM/ELIXIR FOR THE THROAT CHAKRA

BLUE SAPPHIRE (SATURN)

Blue Sapphire resonates with the throat chakra. It assists the throat chakra to open up to the infinite void of space and the eternal rhythms of time. It supports the throat chakra to transcend boundaries and yet communicate and define space and time relative to the development of one's individual consciousness.

Sapphire also resonates with the planetary frequencies of Saturn. It is a slow, steady, powerful planetary influence that carries the authority of ancient wisdom. The gem cultivates the virtues of compassion, selfless service, maturity, accountability, and loyalty. Blue Sapphire reinforces the Saturnian influence that guides one to see the unifying and potent truth in practical reality. It opens the channel of communication for the heart to find its voice and purpose through the throat.

Blue Sapphire attunes a person to his or her inner mystical nature and encourages perseverance to accomplish one's goals. The gem activates the innate gifts of the soul and supports the manifestation and expression of the individual's unique soul attributes. The gem assists in grounding one's personal and cosmic talents in a practical manner that will yield a deep sense of satisfaction. Blue Sapphire cultivates a steady and constructive disposition that authenticates one's commitment to *dharma*, or purpose.

The ancient mystical knowledge kept hidden from relative consciousness is bound in referential time. As the soul matures, time codes are lifted and freed. This process can be enhanced through devoted spiritual practice and activated by the influence of Blue Sapphire and attunement to Saturn, which governs longevity. One's personal astrological blueprint and rhythms of time are all factors in this unique unfoldment.

Blue Sapphire has a beneficial influence on the nervous system; it cultures a deep sense of peace, tranquility, and harmony, which assists the soul in deepening one's experience of both dreamtime and life, especially on the subtle feeling levels. Blue Sapphire guides the heart and mind into the mystical realms, which require the soul to seek contemplative moments and a transcendent perspective on life. **In the vast space of personal and transpersonal solitude, the soul learns how to sustain relative existence while entering mystical realms in which boundaries are illusory and definition loses meaning.**

Saturn is the lord of time. It governs the reality of time and the mechanics of how dimensional worlds (*lokas*, or planes) are laid out according to the laws of time and space. Through initiatory processes known only to the soul, one is made ready for entry into the mystery school of the inner sacred.

One of the markers on this journey is a sense of profound grief engendered by a break from identification with the limited egoic mind. The psyche experiences the unfathomable void, or abyss, that is encountered as one releases limited, attachment-based perception and enters an intimate relationship with the Godhead.

Blue Sapphire elixir addresses the grief arising from the loss of the personal self. As transpersonal awareness expands, transcendental time swallows the assigned meanings one has given to physical reality. Grief is a portal in the throat chakra for one to let go and open into a vast, empty space; this is the abyss of nothingness accompanied by primordial feelings of aloneness. In the emptiness, one awakens to the spacious intelligence for creating new life and possibilities. Blue Sapphire carries intrinsic threads that nourish the soul at this stage of realization.

Blue Sapphire supports the soul in shifting the currents of time that metabolize personal event streams. This shift is towards a timeless, fluid reality. Unshakable faith is a compass through the abyss, the backdrop that allows the personality to surrender control of time as an artificially measured quantum. The gem aids one in breaking free of the repetitive nature of time and entering a suspended state of superconsciousness.

This is a felt reality that promotes the subjective and objective speeding up or slowing down of the rhythms of time. Time either compresses or expands to where ultimately, the personality meets up with the soul. In this meeting, the soul is realized and imprinted on the field of mind/body consciousness. Blue Sapphire elixir aids in erasing *samskaras* by liberating the light of consciousness locked in time and focusing it upon the karmic lessons/stresses held in the nervous system.

Blue Sapphire opens the pathway of the heart that longs to merge with God the Beloved. It seduces the mystical traveler into the den of the transcendent. This causes a collapse or breakthrough that encourages the illumined ego to enter the sanctuary of forgiveness, in which the individual is immersed in a heightened state of self-acceptance and divine love. The mystical quality of the gem infuses the mind with humor, which pierces the veil of the relative, illuminating the absurdity of earth-bound duality. In this state of singularity, the throat chakra can literally open and sing the song of joy through life.

The Saturnian Blue Sapphire excavates the psyche, freeing one from old or outdated belief systems, functions, and thought-forms. It scans the mind for "free-radical" thoughts and reshapes them into new forms of understanding and wisdom. "Free-radical" thinking unhinges the mind from its structures, conditions, and definitions of reality. The enslaving boundaries, limitations, and resistances to life now turn the ego outside in.

As forms, functions, images, and language fade into the background, the ego grapples with its own perceived death. There ensues a dying to all known aspects of self-definition. The grasping and attachment to previous forms, structures, and limitation no longer define life. The void of space within the throat chakra becomes an open, spacious, and clear palette to allow the impulses of the source of creative intelligence to formulate new realities of being and expression based on the universal vibratory frequencies of love: in other words, a heart-throat articulation.

This slipstream process leads into the transcendent, in which silence resides in the timeless reality of Being. There is no knowing beyond the Present; the measurements of personal time collapse into an expanded here and now. A type of transpersonal centeredness develops as one recognizes past and future points of reference converging into a moment of pure awareness. The breath, settled in transcendental silence, knows the eternal Now.

Blue Sapphire attunes consciousness toward the mysteries of life, turning the mind away from the fluctuations of common thought. The psyche leans into a felt reality of pure existence that brings tranquility to the nervous system and creates a deepening contact with the soul. Life and death share a nondual ground state in which one does not preclude the other. The instinctual fear of death resolves itself in the awareness of silence and the eternal currents of the breath.

Blue Sapphire creates a steady state of calm, clear peacefulness. One learns to enjoy the knowledge procured through the exploration of multi-layered forms of existence; the soul is intelligently informed in its quest to comprehend all facets of human experience. Through humor, curiosity, and wonder, the soul becomes capable of exhibiting all of its inherent virtues, including patience, mercy, justice, honor, and sincerity. The elixir helps one to develop a sense of innate responsibility, which encourages action for an all-encompassing good.

Blue Sapphire strengthens the nervous system and the physical structures of the body: the skeletal system, bones, nails, and teeth. It aids in stilling the active mind, pacifying the air element and reducing anxiety. It assists the soul in deepening the creative expressions of purpose, thus opening the throat to project its radiance of vibration through speech.

Blue Sapphire cultures a contentment that fosters nonattachment to material reality, people, places, objects, events, and expectations. In the space of contentment, self-acceptance of "what is" deepens the experience of pure love. Maturity in self-acceptance creates stability and wisdom. The full awakening of these attributes helps to transform the controlling mechanisms of the immature mind, which constrict the throat, thus eliciting trust in the spacious wonder of the void. This wholeness of spirit provides a clear background for the intrinsic light of the soul.

FLOWER ESSENCES FOR THE THROAT CHAKRA—THE GENESIS STARGATE

[Note: This is the author's Star Matrix planetary formula. The synergy of this blend of flower essences facilitates the opening of the throat chakra, often referred to as the second birth canal. Each essence geometrically weaves the celestial opening of the associated planetary elements through the subtle bodies.]

SUNFLOWER (*HELIANTHUS ANNUUS*—SUN)

Sunflower activates one's sense of "I," shifting the identity from the personal "I" to the transpersonal "I Am" Presence. This stage of development is grounded in the solar masculine principle of the radiant Father godhead.

Sunflower represents the pinnacle of the upward movement of the solar force. The solar force is the governing celestial and central authority within the physical brain; it functions as the director of the whole mind/body complex.

Sunflower enhances the higher mind to directly cognize knowledge from the invincible Truth. In the phenomenological field of action, the soul awakens to how words carry a synchronized and potent reality from the Sun, a living, interactive archetype.

MUGWORT (*ARTEMISIA DOUGLASIANA*—MOON)

Mugwort activates the dream-well of the psyche. Mugwort essence opens the visionary door that leads the psyche into the Queen's Chamber, where the lunar forces govern. This is the realm of intuitive psychic energies and the subconscious.

As the psyche navigates the depths of the subconscious realms, psychic powers increase, engendering the need for clarification and discrimination. Mugwort heightens sensitivity and lucidity, revealing a level of spontaneous insight that appears random in character but actually expresses a pure level of organization. This leads to a synchronous superconscious state that springs out of a sequencing process that is ordered by the rhythms and tides of pure felt intelligence.

The synergy of Sun–Sunflower and Moon–Mugwort brings into balance the two primordial principles of life. Sunflower and Mugwort harmonize the masculine and feminine wave formations into a non-dualistic state of unification. **Sun and Moon coalesce to form a field of cosmic intelligence that is built upon direct cognition, knowing, and a receptive yet penetrating lucidity.** Inspiration is empowered to serve the pursuit of creative intelligence as it nests in the stable architecture of Divine Mind.

COSMOS (*COSMOS BIPINNATUS*—MERCURY)

Cosmos is one of the most important essences for the development and cultivation of the throat chakra. In mythology, the energy of Cosmos is contained in the messenger of the gods: Mercury, or Hermes. The mercurial energy of Cosmos enhances the neuro-network of communication. It opens the pathways between the heart and throat chakras, enhancing the articulation and synchronizing the felt impulses of intelligence seeking to be expressed through the throat and fostering their expression to unfold in a warm, heart-centered transmission.

This process of alignment between heart and throat establishes the dimensional pathways in which sound vibrations are organized in sacred geometric patterns. **The geometric patterns contained in the sound at the most primordial levels can efficiently translate and exchange data intelligence between personal and transpersonal awareness.** As awareness grows beyond the range of personal reality to include the transpersonal truth of felt divine intelligence, the ability to articulate this level of cognition takes on an objective, spiritual vantage point.

Cosmos serves to articulate the finest feeling value of the sacred spaces of the heart and translate it into the expression of the spoken word. The unification of heart and throat amplifies the *akashic* element of space, which is fundamental to creative expression and manifestation. The paradox of the fullness of creation, as felt in the sanctuary of the heart and the void of infinite space, is experienced through the throat, finding reconciliation in the communication of the voice of the whole body.

STAR TULIP (*CALOCHORTUS TOLMIEI*—JUPITER)

The three planetary energies of sun, moon, and Jupiter harmonize as a triune function feeding the subtle structures of the light body. The associated flower essences—Sunflower, Mugwort, and Star Tulip—are conduits for these planetary forces to be awakened within the psyche and subtle structures of the light body.

Star Tulip essence attunes the senses to perceive subtler inner vibrations of information and to distinguish the source of this information. The sensitizing and expansive energy of Star Tulip enhances communication with one's personal guides, teachers, and masters on the inner planes. This process of opening to finer levels of spiritual and psychic perception is balanced through the union of the sun and moon principles.

As the throat chakra is cleared and opened, the light of consciousness can move dynamically, ascending through this spiritual gateway and piercing the third eye chakra. Star Tulip essence opens the spiritual eye to higher knowledge, wisdom, and realities, transcending duality and converging into singularity. It resonates with the celestial codes of intelligence that penetrate deep into the third eye center. As the throat chakra and third eye articulate in union with each other, one gains a big-picture view of the potential of their destiny.

INDIAN PAINTBRUSH (*CASTILLEJA MINIATA*—MARS)

Indian Paintbrush activates and grounds the masculine principle. This essence stabilizes the creative force as it is birthed and helps direct the fiery impulses of action to manifest one's visionary goal. Indian Paintbrush feeds the feeling body with renewed vitality, stamina, and practical expression to bring fruition to one's envisioned goals.

This essence harnesses the planetary power of Mars, the red ray of vitality, and infuses the etheric and cellular levels of the body with vitality. This infusion of vitality sparks inspiration and an ability to sustain a focus of will. The focus of will generates an alignment of innate intelligence and the grounded practical forces that bring about the fruition of creative action for manifestation.

CALIFORNIA WILD ROSE (*ROSA CALIFORNICA*—VENUS)

As spirit makes its journey into matter, it is in the *akashic* realm of the throat chakra that the life-force energies begin their translation into the four elements (air, fire, water, and earth), giving rise to form.

California Wild Rose anchors this process of fusing spirit with matter, enhancing the senses and thus enlivening the subtle feeling body. Through the enlivenment and subtle refinement of the senses, the feeling body establishes a deeper resonance with the experience of beauty and appreciation for life.

As the soul is fed, a dynamic, interactive process lifts the individual into realms of light, thus eliciting an ecstatic experience of beauty. This phenomenon strengthens the unifying bonds of spirit and body to allow for fuller participation and joyful enthusiasm in life, expressed through the articulation of the heart and throat chakras.

California Wild Rose infuses the heart with Venusian energies, uplifting and aligning the body/mind/spirit with one's originating pure light. One grows in the realization that the purpose of the human form is to experience the Divine in all its diverse forms and unique and artistic expressions.

SAGUARO (*CEREUS GIGANTEUS*—SATURN)

The throat chakra governs the aspect of space (*akasha*); Saguaro unlocks the referential boundaries of time. As one is freed from referential habituation, the canvas of space in the throat chakra is equally freed from referential boundaries, thus unlocking an unlimited potential for creativity and self-mastery.

Saguaro cactus is a keeper of time intelligence. The historical records of ancient intelligence residing deep within the core of earth's subtle matrix are held within the wisdom of this plant essence. Saguaro establishes the nobility of guidance sourced from the rhythms of time.

The subjective personal element of time is often experienced in the mind/body complex as an overseer/authority extending its limitation, perceived control, or power over the psyche. This felt condition leads to resistance and rebellion against the authority principle. The spiritual authority principle is confused with the personal authority programs and conditions of the past.

Saguaro essence cultures the *soul's* domain of authority, which has jurisdiction over the psyche. As the persona matures, it relinquishes the habitual references to the false authority that defines time-bound reality. Thus Saguaro allows the psyche to free-fall out of the fixed past and catalyze the ancient wisdom seer into the future-now seer. New points of personal destiny are discovered through a recalibration of how the individual perceives the difference between past, present, and future.

To seek authority of spirit, the body/mind complex must free itself from the historical imprint of falsely imposed authority figures, whether they be parents, teachers, siblings, or legal structures. These imprints are held in the cellular structures, personally and collectively. With the vibrational support of Saguaro, the psyche becomes free to navigate its original territory by clearing interference patterns based in limiting concepts of authority. The individual is self-empowered and becomes capable of mining the gold from the spiritual repository of collective consciousness.

CALENDULA (*CALENDULA OFFICINALIS*—SUN AND PLANETARY HARMONIZER)

Calendula empowers the spoken word with the healing presence of God's creative force, attuning the individual to the radiant power of the Logos. As one draws closer to Source, the intelligent governing force of nature's order is cultured in the physiology. As one expresses the presence of life through the spoken word, the sound value carries Nature's voice, which holds the power either to support evolution and creation and/or disintegrate the structures of life.

Calendula catalyzes awareness to manage and master the internal and external voiced energies. It unifies the creative principle in the solar plexus chakra with the voice in the throat chakra, which vibrates space, helping one to manifest directly out of higher octaves of intelligence.

THE THIRD EYE CHAKRA

The sixth chakra, the *Ajna* (authority, unlimited power) center, located between the eyebrows, governs the pineal plexus. The third eye center is also understood as the mind chakra; it resonates with one's psyche in its conscious and unconscious aspects. The integration of cosmic mind and psyche actualizes illumined insight and strengthens intuitive clarity. **The challenge for the mind is to transmute the personal mental field (thinking mind) into a transpersonal level of awareness (cosmic mind).**

The third eye center is the abode of the light of consciousness. This center is responsible for the quality of spiritual seeing through which we receive knowledge, insight, and wisdom. The third eye center is the portal enabling one to travel beyond duality to the unbounded state of singularity. The Ida and Pingala, the two channels of energy that run along the spinal column, are joined at the third eye center. The Ida, or solar force, and the Pingala, or lunar force, are the polarities that become unified in the opening of the third eye.

On a subtle level, the third eye center functions as the spiritual eye, or "third eye." The pineal gland, which regulates light in the physiology, is derived from a third eye that is developed early in the embryo. The pineal center transmits the chemical messengers and specialized hormones that distribute the light of consciousness to human form. It influences the endocrine and central nervous systems.[9]

The third eye center is referred to as *sat-chit-ananda*: being, consciousness, and bliss. It is a state of non-duality, or unity consciousness.

The rising of the *kundalini shakti* to the third eye begins a process of integration between the crown chakra and its higher counterparts. With this process comes the possibility of psycho/spiritual liberation, a nonreferential state of awareness free from conditions. The individual prepares to go through the many stages of cosmic marriage that unite the feminine and masculine principles in holographic awareness.

The richness of the resulting growth of consciousness opens channels for communication and relationship beyond human intelligence. Through the holographic field of the soul, relationships of a celestial and angelic nature are more fully established.

Within the abode of the third eye center, one transcends time and space, liberating the soul to travel transdimensionally. A symbolic representation of this process is depicted in the caduceus, the two wings representing the ability to fly in both this world and beyond.

Through the third eye center, one opens to holographic awareness, simultaneously perceiving the life of the soul on many planes of reality and living in full unification in the cosmic self. And since evolution is eternal and infinite, this state is only a gateway to the development of even more advanced levels of self-mastery.

Bio-Resonant Remedies for Mastering the Third Eye Chakra

Planetary Gems/Elixirs—Diamond and Cat's Eye

Flower Essences—Queen Ann's Lace, Cerato, Star Tulip, Angelica, Shasta Daisy, Beech, Holly, and Lotus

This group of flower essences and gem elixirs cultures the divine nature that opens the door of the third eye to spiritual sight, shifting awareness from a personal to a transpersonal dimension. The change from fixed to fluid parameters begins to culture illumined insight, knowledge, and wisdom. The fluid mind, transcending judgment, can free itself from the conditions that dominate personal intellect. The common mind is suspended, allowing an opening of space and a release of fixed time that transmutes the habitual pathways of perception and function.

As one relinquishes the control mechanisms of the intellect, the soul aligns with its spiritual nature. The human experience steps off the platform of relative time and space, and the presence of one's personal guides, inner teachers, and Ascended Masters becomes known through the heart and the third eye center.

This group of flower essences integrates the physical, mental, and emotional bodies, supporting the opening of the higher chakras. When one surrenders the boundaries of belief and becomes humbled by the mysteries of life, the power of one's divine nature can emerge. Impulses from the spiritual realm lift the body to a state of godliness. Awareness shifts from ordinary perception in waking consciousness to a subtle, more expanded, multi-dimensional plane. Unification is realization through the still sanctuary of the Holy breath. As one's spiritual nature matures, impulses of intelligence are articulated from the primordial level.

As perception travels inward through the use of this group of gems and flowers, the radiant heart seats itself in the depth of Beauty. Perception of the inner and outer worlds becomes full with luminescent light, and subject and object are one in the Holy Breath. One realizes the ever-present God force in all life.

PLANETARY GEMS/ELIXIRS FOR THE THIRD EYE CHAKRA

DIAMOND (VENUS)

Diamond cultivates the opening of the third eye. It cleanses and purifies this sixth chakra, creating clear, light-filled spiritual vision. It clears the subtle bodies, especially the emotional and mental bodies, facilitating an alignment of the persona with the soul.

Diamond vibrates and emanates in pure colorlessness and tone with the planet Venus. Its healing influences vibrate along the frequencies of universal love, purity, compassion, and absolute beauty. The clarity or grade of flaw-lessness of a Diamond enhances its power to radiate the universal white ray of light. Its energy is powerfully invigorating and clarifying. Depending on the astrological placement of the planet Venus, Diamond can have a very beneficial influence in balancing and strengthening the heart.

The clear and flawless Diamond is the pinnacle of perfection, and the Diamond elixir emanates the full spectrum of light. It opens the channels to the originating source of light within, radiating the light of light, omnipresent and omnipotent.

Diamond offers all the possibilities of pure radiant light by embodying the most compressed crystallized form. **All terrestrial life is carbon-based, and Diamond is the hardest, most compact crystalline form known on the planet, the highest alchemical expression of carbon.** The Greek and Latin words for diamond translate as "invincibility" and "the unconquerable."

In its rarefied, crystalline state, Diamond transmits a strong physio-energetic influence that stabilizes and refines the cranial field. Specifically, it supports the natural adjustment of the cranial field. It has an affinity for the midbrain, facilitating communication between the left and right hemispheres, thus creating a potent and radiant ecofield. It enhances the functioning of the limbic system, which processes emotions. And it attunes one's auric field with the celestial qualities of Venus at its highest expression—beauty, grace, and the refinement of feeling—thus supporting the evolution of one's creative intelligence.

Diamond also balances and enhances the function of the pituitary and pineal glands. The pineal gland is the master gland for regulating and processing light. In individuals of advanced spiritual integration and development, it is the gland that produces soma, the liquid light that feeds the subtle and physical bodies. It is the gland that nourishes the light body, creating a bridge between the human and the Divine.

Diamond supports the physiology to function in a superconductive manner. It is the master elixir for removing energetic patterns and blockages created by disease entities and thought-forms. The cosmic frequencies of Diamond have the ability to disperse subtle levels of toxins and transmute them into light. Diamond's range of influence reaches into the highest spiritual realms. The gem supports the physiology in creating a renewed energetic platform that embodies higher vibrational knowledge by transducing and anchoring it into the physical plane. This catalyzes a profound level of clearing and transformation.

Diamond elixir creates a crystalline light matrix that interfaces with the human light body. It aids in accessing and conducting the higher energetic principles of consciousness that support the translation of spiritual information.

The crystalline structure of the physical diamond manifests as an octahedron and carries the power of a cube, the most stable Platonic solid. As we saw in earlier chapters, a Platonic solid is a sacred geometric form whose meaning is derived from its inherent mathematical values. The cube functions as the founding father of creation, as it pertains to physical/energetic reality. It serves as a self-contained building block that can prevent other energetic influences from entering its structure, protecting one from negative mental activity. In the cube, the focalization of energy towards the center point supports concentration and stability of the light of consciousness within.

Diamond elixir amplifies higher levels of organization that potentially enhance biological and physical intelligence. Humanity is destined to become the diamond body, individually, collectively, and terrestrially. As a race, we will become capable of emanating the purity, clarity, innocence, and strength of the dynamic celestial light of the Diamond.

CAT'S EYE (MOON'S SOUTH NODE, KETU)

Cat's Eye correlates to the third eye, supporting the light of consciousness to perceive reality closer to the source of its origination. It clears the memories and mind of the habit of seeing life through a linear pattern. It allows the light of consciousness to embrace the wholeness of life, thus seeing through the camouflage of form.

Cat's Eye carries a bio-resonant frequency correlated with Ketu, the moon's south node. **Ketu has the capacity to bring one into a dynamic relationship with one's inner mystical life.** Ketu creates a witnessing state of nonattachment to life events. The soul is liberated to move in the direction of transpersonal levels of realization. The placement and timing of Ketu in one's astrological chart directs the soul's capacity to attract the grace of *moksha*, liberation from the cycles of rebirth and karma. Cat's Eye assists the psyche to overcome the fear of death, physically and psycho-spiritually.

One of the animal totems for the moon's south node is the snake. At the base of the spine, an archetypal energy pattern of a coiled snake lies poised in the sacral well. It awakens due to spiritually generated psychic energies often referred to as *shakti kundalini*. The shakti is conducted through the liquid medium of the cerebral spinal fluid and pumped to the brain by the breath of life. It then sends electrical charges throughout the brain, awakening the psychic healing potential that can transmute limited beliefs and core emotional conditioning that rob one's originality.

Cat's Eye ameliorates emotional tensions, impulsiveness, and fanaticism, revealing the motivating factors for such conditions. It attracts one to the mystical nature of life and the secret or hidden occult sciences that delve into the forces of creation. When used during auspicious times of transformation, the stone assists one to see beyond the binding influences that arise from habituated patterns of spiritual belief. One cultivates the singular vision of an awakened third eye.

Cat's Eye has a stimulating influence on one's psychic energies, but one must be cautious as to the timing and appropriateness of the use of this stone. It has the potential to activate one's shakti force and open the third eye, increasing intuition and refining other senses. It helps to develop compassion and other subtle sensitivities. However, in some cases, it may cause hypersensitivity and open a person to more information than he or she is able to comfortably process. When one has not mastered the shadow self, psychological distortions and confusion may arise.

Cat's Eye assists in developing a sharp psychic vision that penetrates to the truth of pure existence and being. It enables the traveler to pierce the veil of the shadow of death. It empowers individuals to use their creative psychic powers (shakti) to face death with greater equanimity, even fearlessness. The individual becomes open to the eternal life-giving power of shakti while embracing the possibility of physical death.

Cat's Eye cultures a refined discrimination through enlivening the undercurrents that might otherwise unconsciously feed mistaken notions of self-aggrandizement. This frees the soul to move beyond a comfortable orbit of personal belief and support, allowing for an alchemical transmutation of cherished personal belief structures and an unmasking that reveals the soul's true nature.

Cat's Eye can also assist an individual encountering the dangers that lie within the realm of the highly developed spiritual psyche—that is, the delicate use and subtle attachment to spiritual knowledge and practices, such as self-inquiry, contemplation, philosophies, beliefs, and language, which *can* become entrapments on the path of liberation. For example, an individual may become attached to the notion that the work, time, and demands of spiritual life and practice are to be redeemed for a particular spiritual reward. Or the spiritually empowered intellect may be mistakenly attached to the refined egoic structures that lead to a sense of entitlement.

Another challenge is the addiction to language as a point of self-validation and self-definition, which can indicate a fear of death and an attachment to the *thought* of who one is. Eventually one recognizes the limitations inherent in such descriptive functions and points of reference.

By introducing Cat's Eye at prescribed astrological times, the individual finds himself or herself naked at the doors of transpersonal reality. The higher powers that define greater levels of psychic discrimination become more accurate and available. The permeability of the psyche towards the invisible truth that is at once expressible and inexpressible can now form the basis for a highly original linguistic expression.

Divine grace escorts the soul into this transformational process of dying to one's self. **The gate of entry into the life of liberation requires one to be in the eternal death of life and to live the full glory of life simultaneously.** From this vantage point, death has no meaning. The value of divine love becomes the all-permeating, sustaining energy of life. This is the greatest teaching of Cat's Eye.

FLOWER ESSENCES FOR THE THIRD EYE CHAKRA

QUEEN ANNE'S LACE (*DAUCUS CAROTA*)

Queen Anne's Lace balances the emotional body through an alignment of the whole chakra system. It weaves a lattice of light that communicates between the upper and lower halves of the human body. This alignment facilitates an opening into the third eye, refining perception of subtler levels. The psychic/spiritual frequencies of energy are balanced and integrated with the earth energies.

This gentle process clears old perceptual patterns and distortions in the psychic/intuitive realms, allowing the light of consciousness to permeate the field of awareness and dispel illusion.

CERATO (*CERATOSTIGMA WILLMOTTIANA*)

Cerato cultures a transcendental level of trust emerging from an innate knowingness of the unshakable truth. As one continues to open to inner psychic and spiritual perception, there sprouts a need to culture a deep sense of balanced responsibility and unshakable trust. Cerato strengthens the knower from the level of the solar plexus, supporting personal confidence.

With the development of the third eye, one is able to see through the surface level of information into what is real in the unseen world of spirit. Cerato expands the range of insight through the structure of consciousness as it moves towards clear perception. Cerato enables one to see the symbolic messages layered within life's events. Its indigo color vibrates the pineal gland, sensitizing it to light-coded information that is accessed through the spiritual-eye center.

STAR TULIP (*CALOCHORTUS TOLMIEI*)

Star Tulip refines the sensory channels to receive and recognize subtle intelligence present to us on the inner levels of life. It focuses awareness to open and clear the psychic faculties to receive guidance from one's inner teachers, angels, guides, and Masters. The eye of spirit opens to a living light, color, and sacred formless Presence.

Star Tulip supports one to gain awareness in this holographic reality. This cross-dimensional awareness of life allows the soul presence to be supported and at home in the multiple worlds of experience.

ANGELICA (*ANGELICA ARCHANGELICA*)

Angelica flower essence creates a lattice in consciousness that facilitates the perception of information from the higher worlds. One learns to attune to his or her guides and angelic assistants.[10] Angelica facilitates the lifting of the veils between the physical and nonphysical worlds. It has the capacity to engender interdimensional experience, leading to an expanded use of the light body.

Angelica strengthens the telepathic and empathic bonds with the angelic realms. It creates a strong field of protection and benevolence for the journey through the subtle worlds of creation. Angelica, Star Tulip, and

Queen Anne's Lace together activate a powerful bio-resonant field to focus awareness on opening of the third eye chakra. These flower essences enhance the refinement of perception that nourishes the light body, releasing constrictive feelings in the emotional and physical bodies.

SHASTA DAISY (*CHRYSANTHEMUM MAXIMUM*)

Shasta Daisy flower essence supports communication between the right and left hemispheres of the brain. The wave-forms become orderly and coherent; the conscious and subconscious mind fields are then able to produce an all-encompassing functioning of wholeness.

Creative intelligence is upheld through a celestial blueprint founded on the informative mathematics of universal causality. **Shasta Daisy stretches the fabric of consciousness, enabling the higher mind to clarify and synthesize information from multiple levels of perception and insight.** The essence opens the mind to a deeper level of symbolic meaning realized from soul wisdom.

Shasta Daisy softens the structure of the common mind, thus culturing a shift into higher levels of intelligence. This shift allows the individual to organize and synthesize a broad spectrum of information. The information streams funnel down to a single, focused unit of unified practical comprehension. This process creates a more cohesive level of holistic memory storage that serves as timeless wisdom.

There is a direct correlation between the structural signature of Shasta Daisy and its spiritual significance as a flower essence. The white petals represent an array of information channels that converge into the yellow center in an orderly display of the Golden Mean spiral. The divine proportion of nature as it spins out of the Golden Mean spiral unfolds the mathematical mysteries inherent in creative intelligence.

BEECH (*FAGUS SYLVATICA*)

Beech cultures the heart/mind to embrace diversity in life. A felt appreciation for differences sheds new light on attitudes and behavior. This essence expands the mind, thus releasing conditioned patterns of analysis and judgment. Transmuting these conditions of mind is essential to awakening the clear perception of the third eye.

As the common mind clears the pathways of habitual ill use of the intellect, the higher mind gains the dexterity to receive pure impressions from the soul. This results in a deep acceptance of life, and all its incomprehensible aspects no longer frighten the psyche, which previously would have retreated into its protective mechanisms of control and the habit of justifying.

Beech softens the membranes of the ego, opening the individual to new dimensions of perception in which he or she is able to discern finer levels of beauty, goodness, and truth—the virtues gained through seeing with the spiritual eye.

HOLLY (*ILEX AQUIFOLIUM*) (SEE ALSO HEART CHAKRA)

Holly supports the light of consciousness generated within the heart to penetrate the third eye, opening it to an unconditional state of perception based on the purity of felt love.

The heart is the filtering chamber for the communication of the light filaments that pass between the worlds. Love holds the passport that allows for the cross-dimensional communication of information to be translated, received, and sent. The unconditional heart is a functional focal point for navigating in a space/time reality.

LOTUS (*NELUMBO NUCIFERA*)

Lotus enhances the synergistic action of all flower blends. It cleanses and aligns the whole chakra system. It opens the crown chakra for the ascension of shakti, the dynamic force of the kundalini energy.

THE CROWN CHAKRA

The crown chakra, *Sahasrara* (thousand-petaled lotus or empty void), is located at the top of the cranium. The crown chakra resonates with the pituitary gland (the master gland regulator), the nervous system, and the mind. The human brain contains over 13 billion interconnected nerve cells, creating a system of connection that rivals the connective pathways of the atoms in the universe. The mind has been found to be 100,000 times more sensitive to its internal environment than its external environment.[11] Judith calls this a place of "withinness," capable of accessing dimensions of non-locality in time and space.

As the unity value of consciousness becomes more established, the activity of mind is quelled by the expansion of light/being. Knower, known, and process of knowing are merged into one. This creates a style of functioning in which awareness is looping back on itself, eliciting a seamless I/ Thou experience. This unification of awareness sparks the sacred light of the heart, freeing it from the weight of the mind. In this state, the bliss that arises when suspended in pure awareness, or *samadhi*, is experienced.

Cognitive awareness arises out of this silent ocean of transcendental consciousness. Cosmic awareness can then access higher-dimensional information that opens the doorway for manifestation. The crown chakra is the entry point for the divine spark that elicits the formation of the physical body from a causal blueprint. The crown chakra is a portal into the kingdom of light, organized as a geometric representation of divine intelligence. This portal forms a bridge to the higher orders of information. Thus, consciousness reaches out and encompasses multiple planes of simultaneous awareness.

Through the cosmic fields of consciousness hosted by the crown chakra, the mind/body/energy systems are sourced from Supreme Intelligence. The mind/body unit develops a capacity to self-regulate and maintain the regenerative processes. As this transmutation of the physical and subtle bodies occurs, an internal digestive process creates a substance called *ojas*, referred to in ancient texts as the nectar of God. This divine substance nourishes the body and feeds the shakti kundalini's fiery light.

Ojas is produced out of a sublime state of integration and purification in the mind/body/energy system. Ojas transmutes the cellular genetic body into the Christic light body. In this advanced stage of spiritual mastery, one is unified with the cosmic principles that govern the universe within his or her own physiology.

Bio-Resonant Remedies for Mastering the Crown Chakra

Planetary Gem/Elixir—Amethyst

Flower Essences—Lady's Slipper, White Chestnut, Lavender, Star of Bethlehem, Cherry Plum, Impatience, Chamomile, and Lotus

This group of flower essences indicated for the crown chakra cultures a "silent mind." The silence generated through the expansion of the crown chakra creates a spiritual foundation for the lubrication of the bio-resonant fields that feed the subtle and physical bodies. The crown chakra, when fully clear and open, creates a deep integrative state that offers balance to the upper and lower chakra areas. The portal at the top of the head, which opens one to cosmic experience, can then be made stable and viable as a consciousness receptor.

This group of flower essences and gem elixirs allows the inner nature of the mind to settle its awareness in the transcendental field. As the mind learns to establish itself in deeper levels of silence, cycles of repetitive thought associated with stress, worry, and fear are spontaneously released. Silent awareness transmutes the habits of the relative mind. In the silent stillness of mind, there is no activity, no knower, no referential knowledge, and nothing to be known. At this level of autonomous cognition, which underlies the bed of conscious thought, the platform of divine consciousness is restored. Silence in the mind leads to the development of a richer, more cosmic state of creative awareness.

The higher faculties of the mind are capable of both intense, one-pointed focus and mystical, boundary-breaking expansion. Inside this experience lies the divine nature of the human mind, which is open in its natural state to the mind of God. As the personal mind lets go, it no longer needs to think about what will become of it; it is no longer competing with the divine for meaning and attention. Instead, it enters into a spiritual free fall with the divine as its net.

As the mind rests in its true nature of cosmic intelligence, it can spring into action with the coherent power of omnipotent silence. In the silent garden, one is witness to infinite surprises. A silent mind is a dynamic and creative field of consciousness. Having gained the status of cosmic mind, one then manifests according to the will of his or her essence. Essence is the distilled point of soul presence expressing as dharma (living "on purpose").

The flower essences and gem elixirs that support this silent state of mind culture a coherent exchange of information looping between the mental and emotional bodies. This creates a harmonic resonance that synchronizes the electromagnetic field's response to internal and external stimuli. The emotional body gains greater levels of objectivity, resilience, and peace; the mind creates a silent witness that provides profound objectivity in relation to the people and events in its field of interaction.

This group of essences and elixirs strengthens the nervous system, allowing for a transpersonal witnessing of reality that is non-referentially based. This primordial state of the nervous system provides the opportunity for deep rest and an autonomous value of purification during both sleep and activity.

This regenerative principle within the nervous system is a bio-spiritual adaptation that supports evolution. Physical and emotional events glide easily over the nervous system, rather than creating an indelible impression to which the mind and emotions become attached as a point of identification. Neurological pathways are created that allow for higher orders of complexity to be processed. This advancement in the conductivity of intelligence fosters higher order of cognitive functioning. The highly ordered and silent mind liberates the intuition to act as a guidepost to the outer realms of action.

The still point of mind seeds the backdrop for soul knowledge to emerge out of the space/time field of dimensional reality. The still point of mindfulness is both fluid and stable. This paradox of dual function safeguards the ability to maintain balance during intense centrifugal movement in the light body, which occurs when the ascending and descending light of consciousness is radically expanding through the chakra system.

This higher functioning of the mental body is essential for navigating in higher dimensions founded on non-referential reality. **Once the natural (indigenous) mind has claimed its spiritually creative power, it thrives on the unknown and novel possibilities inherent in the palette of space/time.**

The essences and elixirs associated with the crown chakra offer vibrational information and serve as catalysts that support the awakening of the kundalini shakti and the balanced opening of the crown chakra.

PLANETARY GEM/ELIXIR FOR THE CROWN CHAKRA

AMETHYST (SATURN)

Amethyst resonates with the pineal gland, the gateway to super consciousness and the regulatory transducer of light. The pineal gland is considered in many ancient and modern mystical traditions to be the spiritual focal point into the "Cave of Christos" or the "Cave of Brahma." The three axes of

90-degree rotation converge, opening the tunnels to embrace the realization of the "I Am" Presence. These are the divine proportions that constitute the working of dimensional geometry in the human energy field. It is these divine geometric principles that we resonate with in the higher worlds.[12]

Historians have identified Amethyst as the ninth stone of the High Priest's breastplate in the Judaic tradition. Ancient sages associate the Amethyst with the ninth celestial mansion (Sagittarius). In Vedic astrology, it resonates with the planet Saturn, lord of the tenth mansion (mystical and worldly wisdom).

Amethyst connects us to earthly and spiritual potential. It nourishes the physical nervous system and quiets the mind field, integrating the neuro-physiology and the higher centers of the brain. This allows for increased awareness of our subtle spiritual nature and the ancient wisdom of the soul to emerge.

Violet is the highest vibrational frequency visible to the human eye. It has been measured to vibrate at 750 trillion vibrations per second, as determined by how many wavelengths pass a fixed point in one second.

Violet is the invisible color of the skin. The receptor sites in the cellular composition of the skin function as biological translators; coded information in the form of light/color relays vibrational frequencies to the endocrine system, converting them into chemical messengers. The violet ray is resonant with the entire endocrine and nervous system, the cranial field, and ultimately, the DNA.

The spiritual vibration of the Amethyst elixir washes over one's auric field. It fosters a process of surrendering, allowing an opening to the light of truth and cosmic mind. Amethyst catalyzes a transpersonal depth of love and surrender, increasing one's capacity to yield to the flow of love as an act of devotion. The violet light of Amethyst elixir clears and transforms limitations and blocks in the subtle bodies, and it creates an infusion of calm, peace, relaxation, and openness, as well as the expansion of inner light space.

FLOWER ESSENCES FOR THE CROWN CHAKRA

LADY'S SLIPPER (*CYPRIPEDIUM PARVILORUM*)

Lady's Slipper flower essence grounds the energy force of all the chakras by aligning the subtle energy system with the root chakra. When one grounds the higher spiritual frequencies in the root chakra, a radiant life force infuses and sustains the whole body and chakra system. The mind/body complex increases its capacity to build strength and stamina, embodying the vitality of spirit. Body, mind, and spirit can then function in unison, fulfilling one's soul desires and life work.

As one learns how to access energy from the source and manage its flow rate in personal life, a calm, fully present state becomes possible. This depth of energy gives rise to dynamic creative impulses and reliable intuition for action that serves the highest good. These are key principles for being a global participant or leader.

WHITE CHESTNUT (*AESCULUS HIPPOCASTANUM*)

White Chestnut clears the mind of looping patterns of relative thinking. As the mind settles into transcendence, attachments and habituations of personalized thoughts begin to fade. Fixated clusters of emotional and mental energy are transmuted, thus precipitating new perception.

The agitation created by the relative mind is stilled as the essence of White Chestnut. It infuses the mind field with objective space, in which the bound intellect can let go. When the personal mind becomes relaxed and emptied of thought, it has the space necessary to recognize its nature as cosmic mind, a field on which information is imprinted and processed through the nervous system. The natural state of cosmic mind functions as a receiver and synthesizer of higher orders of intelligence.

White Chestnut essence is indicated when evolutionary demands from the soul are calling for a mind shift in terms of transmuting attitudes, perceptions, and beliefs. **This essence sets the stage for the organization of new neuropathways that constitute advanced styles of learning and being.**

LAVENDER (*LAVANDULA OFFICINALIS*)

Lavender nourishes and soothes the nervous system. It is an ally during times of intense information processing. It is especially valuable when the processing ability of the brain/nervous system is attempting to reconfigure and upgrade its ability to handle new information and dispose of the old. Lavender supports the body/mind to ground and integrate the physical and subtle energy of the whole chakra system.

Lavender enhances the organization of refined levels of impulse intelligence that feed the central nervous system and nourish and strengthen the emotional and mental bodies. The soothing influence of Lavender supports and stabilizes the emotional body, thus settling and quieting the air element of the mind. The still point of mind creates spiritual equanimity and vision from a grounded state of being, facilitating the full blossoming of the crown chakra.

STAR OF BETHLEHEM (*ORNITHOGALUM UMBELLATUM*)

Star of Bethlehem is a healing balm that releases imprinted traumatic memory from the cells and subtle bodies. This essence clears the emotional and mental bodies, releasing disruptive patterning that might otherwise cause the individual to unconsciously repeat negative feedback programming. The mind shifts towards a more objective and spacious state, in which it can recognize negative impulses before they re-implant into the nervous system and emotional body. **Star of Bethlehem focuses the light of peace, resolving the discordant energy of disease and setting the foundation for the opening and stabilization of the crown chakra.**

CHERRY PLUM (*PRUNUS CERASIFERA*)

Cherry Plum assists the soul in diving deep into the pool of faith and anchoring Divine Trust. The ego faces the fear of losing control and initially, surrendering to divine power, which leaves the referential mind at a loss. Through the use of Cherry Plum, the presence of the Self is infused into the persona, enabling one to see resistance to his or her own supreme authority within.

Cherry Plum essence allows our stream of inner events to move in a more fluid and graceful direction that transcends personal will. The assembly of events in one's life begins to sequence itself in accordance with cosmic plans and time. Synchronicity permits the soul to rest in a state of profound ease, surrender, and trust.

IMPATIENS (*IMPATIENS GLADULIFERA*)

Impatiens assists the psycho physiology to release its referencing to measured time ("referential" or "psychological" time). It relaxes the stronghold of the intellect's thinking process, fostering a more natural and fluid relationship to time. This opens awareness to the innate cosmic rhythms of time that are governed by the soul. As the individual can "go with the flow" and allow the momentum of time itself to guide the life stream of events, the ego can let go of its anxious drive for accomplishment, which arises from an unconscious fear of death.

Referential time is both a biological and a psycho-emotional felt reality that is genetic, cultural, and species engendered. When psychological time loses its boundaries and becomes seamless, the mechanics of synchronicity govern the creative actualization of life's events. A recalibration of one's past, present, and future trajectory is in constant realignment and up-ordering.

The state of patience allows one to live in time while outwardly experiencing life as a timeless state. Living without the pressures of psychologically measured time fosters unconditional understanding, forgiveness, and compassion, which flourish in the presence of patience. It is from the subjective vantage point of time standing still that one has the space and mobility to view life from all points of reference, an omnidirectional state of consciousness sourced within the awakened crown chakra.

CHAMOMILE (*MATRICARIA CHAMOMILLA*)

Chamomile balances the emotional body while maintaining an objective eye into the event streams of personal life. This essence creates a synthesis in the mind/body's perception that fosters insight into the nature of one's personal experience. This shifts the experiencer from the personal perspective into the transpersonal viewer.

A keen felt awareness into the mind/body complex allows the feeling, sensing attributes of life to be present and nourish the emotional body without overshadowing the visionary light of the soul. This can be understood as viewing personal reality with the eye of the soul. From this vantage point, one is able to digest life's events easily, without the upsets. Chamomile essence cultures a calmness of spirit and acquiescence to the atmosphere of silence as a rich foundation from which to live, thus supporting the crown chakra to remain open.

LOTUS (*NELUMBO NUCIFERA*) (WHOLE CHAKRA SYSTEM)

Lotus is one of the most revered flowers in the world, especially in the Ayurvedic tradition. Spiritually, it is seen as the blossom that resides within the crown chakra.[13]

Lotus has the capacity to unify the vibratory dynamics of any flower essence formula—or it can be taken alone. **It brings the whole formula together in a symphony of harmonics, allowing for a new level of vibratory clarity and originality to emerge.**

Lotus clears and aligns the whole chakra system, facilitating the even flow of kundalini energy through the spinal column, brain, and crown chakra. It awakens awareness of the light at the door, assisting the soul in entering into the domain of Holy Spirit. It is this flower that draws upon the primordial psychic forces for Self-realization.

TRANSGENERATIONAL CLEARING: UNIVERSAL CHAKRA BALANCING

The chakra system, in its highest spiritual order, is a vessel for the awakened holographic human. When the chakras are contracted or damaged, they will continue to reflect recurrent biogenetic memories. The family tree contains historical limbs of memory and belief that hold unconscious genealogical patterns. These memory ideogram patterns are perpetuated by an individual's linear conditioning from past to present to future.

The shift from personal self to transpersonal divinity requires one to energetically and objectively backtrack into the historical data pool of one's roots. This self-investigation includes insight into the biological, social, cultural, religious, and psycho-spiritual processes.

The Transgenerational Clearing formula holds the key for unlocking the stored familial blueprints that inhibit the evolutionary process of an entire family or line of ancestry. Couples who wish to conceive a child can utilize this group of flower essences to clear the psycho-spiritual field of both parents, thus supporting the being incoming or *in utero*. The matrilineal and patrilineal lines of stress that might interfere with the highest level of development of that individual soul can thus be neutralized. As challenges arise in the psycho-spiritual development of the child, these essences can be used again. This process can continue throughout the life cycle of the child and/ or adult family.

The Transgenerational Clearing formula, cognized by the author, hold subtle keys for freeing the heart and soul from fixed personal reference points. The intention is to clear the emotions, attitudes, and beliefs held in the body/mind, invoking a biological and psycho-spiritual metamorphosis.

The propensity toward personal identification perpetuates allegiance to ghosts of the past. The persona houses many faces and subroutines that re-enact one's familial, unconscious, historical events on the screen of the present. The inherited characteristics that bind the identity to the traditions, beliefs, and attitudes of one's parents create a form of ancestral possession, constricting evolution.

The Transgenerational Clearing formula allows one to take a profound look into the mirror of one's personal structure, revealing the architectural blueprints and sources that form the underpinnings of the psyche. The repetition of limiting conditions and patterns previously held in endearment find their way to the surface of reality. This process of self-reflection is fundamental to the personal transformation necessary to unlock the holographic psyche.

Transgenerational clearing cultivates the soul's realization. One learns how to access the codes inherent in the superconscious dimensions of the DNA, which inform the individual how to live independently of family or cultural conditioning. The effectiveness of these flower essences can be enhanced when a cluster of family members is committed to transforming their ancestral background. The synergistic potency of the Transgenerational Clearing formula offers a clearing for each chakra and may also be combined with specific essences and gem elixirs indicated for each specific chakra.

The soul is the playground for multiple life experiences and forms that carry memories of all that has gone "before and after." **The soul is not bound by time or space. It freely traverses dimensions in search of timely opportunities.** Once the soul is cleared of overlays of imprinted memory, the authentic self is free to emerge in its true nature. The soul seeks a pure, dynamic, and receptive environment to open into its full potential. It seeks to utilize the body it has created without prejudice.

The journey into the dimensions of the chakras inevitably brings one face-to-face with persistent memories, fears, and unresolved issues from our own genealogy. These influences activate the trajectories of the future and can give rise to precognitive information, which for some may lead to psycho-physiological distortions. However, these conditions and trajectories can be resolved by restoring the inner knowledge of Self through the Transgenerational Clearing formula, which assists the psyche in resting in the eternal gap of non-referential living.

As the psyche opens to an unencumbered experience, it gains an objective momentum to discern soul-level truth from illusion. The intelligence of nature gained through the formula's essences generously enhances the positive cultural and genetic tendencies of the family tree while encouraging the release of characteristics that inhibit one's soul potential. **The Transgenerational Clearing formula empowers the authentic liberation of one's being to individuate as a unique and unfettered soul.**

The light of awareness engendered by the Transgenerational Clearing formula brings insight into the thought forms and behavioral tendencies of one's lineage that have created overly dominant or submissive inner dramatization. The imprinting of culturally based suppositions can create an internal pressure that cloaks the natural tendencies of the soul. As one begins to understand the matrilineal and patrilineal associations that govern unconscious behavior, psycho-physiological constructs are resolved. The heart and mind become more integrated, thus balancing the primordial feminine and masculine principles that describe personal reality.

These principles traditionally represent the flowering of receptivity combined with the drive towards catalytic action. When the individual is removed from the programming of persistent biogenetic memory, the soul can move beyond even gender-based conditioning and act freely.

The Transgenerational Clearing formula enhances the coherent emotion of love, creating a platform for breaking attachments and conditioning and opening pathways to a new, authentic, and individuated paradigm. The heart is the conduit through which the giving/receiving principles can be expressed; it is the "mixing chamber" through which the receptive and creative energies can be integrated with wisdom and compassion. The balanced integration of masculine and feminine widens the path for the presence of soul.

Transgenerational Clearing essences are organized in consciousness with the intent to fuse spirit into matter. Matter follows thought and intention. The Transgenerational Clearing formula activates the unification of soul through the heart chakra. When this intention is felt and imaged in consciousness by the formula developer and the user, a sacred geometric structure organizes and delivers a focused power of intention that is conveyed through the bio-resonant substances used.

Each essence unfolds the intelligence of the God force packed within sacred geometric form. Geometric expressions are visual and mathematical concepts from the godhead intelligence. They are the language of light/time/space, unfolding the mechanics of creation.

Bio-Resonant Remedies for Transgenerational Clearing

Planetary Gems/Elixirs—Cat's Eye and Diamond (See Third Eye Chakra). Either or both of these may be added to the Transgenerational Clearing formula.

Flower Essences—Sunflower, Mariposa Lily, Holly, Walnut, Wild Oat, and Joshua Tree

FLOWER ESSENCES FOR TRANSGENERATIONAL CLEARING

SUNFLOWER (*HELIANTHUS ANNUUS*)

Sunflower embodies the solar force—the masculine archetype. Its radiant solar energy and guiding light facilitate the strengthening and healing of one's relationship to Father.[14] It assists in identifying how the father characterization has been played out through the revolving doors of our ancestral psyche.

Sunflower's light force melts the ego's veils of perception, revealing deeper levels of the soul. It balances the ego, yielding power to the higher Self. The ego becomes less attached and identified with the biological imprinting or lack of that imprinting from Father.

The radiant sun compassionately guides the actions and momentum of life in an evolutionary direction. Sunflower heals areas in our life stream where the solar energies have either been overpowering or lacking in strength. It sustains the individual through self-fulfillment and authentic power, bringing about warmth and compassion to restore balance. It elicits the core power of Self, while the psyche is experiencing the dissolution of the personal "I."

Sunflower directs awareness to the center point of Being so that one may gracefully realize one's authentic essence, the true Self.

MARIPOSA LILY (*CALOCHORTUS LEICHTLINII*)

Mariposa Lily represents the primordial Mother archetype.[15] The expression of Mother Divine in nature takes on many forms. Mariposa Lily brings forward the cradling, embracing, and receptive gestures that culture unconditional love, supporting compassionate action. Through the powerful process of rebirth that this essence elicits, one enters an all-encompassing divine embrace. Subsequently, one is gradually weaned from one's biological parenting process relative to the biological mother, thus shifting to an internal re-parenting process guided by the soul.

Mariposa Lily is empowered to heal through the creative force and delicacy of feeling evoked by the Divine Feminine. The process of self-realization is sustained through the stability and safety of the intuitive insights gained through the feminine archetype. Mariposa Lily connects us to Mother Earth, giving rise to the forces of nature that support the individual in love, nurturance, and abundance. The receptive, flowing balance of the heart center is enlivened.

The feminine principle encourages us to unite with and embrace life without being bound by it. Mariposa Lily supports right relationship between mother-child; the adult persona that has not healed its relationship with Mother can now reunite with the Divine Female archetype.

Mariposa Lily helps release contraction, possessiveness, and emotional neediness, which arise due to feelings of being unloved and abandoned. It helps us to establish our connection with Nature (Divine Mother), which allows grace to flow within us. As we gain the courage required to forgive those forces that have not adequately expressed maternal love, we unite with the Mother and enter into the gift of Her bliss.

HOLLY (*ILEX AQUIFOLIUM*)

Holly is a powerful clarifying agent for the feeling level of the heart. Dr. Edward Bach, pioneer in the research and development of flower essences, viewed it as a key to unlocking the seat of the soul, which resides deep at the base of the heart. Holly transmutes emotion to create a steady state of love, compassion, understanding, and unity.[16] It is essential for authenticating one's unique soul essence independent of genetic, environmental, and cultural conditioning.

The purification of the heart catalyzed by Holly leads one toward a deep inner synthesis of life experience. It moves us gradually toward an objective reality of nonattachment and truth, which liberates the unconditional feeling levels of the heart. This heart-centered reality of soul is the grounded state of being a holographic human.

Plants are the heart of nature; they live life on an electromagnetic sensory feeling level. In the plant kingdom, Holly is the embodiment of a subtly refined expression of unifying love. It facilitates the unwrapping of the shields that bind the heart. This unwrapping of the heart allows it to expand and break the boundaries of consciousness. The heart that is free exhibits a perpetual spiral-type vortex that infinitely expands one's capacity to love.

Holly adjusts and integrates the layers of the heart. The link-up and alignment of the heart with the third eye, or *ajna*, center unfolds spiritual sight and wisdom. This disengages one from the trauma of past events and memories that affect physical, emotional, and mental health. As access to the base of the heart deepens, a clear experience of psychological and spiritual security is established.

The heart is pivotal in its ability to retrieve the message units of time; Holly acts as a spiritual lubricant, opening the heart to this experience of "all-time." In this way it serves the transgenerational clearing process by removing the binding element of psychological time created by cultural and familial conditioning. **Holly returns the individual to a place within that is innocent, free, unconditional, and undetermined. Holly is a magical moment.**

WALNUT (*JUGLANS REGIA*)

Walnut, another key flower essence identified by Dr. Bach, helps us release our attachments to people, places, and events that no longer serve our evolution.[17] Walnut is the karmic link breaker that dissolves the habituated behavior patterns transmitted to us through our genetic lineage. It creates the emotional space to reflect and choose our responses to life's opportunities and challenges.

Walnut facilitates a healthy process of individuation, creating the autonomy necessary for periods of great shift or life transition. It combs the auric field, clearing and freeing us to make leaps in consciousness that can release inhibiting boundaries and move us into a sense of liberation that restores our ability to follow our own destiny.

Walnut helps us to let go of preconceived expectations and programs we have taken on from our families of origin and institutions such as school systems. With autonomous vision, we can go beyond the conditions and beliefs that limit our perception of what life ought to be. Walnut empowers the soul, strengthening our ability to express our true essence.

WILD OAT (*BROMUS RAMOSUS*)

Anyone on the path of transgenerational clearing must ask himself these important questions from the level of the soul: Who am I? Why have I incarnated on this planet? What are my unique gifts and talents? Wild Oat helps answer these questions, attuning us to our life purpose and catalyzing us to manifest it.[18]

Each individual soul is encoded with cryptograms of information that identify one's purpose on both a personal and collective level. Wild Oat helps the individual to access these codes and translate them, first on the level of enhanced sensibility (or psychic, intuitive impulses) and then on the level of action.

Wild Oat opens an energetic channel of communication from the solar plexus chakra through the heart and third eye. This unfolds the impulse of the Will that is directed from the higher Self, infusing the individual with illumination, guidance, and a sense of purposeful service. Wild Oat enables us to wake up to this realization and to have the stamina and discipline to follow through on what we know to be our true calling.

JOSHUA TREE (*YUCCA BREVIFOLIA*)

Joshua Tree, a desert plant, has a longevity that often stretches beyond a half-millennium. Joshua Tree essence holds the key to unlocking the ancestral codes of the past and redirecting the psychic familial patterns toward new cosmic forces. Joshua Tree cleanses the soul's scars (*samskaras*) and frees the individual from the historical limitation of the ancestral bloodline. This process opens the psychic birthing canals, cultivating an independent core identity structure that is empowered by the soul to actualize its higher human potential: the holographic human.

8

HIGHER TECHNOLOGY
FOR HIGHER CONSCIOUSNESS
The Birth of Bioactive Techno-Intelligence

*In this electronic age we see ourselves being
translated more and more into the form of
information, moving toward the technological extension of consciousness.*
—Marshall McLuhan

The potential for acceleration of planetary awareness has never been greater. Through the enhanced communication elicited and facilitated by the Internet and mass-communications networks such as social media, we now have an unprecedented capacity for global interconnectedness, as well as the shared brilliance of mass consciousness.

Systems of technological organization are now being inescapably woven into human reality. Technology has become an extension of human functioning. The impulse of a thought can move an artificial limb or command a remote device such as a television. It is no longer a matter of technology being seen as something foreign to our human identity; the question for humanity is, how do we live in harmony with technology and preserve our humanity?

The information/communication revolution is of a different order of business than the Industrial Revolution of the previous century. Humanity has crossed a threshold where higher consciousness and higher technology have become indivisible. A spacious opening in the landscape of the collective holographic psyche is supporting the human nervous system to process the vast pools of data that have become available to us. The fabric of our actual functioning as human beings is changing to equip us to handle the speed, efficacy, and neural challenge of modern technology. **Our mandate is to create a bio-resonant signature for human consciousness that is more than mechanical and of a higher order of human than we have previously known.**

In view of this dynamic upgrade occurring in our central nervous system, the new balance point of human and techno-reality will involve a collaborative union between the superconscious mind and the lightning-fast internal circuitry involved in high-level information and cognitive processing.

This union, which is rapidly becoming synonymous with the modern world, will stretch the boundaries of human possibility, and it will have the potential to lead to a type of freedom never before seen. Technology, while at first seeming to involve greater interplay within the conceptual field of the mind, has the capacity to break our boundaries of perception and lead us directly to a more complex and open-ended engagement with our inner and outer landscapes. Cosmically infinite energies are becoming accessible through the union of technology with internal human systems of direct, spontaneous cognition.

The techno-human interface is an emerging frontier in which human consciousness is offered the opportunity to transcend dualistic and opposing forces. **Human beings are becoming able to incorporate technology into their lives as a living process that serves cognitive/spiritual functioning.** Fused directly with thought, feeling, and consciousness, technology will also provide fertile ground for higher states of health and longevity to flourish.

This techno-evolutionary process requires that technological advances become more human centered and animated in nature. We have, to a large extent, enslaved technology as we have attempted to enslave the human spirit—satiating our senses, indulging our fantasies and desires, and keeping us separated from our heart-centered human nature. What now awaits human consciousness is the awakening into the pure spiritual intention out of which consciousness-based technology can be birthed.

Evidence of this process can be found in a computer-generated bio-scalar-wave technology, one of the most direct and profound technologies I have encountered to this point to support the advancement of the holographic psyche. In this chapter, we will explore the use of such technology for health and the development of higher states of consciousness—in particular, the Energy Enhancement System (EES), which exemplifies the possibilities for human evolution and realization through the use of consciousness-based technology. I have set up numerous EES "chambers" around the country, trained and guided many people in their use, and for several years personally conducted healing sessions, programs, and events in the EES. My home has included an EES chamber for many years, affording me vast experience and understanding of beneficial and evolutionary use of scalar technology for the development of higher consciousness and health.

THE BIRTH HATCH FOR TECHNO-INTELLIGENCE

Computer technology is one of the greatest advances of our generation. Its capacity to process data at very high rates of speed and assimilate seemingly incongruent levels of information is extraordinary. However, in its present state, our technology is essentially "cold" in nature. It does not yet have the capacity to simulate the feeling, understanding, and consciousness-generating attributes of human intelligence. This is due in part to the need for more advanced software and superconductive high-tech chips, but it also has to do with the actual waveforms that are the basis of consciousness-based technology. The traverse linear waveform currently imprinting the Earth is the electro-magnetic Hertzian wave that results in harmful "EMFs."

These waveforms have a limiting and toxic effect on the human psycho-physiology. Due to its inability to support a more coherent and flexible avenue of response, the Hertzian wave elicits modes of conduct that limit the development of true freedom and originality. **The very nature of the Hertzian waveform creates an energetic architecture that lies at the basis of our incoherent, dysfunctional, and materialistic social order.**

The shift to more humanistic, wisdom-based technology that truly enhances human development and interacts with consciousness is rapidly advancing. Leading this shift is scalar-wave technology, found in healing systems such as the EES developed by Dr. Sandra Rose and the Stillpoint Scalarwave Lasers developed by Paul Weisbart.

The EES in particular creates a birthing field through which human intelligence and techno-intelligence can develop a symbiotic merger at an energetic core level. EES technology, operating out of the binary system inherent in present software methodology, has the unique capacity to convert inherently dualistic code into a unified field of singularity, also known as the zero-point field of infinite correlation and potential.

The EES points the way to a powerful and harmonious new technological system that is profoundly life enhancing. It creates a dense field of highly coherent and permeable energy that is physically experienced by an individual sitting in its field. The resultant elevation of awareness, freedom from anxiety and problems, and sense of universal wholeness transcends the limitations of other modern technological models.

HEALTHY BIO-SCALAR FIELDS: A LIFE-SUPPORTING TECHNOLOGICAL ADVANCEMENT

Scalar waves are a well-known phenomenon described in astrophysics, geology, and hydrodynamics. Many emerging healing-technology systems can generate scalar waves to intelligently interface with one's living bio-interactive fields. These newly created systems are benevolent in their orientation. They can be programmed to carry multiple layers of coherent, creative, intelligent, and orderly information that directly enhances our natural intelligence.

Scalar-wave technology can escort us into the future of interactive consciousness development. Through this human-techno window, civilization can pass into the domain of our collective higher Self.

According to *The Barron Report*, the standard definition of a scalar wave is as follows:

> [A scalar wave is] a wave created by a pair of identical (or replicated) waves (usually called the wave and its anti-wave) that are in phase spatially, but out of phase temporally. That is to say, the two waves are physically identical, but 180 degrees out of phase in terms of time. The net result is that scalar waves are a whole different animal from normal Hertzian waves. They even look different, like an infinitely projected Moebius pattern on axis.
>
> Scalar energy differs from standard Hertzian electromagnetic fields in a number of important ways. First, it's more field-like than wavelike.

Instead of running along wires or shooting out in beams, it tends to "fill" its environment. This is important for applications of the technology for embedding products with scalar energy. Second, for many of the same reasons, it is capable of passing through solid objects with no loss of intensity.[1]

Quantum-mechanical analysis of biological processes has revealed that biological systems are nonlinear in nature. Scalar waves generate a "standing wave analogous to a sound wave, where one particle bumps the neighboring particle and forwards the impulse only."[2] Scalar waves exist outside of relative space/time, so they do not decay or lose intensity.

The nonlinear wave propagates throughout the body via the crystalline lattices of the elaborate collagen network. The human body has crystalline structures in every cell wall that are capable of holding a charge. When functioning at its maximum health potential, every cell ranges from 70 to 90 millivolts. Disease and aging occur when the cellular energy depreciates to levels below this range; scalar waves support healthy cellular functioning within this range.

The self-replicating signature of scalar waves is reminiscent of the multiple helical structure of DNA as it folds in on itself. Quantum-mechanical models describe subatomic particles that can store and carry biological information along helical macromolecules like DNA. This indicates that scalar energy is capable of imprinting itself in the DNA.[3]

Research conducted at the Max Planck Institute of Germany indicates that microorganisms exposed to scalar fields have increased activity of the RAD-6 gene, which codes for proteins involved in DNA repair. Scalar waves facilitate a bidirectional communication between the nervous and immune systems, as well as increase whole-brain hemispheric functioning.[4]

Scalar waves have the ability to carry information. They travel faster than the speed of light and, as noted previously, do not decay over time or distance. Scalar energy can be created many ways, including electronically, magnetically, and optically using rhythmic sequences and phase patterns projected visually. These techno-healing tools create a multiple-field, scalar-energy matrix—a life-enhancing resonance field that can even be generated by computers programmed with advanced algorithms, chaos theory, and fractal geometry.

As mentioned in the previous section, one such system is the Energy Enhancement System (EES). In the EES, computers are laser calibrated in sacred geometric patterns such as the square, the octahedron, and the Golden Mean rectangle—celestial architectural structures known to uphold coherent fields of energy. This replicates the sacred geometric knowledge inherent in all creation, experienced most notably in "power spots" and "energy vortices" in natural settings, and in manmade structures such as indigenous medicine wheels, Buddhist sand paintings, and religious buildings such as cathedrals, temples, and mosques.

This language of geometry, which is used to imprint the EES scalar field, unpacks light-coded information that can then create a bio-resonant interface with human intelligence. The highly dense coherent fields generated in the scalar energy matrix entrain and recondition the mind/body complex to recalibrate to its optimal state: a light/energy matrix undisturbed by the resistance of conscious and subconscious belief structures, thought forms, and emotional conditions. In a pure state of Presence, disturbances and limiting resistance patterns held in the subtle structures of one's energy bodies are neutralized.

This paradigm shift involves a nonlinear regulatory network in the mind/body with properties best described by quantum physics. The individual's ability to function unconditionally is sourced from the zero-point energy field of unlimited energy potential. This field is defined as a non-localized phenomenon that carries information at infinite velocity and correlation. The electromagnetic aspect of the wave is cancelled due to destructive interference patterns that reveal scalar-wave field effects. The result is that we can move into a state of fluid response and mastery that allows us to function as a whole entity, not driven by the dualistic nature of life.

Eldon A. Byrd explains the significance of scalar information this way:

> Because "propagation" of scalars is independent of the two physical quantities electric permitivity and magnetic permeability (which are linked with the speed of light), scalar information is not limited to the speed of light. Scalar potential is an instantaneous potential, although scalar information can ride piggyback on EM waves, thus slowing it down . . . . Thus it is possible that we live in a universe filled with information fields

operating at all frequencies; subtle fields not yet detected by instrumentation; fields that link all life forms. These fields were described by the great mathematician Dirac[5]

When the human body enters a scalar-energy field, the subtle energies of the individual become aligned with Source. This catalyzes the mind/body complex to have an optimally adaptive process that leads to a state more representative of its original quantum-mechanical matrix.

UNDERSTANDING THE MECHANICS OF SCALAR WAVE REGENERATION

Scalar waves create a self-generating dynamic that references directly to Source. They multiply through a generative self-replicating process that produces an overlapping wave phenomenon. Thus, two scalar fields wrapped around each other will produce another set of scalar fields and can never configure to produce EM or other types of harmful bio-resonant fields.

They can, however, naturally interact with the nonlinear fields of biological organisms, so that they can directly affect and respond to anomalies in the genetic code of biological life forms. Scalar fields are not the source of change in the organization of DNA but are the carrier waves for information to enter into the biological field(s). In other words, the scalar field itself is innocent of information or specific effect. Healthy bio-resonant information—such as the bio-geometric signatures of the body, Solfeggio frequencies, light, color, botanical essences, and gem elixirs—all uphold and nourish the original blueprints of our species.

Biological fields contain a signature that is capable of detecting, retrieving, and organizing scalar field–based information. Because biological fields are inherently interactive and self-organizing, they contain codes that make it possible for all intelligent life to be founded from a common database, or source intelligence, that is constantly regenerative and responsive to new input. This responsiveness is what catapults a biological organism to synthesize higher fields of intelligence and be able to recognize other dimensional frequencies or variants.

"Information scalars" are not presently accounted for in the foundation matrix of theoretical physics. **Biological organisms broadcast information** through their own scalar interface, interacting with all intelligent life forms simultaneously and multi-dimensionally. This is the foundation of the mechanics of collective consciousness. This gap in understanding the purpose of life and its interwoven system of shared information has created a deep vacuum in our modern paradigm of medicine, of biology, of technology, and ultimately, of the nature of the universe.

Scientists such as Eldon Byrd, who have embraced a more nonlinear aspect of thinking, seek to initiate a new form of mathematics and physics that would not be limited by our present understanding. Byrd seeks to bring recognition to biological information transference as a highly novel mechanism of significance for the propagation of a new form of analysis/synthesis. He seeks to show that it is not a matter of energy transfer that is of most concern but rather a leap into seeing how mathematics can describe the complexities of information transfer in all of its levels, including quantum mechanical. In other words, Byrd sees information as the ultimate quanta.

Einstein's General Theory of Relativity concerns itself exclusively with gravitational fields. It is not able to predict the existence or structure of any other field, including EM. Says Byrd, "Both the General and Special Theories of Relativity assume no instantaneous action at a distance; however, the Special Theory does not exclude massless *information* transfer. It is from this concept the notion of scalars as information carriers emerges."[6]

A QUANTUM SHIFT FROM LINEAR TO NONLINEAR BEING

Scalar waves are an effective carrier of information that positively influences psycho-emotional and conceptual insight. As we become anchored within the singular, universal source of the infinite unlimited energy potential facilitated by a scalar field, it becomes possible to shift our awareness into other dimensions of perception.

A system such as the EES creates multiple bio-active scalar fields that impact the human system at its core level, creating a high degree of psycho-emotional resonance that illuminates the subtle celestial architecture of the mental and emotional bodies. The individual ego views the natural mind as a field of influence within the underlying core identity. Within the scalar field, a spontaneous shift to a more creative and uplifting pattern of cognitive activity can take place. Belief structures that exist solely to encapsulate personality/mind and that habitually reference past and future do not have a life-supporting value in a scalar field. When the identity-bound mind is released from its security-based sensibility, a direct physiological experience of buoyancy and psycho-emotional freedom is generated.

Ordinarily, human beings are held captive by linear emotions such as grief, anger, jealousy, fear, worry, anxiety, and self-hatred. Linear emotion creates a closed loop that feeds on itself, creating endogenous toxins and a buildup of fixed psycho-structures. An individual finds it difficult to break free from past timelines that reinforce reactive states.

However, when exposed to healthy scalar fields over time, the individual gains the freedom of space to be able to experience an unlimited, open-ended emotional state in which love, gratitude, peace, forgiveness, and Presence cultivate a deep liveliness of spirit. The emotional and mental bodies are able to maintain a core level of neutrality, centeredness, and balance. Emotions are not limited to either the flat plane of the transcendental field or the ups and downs of the relative mind.

During a scalar healing session, one is encouraged to witness, or observe, when a particular negative event or emotion arises from the past; the inner self is able to identify the extent to which this emotion continues to limit the life force. The consciousness then has the opportunity to effortlessly recalibrate the event in light of neutrality, witnessing, and new vistas of insight. There is a junction point between the time of the event and its possible future trajectory that provides a window for transformation and freedom from the past event.

Upheld by the coherence of the scalar-field environment, the individual is able to pick up the new trajectory and work with it in subtle awareness. Personal reality is magnified by feelings of compassion, kindness, and tolerance. These states kindle avenues of self-acceptance and feelings of positivity and renewal. At this stage, one finds the mind/body is flooded with receptivity to divine input, which transmutes the past and creates a state of unconditional truth, free of fear.

During an EES healing session, events imprinted in the psyche or hidden in the subconscious will come to the foreground of awareness for reexamination and resolution. This is followed by a heightened self-awareness that reveals choice points in the life trajectory. The choice to enter into a sublime state of surrender emerges. The individual gains the objectivity to witness the constructs of linear patterns as having a beginning and end point that loop and repeat. At the end of the timeline, there is a window of opportunity that lies in the spacious feeling of consciousness opening into the neutral zone—a non-reactive, non-referential state.

This neutral zone functions as the counterpoint or resolution—thus dissolution—of habituated or past feelings of, for example, remorse, guilt, or fear. In the stillness of the neutral field, consciousness is gradually flooded with a sense of tenderness, forgiveness, and kindness. The individual grows in his or her capacity to be sensitive to the divine Presence and to be present in the now. The physiology is imbued with a powerful receptivity towards well-being and a reverent experience of Oneness. Answers to questions that have been a recurrent source of discomfort for the individual find inner resolution. There is a greater level of courage to face personal truth with dignity, strength, and peace.

Emotions are packets of stored kinetic energy that, when embedded in the physiology, can either elicit profound states of knowing or powerfully inhibit our clarity and sense of purpose. When emotions are illumined by the light of consciousness, they are loosened; no longer held tight by the body/mind, they do not bind the individual to a fixed temporal trajectory. Linearity is pierced by awakened consciousness, freeing the individual to shed a comfortable sense of identity and release the need to defend past behavior. We gain the ability to free ourselves from the imprisonment of guilt or over-weighted responsibility, while being duly accountable for our actions.

As an individual bathes in the multi-fields of the EES, he or she breaks through the boundaries of linear thinking by freeing the physiology to expose radical new levels of cognitive functioning. These levels go beyond our normal notions of seeing, knowing, and feeling, stretching intelligence so that it can operationally self-perfect. As the experience of a beneficent, omnipresent force enters the superstructure of the psyche, it oversees the mind in a timeless process towards gaining lasting liberation.

FREEING TIME AND SPACE: SCALAR FIELDS AS HIDDEN LIBERATORS

Psychological (linear) time fosters a bound state that imposes parameters on the psycho/emotional body. Once an individual is able to leave linear time and still maintain the coherence of Self, there is less need to cling to a false sense of security that binds the identity. One can feel grounded, awake, and functional, able to enjoy a full range of emotion and spontaneous intuitive action that is not embedded in past models of conditioned behavior.

The process of linearity in our personal timeline is based on the conformity generated when beliefs become rigid laws empowered by reason. Once loosened, such beliefs fall away, allowing for deeper inner systems of precise calibration that place us closer to our own innate cosmic time clock.

Scalar-wave fields enhance life-force energy in a way that expands our sense of reality. The two waves that characterize a scalar wave (the wave and anti-wave) create a seamless and timeless non-localized reality, supporting psycho-spiritual awakening to singularity—a unified state of being beyond the linear, dualistic nature of life.

As an individual is infused with healthy scalar fields, a bio-resonant entrainment occurs with the naturally occurring scalar waves that compose our human body. DNA itself is a scalar wave. The chakra system functions as a scalar wave. Our thoughts are scalar waves (they're faster than the speed of light). Steeped in an externally generated scalar environment like the EES, we become realigned with our original state of divine being.

The opening in space/time that occurs when one is exposed to healthy scalar fields has the capacity to shift the individual into a new style of functioning beyond the personal and linear. This shift into zero-point referencing creates a gap or point of origin that parallels the grail points (master points) in the human energy body. These grail points are like transformer stations between the unmanifest and the manifest state of reality. These points are vortices of intelligence that are both superconductive and super glue–like, synchronizing the mind/body/spirit.

The wave and anti-wave are out of phase, in time, by 180 degrees. This accounts for the quantum timing variables. The scalar wave exhibits the same wave function as the DNA helical waveform. Its two aspects intertwine along an axis point that allows for the counterbalancing of negative and positive, a neutral point of singularity.

Like the chakra system, scalar waves have infinite correlation expressed as a unified field. When the two waves cross, they are expressed as a zero-point field—that is, the null effect that occurs when a positively charged wave and a negatively charged wave intersect and cross over each other. This intersection, or gap, creates a field—a neutral zone that opens a timeless, transpersonal, non-localized realm of existence. It is this opening in space/time reality that realizes the infinite as the present. This highly dense, coherent, generated scalar field literally lifts the individual into a new style of communication that is beyond a personal, linear reality free from conditioning. Infinity is the frequency of Love and Oneness. It provides the fundamental underlying intelligence inherent in spiritual and physical health.

SEVEN STEPS OF CONSCIOUS HOLOGRAPHIC HEALING USING SCALAR TECHNOLOGIES

It's been observed through specialized oscilloscope instrumentation conducted by John Orava, physicist and consultant to the Department of Defense and President of Bio-Physicists Foundation, that the EES environment is an infinitely correlated neutral field capable of enhancing human potential. It has the capacity to expand our sense of reality, free us from limiting beliefs and attitudes, and align us with our divine nature to experience Oneness. It does this through "counterpoint unification," a consciousness-based process that naturally and spontaneously emerges out of the scalar-field phenomenon itself.

Counterpoint unification, the dissolution of opposites, is ideally facilitated through the practitioner/client interface. It may also occur naturally and spontaneously with the growth of higher states of consciousness. This is because an experienced EES practitioner is entrained in a state of harmonic resonance with the Field; the process is very lively within him or her. Transformation for the client occurs through bio-resonance with the practitioner as well as holographically in the zero-point neutral field.

Feeling into the pulse and rhythm of the environment, the practitioner holds a still point while transmitting the unconditional felt truth of love into the environment and directly to the heart center of the client. This elicits change in the most natural, efficient, and elegant manner.

In light of my own experience and witnessing, the following is a series of seven active steps of awareness that support a transpersonal approach to self-actualization through the EES. The seven active principles are nonlinear; they will randomly arise from the inner order of the governing soul. This seven-step process may also unfold sequentially or in partial steps, skipping around.

Upon entering the multiple fields of the EES, one enters a sacred space and time that has been prepared with conscious intent for actualizing full-spectrum health and one's highest soul potential. The innocent feeling level of openness, honor, and gratitude invoke Presence and allow for the healing power of grace to flow. A paradigm shift of personal and planetary health, regeneration, and transformation unfolds and takes its course.

The seven steps of awareness are described in the following sections.

1. Notice Everything and Expect Nothing

The participant or group is invited to sit comfortably and observe the internal reality of the mind/body. Participants are encouraged to be simple and receptive to inner listening. As an individual observes and follows his or her thought streams, there is a natural tendency to evaluate or identify with thoughts as they spontaneously arise—this is "common mind" thinking.

In the scalar healing environment, higher states of mind emerge. "Thinking" thoughts, constructs of the ego, begin to fall to the side, disappearing before they are formed or before they can become attached to their familiar landscape in the psyche. Such ego constructs become obsolete as one's newly organized energy matrix presents itself. It is important to surrender resistance and move toward the greatest flow of expansion into a felt positive response that leads to unconditional and holistic truths.

As the awareness settles, the user is immersed in the neutral zero-point environment. The polarized fields collapse to the zero point and neutralize constructs in the mental/emotional field that inhibit fluidity in the physiology. A cushion or buffer is created that eases stress in the psycho/emotional environment. Self-awareness is increased as the mind field is freed from the clutter of "thinking" thoughts related to limiting belief structures and traumas. **One begins to rest in a mindless, silent state of awareness.**

2. Open to the Power of Intention

The EES's unified-field environment creates a type of magnetic attraction to Source that is physically identifiable. The depth of authenticity elicited in this environment supports the establishment of pure intention at a visceral level of feeling. Intention is not formulated from the thinking mind or desire. Intention arises from the soul-level impulses of communication with one's own holographic field of awareness.

Pure intention is experienced on the level of the heart and is a felt sense of clarity. As one allows attention to rest upon the intention, an expansion and magnetic power become activated. This process sets up an alignment of events that yield synchronicities to advance and support the higher potentiality of life. Notable outcomes may include physical healing, vital energy enhancement, increased organization and productivity, greater happiness, open communication, creative realization, and sychronicity as a random path to advanced organization.

3. Receive an Inner Question, Receive an Inner Answer

In a state of witnessing, or pure observation, a spontaneous and parallel process arises. As the mind settles and rests in the field of conscious awareness, one often will be given a question that has been held in the depth of the heart/soul. In that instant of receiving the question, an answer is simultaneously received in one seamless step.

Both the question and answer are presented from the tableau of the higher Self. The scalar environment mirrors one's inner sacred spaces of Self. In this atmosphere, personal intention and prayer are in deep resonance and alignment with the divine universal plan. The question-and-answer phenomenon is a unification of knowledge that is sourced through the functioning of the whole brain.

In the wholeness of the moment, both question and answer unify, giving rise to direct cognitive knowing. At the point of knowing or realization, transformation, healing, and miracles unfold. Some outcomes are more immediate; others will unfold in their own time.

As one bathes in the field, the power of the heart generates spontaneous desires that are in alignment with the core Self. The individual enters a state of timeless patience in which both the subject of inquiry and the keys to unlocking the answers are simultaneously revealed. Information is presented in a clear, relaxed manner that generates an alert attention to what is most true. In this atmosphere of deep rest, the individual is drawn into the still point of awareness, where the mind becomes quiescent and Presence is highly active.

4. Learning the Language of the Soul

The soul speaks in feeling, imagery, and inner voice awareness. The instructive capacity of the soul is expressed through a repertoire of coded imprinting, using light, sound, geometry, kinesthetic body sensing, feeling, and direct cognitive impulses. The soul uses the quantum energy matrices within its auric fields to communicate with the conscious mind and personality structure to turn on the light of insight.

The soul's field matrix is holographic. It is imbued with the life-force signature from a primordial, pre-linguistic level, as well as a highly intelligent information matrix that is intrinsically integrated into multiple dimensions.

As one innocently observes thoughts and/or emotions as they arise in awareness, a pause in time occurs and awareness opens a space that reveals meaning and significance. The illuminated moment brings insight. Thought and emotions are a direct result of unwinding a pattern of stress, thus opening into the clear silence of inner space and balancing upon the still point.

When the thinking mind and/or emotional patterns persist, they signal that information essential to the health and development of the individual is locked within these mind/body sensations. From this point, one can gently bring awareness into the body and allow the self-inquiry process to become activated. One can observe what questions arise or ask for a question that will facilitate insight into the condition of the thinking-feeling pattern.

Thoughts and feelings are packets of information that contain key insights into the nature of your personal reality. Once the light of awareness illumines the mind, attention is free to go into creative space.

As individuals grow in the fullness of their potential, they become infused with the power of Presence, a powerful life force that is both hyper-awake and logical in its core cognitive value. Thus one learns to master the transpersonal landscapes of the soul's holographic dimensional life.

5. Surrender the Need to Know: Not Minding

As one allows time to pass through the mind/body unit, not holding onto or resisting any experience, one surrenders to non-referential beingness. This means being, for even a split second, without a familiar locator point in any particular space or time reference. In the EES scalar fields, time and space alter in one's favor, slowing, stopping, disappearing, speeding up, opening, or closing. In this seeming freefall, ultimately an eternal still point, or suspension, lifts the mind out of its reference points and transmutes conditions and experiences of pain and suffering, thus fostering an internal core of solidity. The mind/body intelligence will intelligently manage the process according to the capacity of one's nervous system.

The element of willingness, coupled with courage, sets the stage for growth in consciousness. Whether the situation is a personal dilemma, a problem of ethics, or a political or social question, it is human tendency to struggle to find the faith to let go, to surrender to the nakedness of what is. However, from the emotional freefall that accompanies the state of surrender, a sense of relief and comfort emerges as one accepts unconditionally that life's circumstances or secrets will not yield to any forced efforts to change. From this vantage point, the soul recognizes that there will be no end to the journey, only a different experience of what is. Thus the personal identity structure is freed and rests in the peace of not minding.

In the state of not minding, meaning becomes wholly original and non-referential. Reasoning and meaning become more autonomous, while the buffer zones of dimensionality no longer have the capacity to limit higher intelligence. The feeling that something "just is" or "will be" is not a passive recognition, but a dynamic entry into the creative power of the Divine. One finds comfort in the essential rightness of life and is bathed in a profound sense of awe about how the pieces of life are put together—without being bound to any particular conceptual constraints. The question of "why" recedes into the mind and heart of God.

6. Quantum Neutrality and the Intelligent Heart

As one stays open and allows the personal identity to merge with awareness as a non-localized field, there is no need for referencing space, time, or location. The EES environment encourages one's bioactive energy fields to go into a superconductive suspension state.

This quantum suspension state creates a window of opportunity for the nervous system to break free of established rigidities and stress patterns, thus creating a deeply relaxing, regenerative, and highly creative brainwave pattern for new information, imprinting, and learning.

Through the transmutation of the electromagnetic waves, a singular standing scalar wave is created. As the electromagnetic waves intersect, a resolution of the polarity occurs, creating a neutral experience. This takes place on every level, from the expanded regions of the field of consciousness to the cellular level.

The unification of polarity energies creates a type of superfluidity in the nervous system. This highly conductive state supports a nonlinear, open-ended lifestyle. Insight into the celestial structures that support, enliven, and propel consciousness is activated. One learns by seeing through previous areas of stagnation and extending sight into new vistas.

In the quantum neutral state, one's intelligence becomes entrained with higher harmonic frequencies, eliciting new pathways of knowledge. This generates distinct breakthroughs in the realm of personal freedom. New, expanded truths are realized and conscious choices for new growth emerge.

Through an awakening to what is uniquely authentic, the light of the Sacred Heart permeates personal reality. The transpersonal messaging process, which occurs while one is in the EES healing field, elicits direct cognitive experiences from the nonlinear state, such as compassion, unconditional acceptance, impeccability, and kindness. **Living life as a holistic quantum field generates an open-ended process of transformation within the heart.** This is the platform from which the higher dimensions of one's soul are able to braid into the present.

7. Freedom and Love: Nowhere Else to Go

As you become referenced and resonant with the zero-point field, you will find yourself in a space/time state that is non-referential. In this non-referential state, there is nowhere to go. The Self alone, potently present in the endless now, is free to be in the highest expression of your divine self. The witnessing aspect of mind takes notice of habit—ceasing to search for identity, definition, or forms and thus allowing the bliss and beauty of being to take hold. Contentment pours over you as a shield of invincibility.

This is a felt experience of personal reality that is cultivated as the nervous system reaches subtler levels of refinement and orderliness. When you notice you are dropping into this suspension state, effortlessly open into the junction point between the light of consciousness and the subtle stillness of breath. An inner-generated light springs forth from the well of the divine love frequency. Breath is the life-force presence of God that arises out of the central vortex of the heart. Love is the only transdimensional frequency that has the power to transform all conditions, to communicate between dimensions, and to lift the spirit to new heights previously unknown.

The EES cultivates changes and shifts in the subtle breath, or *prana*. As one bathes in this cushioned atmosphere, it produces pronounced buoyancy in spirit. This highly relaxed, alert state allows one to let go into the transformational power of divine love and light, liberating soul presence. In the open space of love, there is more freedom within choice and there are more options to choose from.

The holy breath—the subtle, nearly no-breath state—elicits transformation and the recognition and release of frequency patterns that bind one to fate. Residual memories may persist, yet the subtle nervous system cultivates a capacity to depersonalize these residual impulse messages.

The internal state of freedom uses architectural light language—that is, divine signature frequencies of one's soul—to interact with dimensional life streams. In the relative human plane, these signatures often are expressed in creative genius, ethical consciousness, or virtues such as kindness, accountability, acceptance, and peace. Since these soul/spirit expressions are unconditional, they directly emit the holographic blueprints of the godhead within.

You are the paradigm shift, the dimensional change. In this shift, temporal expansion and internal volume and space are reorganized. This new optimized level of functioning organizes itself as highly coherent holistic fields capable of eliciting cognitive insight sourced directly from pure intelligence. The EES bioactive field matrix is an entry into the cradle of space/time expansion, where revelation and healing are powerful and can be instantaneous.

The steps of awakening described above are not sequential. They can occur randomly or in clusters. **As one steps into the ever-shifting future of life's trajectories, whose stage is set by the past and present time records of the soul, a kaleidoscope of worlds beyond imagination emerges as potential realities.**

In the human journey that we all share on planet Earth, it is the simplest of choices to stay open to the unlimited power of love, find gratitude for all that is, and remain alert to the mysteries that transcend all boundaries.

NOTES

Chapter 1

[1] Christian Ratsch, *The Gateway to Inner Space: A Festschrift in Honor of Albert Hoffmann* (Dorset, UK: Prism, 1989), 60.

[2] Ibid., 56.

[3] Jim DeKorne, *Psychedelic Shamanism: The Cultivation, Preparation, and Shamanic Use of Psychotropic Plants* (Port Townsend, WA: Loompanics Unlimited, 1994), 22.

[4] Janet Sussman, *Reality of Time* lecture series, 2007.

[5] Dan Winter, *Alphabet of the Heart* (New York: Author, 1982), 35.

[6] B. B. Mandelbrot, *The Fractal Geometry of Nature* (San Francisco: W. H. Freeman, 1982).

[7] Winter, *Alphabet of the Heart*, 35.

[8] Ibid., 39.

[9] Ibid., 42.

[10] Ibid., 48.

[11] Ibid., 44.

[12] Ibid., 12.

Chapter 2

[1] Michael Tierra, *Planetary Herbology* (Santa Fe, NM: Lotus, 1989), 37.

[2] Vasant Lad and David Frawley, The Yoga of Herbs (Santa Fe, NM: Lotus, 1986), 5.

[3] Tony Nader, *Human Physiology: Expression of Veda and the Vedic Literature* (Vlodrop, Netherlands: Maharishi Vedic University, 1995), 4.

[4] Ibid.

[5] Walter Holder Capps, *Seeing with a Native Eye* (New York: Harper & Row, 1976), 9.

[6] Matthew Wood, *The Magical Staff* (Berkeley, CA: North Atlantic Books, 1992), xiv.

[7] Capps, *Seeing with a Native Eye*, 39.

[8] Ibid., 31.

[9] Ibid., 17.

[10] Ibid., 55.

[11] Virgil J. Vogel, *American Indian Medicine* (Norman: University of Oklahoma Press, 1970), 15.

[12] Ibid., 22.

[13] Vogel, *American Indian Medicine*, 26.

[14] Ibid., 6.

[15] Yaya Diallo and Mitch Hall, *The Healing Drum: African Wisdom Teachings* (Rochester, VT: Destiny Books, 1989), 15.

[16] Ibid., 56.

[17] Ibid., 134.

[18] Ibid., 117.

[19] Ibid., 11.

[20] Malidoma Patrice Somé, *Of Water and the Spirit: Ritual, Magic, and Initiation in the Life of an African Shaman* (New York: Putnam, 1994), 203.

[21] Ibid., 20.

[22] Luis Luna and Pablo Amaringo, *Ayahuasca Visions: The Religious Iconography of a Peruvian Shaman* (Berkeley, CA: North Atlantic Books, 1991), 10.

[23] Ibid., 12.

[24] Richard Evans Schultes and Albert Hoffman, *Plants of the Gods* (Rochester, VT: Healing Arts Press, 1992), 120.

[25] Luna and Amaringo, *Ayahuasca Visions*, 41.

[26] Ibid., 35.

27 A.P. Elkin, *Aboriginal Men of High Degree* (Rochester, VT: Inner Traditions, 1977), 4.

28 Ibid., xvii.

29 Wood, *The Magical Staff*, xii.

30 Ibid., 2.

31 Ibid., 9.

32 Ibid., 15

33 Ibid., 18.

34 Malcolm Stuart, Ed., *The Encyclopedia of Herbs and Herbalism* (London: Orbis, 1979), 22.

35 David Potterton, *Culpeper's Color Herbal* (New York: Sterling, 1983), 6.

36 George Adams and Olive Whicher, *The Plant Between Sun and Earth* (London: Rudolf Steiner Press, 1980), 140.

37 Ibid., 17.

38 Ibid., 30.

39 Ibid., 40–41.

40 Ibid., 146.

41 Ibid., 81.

42 Ibid., 85, 89.

43 Rudolf Steiner, *Spiritual Science and Medicine* (London: Anthroposophic Press, 1948), 47–48.

44 Ibid., 76–88.

45 Edward Bach, *Heal Thyself* (Saffron Walden, UK: C. W. Daniel, 1931), 6.

46 Ibid., 11.

47 Patricia Kaminski and Richard Katz, *Flower Essence Repertory* (Nevada City, CA: Flower Essence Society, 1992), 4.

48 Ibid., 3.

49 Ibid., 12.

50 Ibid., 100.

51 Ibid., 25.

52 Machaelle Small Wright, *Flower Essences* (Jeffersonton, VA: Perelandra, 1988), 16.

52 Ibid., 10.

54 Richard S. Brown, *Astral Gemstone Talismans* (Lumpini, Bangkok, Thailand: AGT, 2000), 1.

55 Dan Campbell, *Edgar Cayce on the Power of Color, Stones, and Crystals* (New York: Warner Books, 1989), 125.

56 Ibid., 138.

57 Ibid., 120.

58 Howard Beckman, *Mantras, Yantras & Fabulous Gems* (Hastings, UK: Balaji, 1996), 115.

Chapter 3

1 Michael S. Schneider, *Constructing the Universe* (New York: Harper-Perennial, 1995), 118–127.

2 Ibid., 120.

3 Patricia Kaminski and Richard Katz, *Flower Essence Repertory* (Nevada City, CA: Flower Essence Society, 1992), 19.

4 Terence McKenna, *Food of the Gods* (New York: Bantam Books, 1992), 256.

5 Vasant Lad and David Frawley, *The Yoga of Herbs* (Santa Fe, NM: Lotus, 1986), 5.

6 Deepak Chopra, *Quantum Healing* (New York: Bantam Books, 1989), 248.

7 Christian Ratsch, *The Gateway to Inner Space: A Festschrift in Honor of Albert Hoffmann* (Dorset, UK: Prism, 1990), 66.

8 Herbal Research Publications, *Naturopathic Handbook of Herbal Formulas* (Ayer, MA: Herbal Research Publications, 1995), 12–13.

9 Susanne Fischer-Rizzi, *Complete Aromatherapy Handbook* (New York: Sterling, 1990), 17.

10 Ibid., 222.

11 Janet Sussman, *Timeshift: The Experience of Dimensional Change* (Fairfield, IA: Time Portal, 1996), 3.

12 Wright, *Flower Essences*, 18.

13 Ratsch, *Gateway to Inner Space*, 68.

14 Eliot Cowan, *Plant Spirit Medicine* (Newburg, OR: Swan-Raven, 1995), 58.

[15] McKenna, *Food of the Gods*, 4.

[16] Gurudas, *Flower Essences and Vibrational Healing* (San Rafael, CA: Cassandra Press, 1989), 30.

[17] Kaminski and Katz, *Flower Essence Repertory*, 312.

[18] David Hoffman, *The Holistic Herbal* (London: Butler & Tanner, 1983), 206.

[19] Kaminski and Katz, *Flower Essence Repertory*, 285.

[20] Hoffman, *The Holistic Herbal*, 206.

[21] Ed Smith, *The Herbal Magazine*, 1986, 10.

[22] Christopher Hobbs and Steven Foster, *HerbalGram*, 22, Spring 1990, 24.

[23] Finley Ellingwood, *American Materia Medica, Therapeutics and Pharmacognosy* (Portland, OR: Eclectic Medical Publications, 1983), 204.

[24] Ibid., 483.

[25] C. A. Newall, L. A. Anderson, and J. D. Phillipson, *Herbal Medicines* (London: The Pharmaceutical Press, 1996), 197.

[26] Terry Willard, *The Wild Rose Scientific Herbal* (Calgary, AB: Wild Rose College of Natural Healing, 1991), 257.

[27] Hoffman, *The Holistic Herbal*, 221.

[28] Michael Castleman, *The Healing Herbs* (Emmaus, PA: Rodale, 1991), 285.

[29] Willard, *The Wild Rose Scientific Herbal*, 257.

[30] Hoffman, *The Holistic Herbal*, 233.

[31] Ellingwood, American Materia Medica, 204.

[32] Lad and Frawley, *The Yoga of Herbs*, 170.

[33] M. V. R. Appa Rao, et al., *Journal of Indian Medicine* (August 25, 1973): 9–12.

[34] M.V.R. Appa Rao, et al., *Nagarjun* (July, 1969): 41.

[35] John Heinesman, *Natural Nutrition* (Provo, UT: Woodland Books, 1984), 85.

[36] Hoffman, *The Holistic Herbal*, 210.

[37] A. Y. Leung and S. Foster, *Encyclopedia of Common Natural Ingredients: Used in Food, Drugs and Cosmetics* (New York: Wiley, 1996), 339.

[38] Lad and Frawley, *The Yoga of Herbs*, 103.

[39] Salvatore Batlaglia, *The Complete Guide to Aromatherapy* (Brisbane, Australia: Watson Ferguson, 1995), 142.

[40] Willard, *The Wild Rose Scientific Herbal*, 142–143.

[41] Donald Brown, *Phyto Fact Sheet* (Seattle, WA: Natural Product Research Consultants, 1996), 2–3.

[42] Hoffman, *The Holistic Herbal*, 229.

[43] Willard, *The Wild Rose Scientific Herbal*, 296.

[44] James A. Duke, *CRC Handbook of Medicinal Herbs* (Boca Raton, FL: CRC, 1985), 412.

[45] Public information document (Swedish Herbal Institute, 1990), 1–3.

[46] "Herbal Hall." http://www.herbal-hall.com/

[47] Stephen Foster, *The Business of Herbs* (July–August, 1996).

[48] Hoffman, *The Holistic Herbal*, 222.

[49] Daniel B. Mowrey, *The Scientific Validation of Herbal Medicine* (New Canaan, CT: Keats, 1986), 191.

[50] Lad and Frawley, *The Yoga of Herbs*, 130.

[51] Willard, *The Wild Rose Scientific Herbal*, 215.

[52] H. L. Wagner, L. Horhammer, and R. Munster, "The Chemistry of Silymarin (Silybin), the Active Principle of the Fruits of *Silybum marianum* (L.) Gaertn. (*Carduus marianus* L.)," *Arzneim Forsch* 18 (1968): 688–696.

[53] P. Bergner, *Townsend Letter for Doctors* (Aug/Sept., 1988): 49.

[54] Hoffman, *The Holistic Herbal*, 202.

[55] Lad and Frawley, *The Yoga of Herbs*, 121.

[56] Ellingwood, *American Materia Medica*, 369.

[57] Michael Moore, *Medicinal Plants of the Mountain West* (Santa Fe: The Museum of New Mexico Press, 1979), 117.

[58] Leung and Foster, *Encyclopedia of Common Natural Ingredients*, 66.

[59] Christopher Hobbs, *Echinacea: The Immune Herb* (Santa Cruz, CA: Botanica, 1990), 219.

[60] Lad and Frawley, *The Yoga of Herbs*, 117.

[61] Stephen E. Moring, *Monograph from Echinacea*, 1–3.

[62] Hobbs, *Echinacea*, 1–10.

[63] Moring, "Echinacea," 2.

[64] Ibid., 1–3.

[65] Hobbs, *Echinacea*, 16.

[66] Moring, "Echinacea," 1–3.

[67] Ibid.

[68] Brown, *Phyto Fact Sheet*, 1–5.

Chapter 4

[1] Anodea Judith, *Wheels of Life* (St. Paul, MN: Llewellyn New Worlds, 1995), 27.

[2] Randolph Stone, *Energy: The Vital Polarity in the Healing Arts* (Orange, CA: Pierre Pannetier, 1954), 39.

[3] Lee Hartley, "Make Those Blues Go Away: The Effect of Light on Seasonal Affective Disorder (SAD) and Premenstrual Syndrome," in *Light Years Ahead* (Berkeley, CA: Light Years Ahead Productions, 1996), 101–119.

[4] Norman Shealy, MD, "The Reality of EEG and Neurochemical Responses to Photostimulation—Part II," in *Light Years Ahead* (Berkeley, CA: Light Years Ahead Productions, 1996), 185.

[5] Peter Mandel, *The Practical Compendium of Colorpuncture* (Bruschal, West Germany: Energetik, 1986), 38.

[6] Janet Sussman, Chakra and Energy Body seminar series, 1999.

[7] Mandel, *Practical Compendium of Colorpuncture*, 36.

[8] Ibid., 34.

[9] Ibid., 37.

[10] Vasant Lad and David Frawley, *The Yoga of Herbs* (Santa Fe, NM: Lotus, 1986), 16.

[11] Vasant Lad, *Ayurveda: The Science of Self-Healing* (Santa Fe, NM: Lotus, 1984), 110.

[12] Harish Johari, *Chakras: Energy Centers of Transformation* (Rochester, VT: Destiny Books, 1987), 13.

Chapter 5

[1] Starr Fuentes, with Shirley A. Resler, *Advanced Light Language, Book 2* (Author, 2001), 1–4.

[2] Michael S. Schneider, *Constructing the Universe* (New York: Harper-Perennial, 1995), 89, 249.

[3] Robert J. Gilbert, PhD, *Seven Keys to Creation: Sacred Geometry and the Patterns of Life* (Asheville, NC: VESICA, 2002), 62.

[4] David Allen Hulse, *New Dimensions for the Cube of Space* (York Beach, ME: Samuel Weiser, 2000), 123.

[5] Starr Fuentes, with Shirley A. Resler, *Advanced Light Language* (Author, 2001), 1–5.

[6] Theo Gimbel, DCE, *Healing Through Colours* (Essex, UK: C.W. Daniel, 1980), 35–41.

[7] Starr Fuentes, with Shirley A. Resler, *Intermediate Light Language* (Author, 2000), 19.

[8] Gimbel, *Healing Through Colours*, 28–41.

[9] Fuentes, *Intermediate Light Language*, 20.

[10] Gimbel, *Healing Through Colours*, 30–41.

[11] Fuentes, *Intermediate Light Language*, 12.

[12] Gimbel, *Healing Through Colours*, 30–41.

[13] R. Webster, *Gems* (Cornwall, UK: Butterworth, 1983), 564.

[14] Ibid., 168.

[15] Webster, *Gems*, 127–128.

Chapter 6

[1] Hart DeFouw and Robert Svoboda, *Light on Life: An Introduction to the Astrology of India* (New York: Penguin Books, 1996), 1–3.

[2] Dan Winter, *Alphabet of the Heart* (New York: Author, 1992), 45.

[3] Rudolf Steiner, *Discussions with Teachers* (Hudson, NY: Anthroposophic Press, 1997), 116.

[4] Gregg Braden, *Walking Between the Worlds: The Science of Compassion* (Bellevue, WA: Radio Bookstore Press, 1997), 77.

Chapter 7

[1] Harish Johari, *Chakras: Energy Centers of Transformation* (Rochester, VT: Destiny Books, 1987).

[2] Gregg Braden, *Awakening to Zero Point: The Collective Initiation* (Questa, NM: Sacred Spaces/Ancient Wisdom, 1994), 180.

[3] Mantak and Maneewan Chia, *Healing Love Through the Tao: Cultivating Female Sexual Energy* (Huntington, NY: Healing Tao Books, 1986), 74.

[4] Patricia Kaminski and Richard Katz, *Flower Essence Repertory* (Nevada City, CA: Flower Essence Society, 1992), 384.

[5] Dan Winter, *Alphabet of the Heart* (New York: Author, 1992), 25–29.

[6] Janet Sussman, *Timeshift: The Experience of Dimensional Change* (Fairfield, IA: Time Portal, 1996), 64–66.

[7] Kaminski and Katz, *Flower Essence Repertory*, 340.

[8] Johari, *Chakras*, 73.

[9] Anodea Judith, *Wheels of Life* (St. Paul, MN: Llewellyn New Worlds, 1995), 319.

[10] Kaminski and Katz, *Flower Essence Repertory*, 284.

[11] Judith, *Wheels of Life*, 370.

[12] Robert J. Gilbert, *Seven Keys to Creation: Sacred Geometry and the Patterns of Life* (Asheville, NC: VESICA, 2002), 20.

[13] Kaminski and Katz, *Flower Essence Repertory*, 336.

[14] Ibid., 384.

[15] Ibid., 340.

[16] Ibid., 326.

[17] Ibid., 394.

[18] Ibid., 397.

[19] Flower Essence Services, http://www.fesflowers.com.

Chapter 8

[1] John Barron, *The Barron Report* 10, no. 4 (2001).

[2] Nicole Loeffler, *Pilot Study Report* (2006): 3.

[3] Barron, *The Barron Report*.

[4] Glen Ryan, *Conference Proceedings*, 1988.

[5] Eldon A. Byrd, "Scalars, Part II," United States Psychotronic Association http://www.psychotronics.org/

[6] Byrd, Part I.

BIBLIOGRAPHY

Adams, George, and Olive Whiche. *The Plant Between Sun and Earth*. London: Rudolf Steiner Press, 1980.

Appa Rao, M. V. R., et al. *Journal of Indian Medicine* (August 25, 1973): 9–12.

———. *Nagarjun* (July 1969): 41.

Babbitt, Edwin S. *The Principles of Light & Color*. Secaucus, NJ: Citadel, 1967.

Bach, Edward. *The Bach Flower Remedies*. New Canaan, CT: Keats, 1931.

———. *Heal Thyself*. Saffron Walden, UK: C.W. Daniel, 1931.

Bandopadhyay, M., et al. *Indian Journal of Chemistry* 10, no. 808 (1972).

Barnard, Julian. *Patterns of Life Force*. Bach Education Programme, 1987. http://www.edwardbach.org/Library/LifeForces/_LifeForce.pdf

Barnard, Julian and Martine. *The Healing Herbs of Edward Bach: A Practical Guide to Making the Remedies*. UK: Bach Educational Programme, 1988.

Barron, John. *The Barron Report* 10, no. 4 (2001).

Batlaglia, Salvatore. *The Complete Guide to Aromatherapy*. Brisbane, Australia: Watson Ferguson, 1995.

Becker, Robert D., and Gary Selden. *The Body Electric*. New York: Quill, 1985.

Beckman, Howard. *Mantras, Yantras & Fabulous Gems*. Hastings, UK: Balaji, 1996.

Bergner, Paul. *Townsend Letter for Doctors* (August/September 1988): 191.

Bhattacharyya, Benoytosh. *Gem Therapy*. Calcutta, India: Firma KLM, 1992.

Bissett, N. G. *Herbal Drugs and Phytopharmaceuticals*. Edited by N. G. Bisset. Boca Raton, FL: CRC, 1994.

Botchis, Lilli M., ed. *Plants in the Light of Healing*. Fairfield, IA: Time Portal, 1994.

Boyd, Doug. *Rolling Thunder*. New York: Dell, 1974.

Braden, Gregg. *Awakening to Zero Point: The Collective Initiation*. Questa, NM: Sacred Spaces/Ancient Wisdom, 1994.

———. *Walking Between the Worlds: The Science of Compassion*. Bellevue, WA: Radio Bookstore Press, 1997.

Breiling, Brian J. *Light Years Ahead*. Tiburon, CA: Light Years Ahead Productions, 1996.

Brooke, Elisabeth. *Women Healers*. Rochester, VT: Healing Arts Press, 1993.

Brown, Donald. *Phyto Fact Sheet*. Seattle, WA: Natural Product Research Consultants, 1996.

Brown, Richard S. *Astral Gemstone Talismans*. Lumpini, Bangkok, Thailand: AGT, 2000.

Bruyere, Roslyn. *Wheels of Light: A Study of the Chakras*. Sierra Madre, CA: Bon Productions, 1989.

Byrd, Eldon A. "Scalars, Part II." United States Psychotronic Association http://www.psychotronics.org/

Campbell, Dan. Edgar *Cayce on the Power of Color, Stones, and Crystals*. New York: Warner Books, 1989.

Capps, Walter Holder. *Seeing with a Native Eye*. New York: Harper & Row, 1976.

Capra, Fritjof. *The Web of Life*. New York: Anchor Books/Doubleday, 1996.

Castleman, Michael. *The Healing Herbs*. Emmaus, PA: Rodale, 1991.

Cayce, Edgar. *Gems and Stones*. Virginia Beach: A.R.E. Press, 2002.

Chancellor, Phillip M. *Handbook of the Bach Flower Remedies*. New Canaan, CT: Keats, 1971.

Chase, Pamela, and Jonathan Pawlik. *Healing with Gemstones*. North Hollywood, CA: New Castle Publishing, 1989.

Chia, Mantak and Manewan. *Awaken Healing Energy Through the Tao.* New York: Aurora, 1983.

———. *Healing Love Through the Tao: Awakening Female Sexual Energy.* Huntington, NY: Healing Tao Books, 1987.

Chopra, Deepak. *Ageless Body, Timeless Mind.* New York: Harmony Books, 1993.

———. *Quantum Healing.* New York: Bantam Books, 1989.

Christopher, J. R. *School of Natural Healing.* Provo, UT: B. World, 1976.

Cowan, Eliot. *Plant Spirit Medicine.* Newburg, OR: Swan-Raven, 1995.

Cox, Robert. *The Pillar of Celestial Fire.* Fairfield, IA: Sunstar, 1997.

Culpeper, Nicholas. *Herbal Remedies.* North Hollywood, CA: Melvin Powers Wilshire.

Cummings, Stephen, and Dana Ullman. *Homeopathic Medicines.* New York: Tarcher/Putnam, 1997.

Davis, Rennie. *The Great Turning: Evolution at the Crossroads.* Boulder, CO: New Nations, 1997.

DeFouw, Hart, and Robert Svoboda. *Light on Life: An Introduction to the Astrology of India.* New York: Penguin Books, 1996.

DeKorne, Jim. *Psychedelic Shamanism: The Cultivation, Preparation, and Shamanic Use of Psychotropic Plants.* Port Townsend, WA: Loompanics Unlimited, 1994.

DerMarderosian, Ara, and John A. Beutler. *The Review of Natural Products,* 6th ed. St. Louis: Wolters Kluwer Health.

Devananada, Swami Vishnu. *Meditation and Mantra.* New York: OM Lotus, 1978.

Diallo, Yaya, and Mitch Hall. *The Healing Drum: African Wisdom Teachings.* Rochester, VT: Destiny Books, 1989.

Duke, James A. *CRC Handbook of Medicinal Herbs.* Boca Raton, FL: CRC, 1985.

Elkin, A. P. *Aboriginal Men of High Degree.* Rochester, VT: Inner Traditions, 1977.

———. *The Australian Aborigines.* New York: Doubleday, 1964.

Ellingwood, Finley. *American Materia Medica, Therapeutics and Pharmacognosy*. Portland, OR: Eclectic Medical Publications, 1983.

Elliot, Cowan. *Plant Spirit Medicine*. Newberg, OR: Swan & Raven, 1995.

Essene, Virginia, and Sheldon Nidle. *You Are Becoming a Galactic Human*. Santa Clara, CA: Spiritual Education Endeavors, 1994.

Felter, H. W. *Kings American Dispensatory, 1898*. Portland, OR: Eclectic Medical Publications, 1983.

Fischer-Rizzi, Susanne. *Complete Aromatherapy Handbook*. New York: Sterling, 1990.

Flower Essence Services, http://www.fesflowers.com

Foster, Steven. *The Business of Herbs* (July/August 1996).

Foster, Steven, and James A. Duke. *Medicinal Plants*. Boston: Houghton Mifflin, 1990.

Frawley, David. *The Astrology of the Seers: A Guide to Vedic (Hindu) Astrology*. Delhi, India: Motilal Banarsidass, 1996.

Fuentes, Starr, with Shirley A. Resler. *Advanced Light Language*. Author, 2001.

———. *Advanced Light Language*, Book 2. Author, 2001.

———. *Intermediate Light Language*, Author, 2000.

Fulder, Stephen. *The Tao of Medicine*. New York: Destiny Books, 1982.

Gerber, Richard. *Vibrational Medicine*. Santa Fe, NM: Bear, 1988.

Gilbert, Robert J. *Seven Keys to Creation: Sacred Geometry and the Patterns of Life*. Asheville, NC: VESICA, 2002.

Gimbel, Theo. *Healing Through Colours*. Essex, UK: C.W. Daniel, 1980.

Gladstar, Rosemary, and Pamela Hirsch. *Saving Our Medicinal Herbs*. Rochester, VT: Healing Arts Press, 2000.

Goethe, Johann Wolfgang von. *The Metamorphosis of Plants*. Wyoming, RI: Biodynamic Literature, 1978.

Gurudas. *Flower Essences and Vibrational Healing*. San Rafael, CA: Cassandra Press, 1989.

———. *Gem Elixirs and Vibrational Healing, Vol. 1*. San Rafael, CA: Cassandra Press, 1989.

————. *The Spiritual Properties of Herbs*. San Rafael, CA: Cassandra Press, 1988.

Halifax, Joan. *Shamanic Voices*. New York: E. P. Dutton, 1979.

Hall, Manly P. *Paracelsus: His Mystical and Medical Philosophy*. Los Angeles: Philosophical Research Society, 1964.

Hartley, Lee. "Make Those Blues Go Away: The Effect of Light on Seasonal Affective Disorder (SAD) and Premenstrual Syndrome" In *Light Years Ahead*, 101–119. Berkeley, CA: Light Years Ahead Productions, 1996.

Hawkins, R. David. *Power vs. Force*. Sedona, AZ: Veritas, 1998.

Hawthorne, David, and V. K. Choudhry. *Astrology for Life*. Fairfield, IA: Sunstar, 2000.

Heinesman, John. *Natural Nutrition*. Provo, UT: Woodland Books, 1984.

Herbal Hall. http://www.herbal-hall.com/

Herbal Research Publications. *Naturopathic Handbook of Herbal Formulas*. Ayer, MA: Herbal Research Publications, 1995.

Hobbs, Christopher. *Echinacea: The Immune Herb*. Santa Cruz, CA: Botanica, 1990.

————. *Foundations of Health*. Capitola, CA: Botanica, 1992.

Hobbs, Christopher, and Steven Foster. *HerbalGram* 22 (Spring 1990): 24.

Hoffman, David. *The Holistic Herbal*. London: Butler & Tanner, 1983.

Hutchens, Alma R. *Indian Herbology of North America*. Boston: Shambhala, 1973.

Hulse, David Allen. *New Dimensions for the Cube of Space*. York Beach, ME: Samuel Weiser, 2000.

Iyengar, B. K. S. *Light on Pranayama*. New York: Crossroad, 1965.

Iyengar, B. K. S. *Light on Yoga*. New York: Schocken Books, 1965.

Johari, Harish. *Chakras: Energy Centers of Transformation*. Rochester, VT: Destiny Books, 1987.

————. *The Healing Powers of Gemstones in Tantra Ayurveda Astrology*. Rochester, VT: Destiny Books, 1988.

Johnson, Steve. *The Essence of Healing*. Homer, AK: Alaskan Flower Essence Project, 2000.

Judith, Anodea. *Wheels of Life*. St. Paul, MN: Llewellyn New Worlds, 1995.

Junius, Manfred M. *Practical Handbook of Plant Alchemy*. New York: Inner Traditions International, 1979.

Kaminski, Patricia, and Richard Katz. *Flower Essence Repertory*. Nevada City, CA: Flower Essence Society, 1992.

Katz, Michael. *Gemisphere Luminary*. Portland, OR: Gemisphere Luminary, 1994.

Lad, Vasant. *Ayurveda: The Science of Self-Healing*. Santa Fe, NM: Lotus, 1984.

Lad, Vasant, and David Frawley. *The Yoga of Herbs*. Santa Fe, NM: Lotus, 1986.

Lamb, Bruce F. *Wizard of the Upper Amazon*. Berkeley, CA: North Atlantic Books, 1985.

———. *Rio Tigre and Beyond*. Berkeley, CA: North Atlantic Books, 1971.

Lee, Seung-Heun. *Brain Respiration*. Seoul, South Korea: Han Mun Hwa, 1998.

Leung, A. Y., and S. Foster. *Encyclopedia of Common Natural Ingredients: Used in Food, Drugs and Cosmetics*. New York: Wiley, 1996.

Loeffler, Nicole. *Pilot Study Report* (2006): 3.

Luna, Luis, and Pablo Amaringo. *Ayahuasca Visions: The Religious Iconography of a Peruvian Shaman*. Berkeley, CA: North Atlantic Books, 1991.

Mandel, Peter. *Esogetics*. Sulzbach/Taunus, Germany: Energetik-Verlag, 1993.

———. *The Practical Compendium of Colorpuncture*. Bruschal, West Germany: Energetik, 1986.

Mandelbrot, B. B. *The Fractal Geometry of Nature*. San Francisco: W. H. Freeman, 1982.

McKenna, Terence. *The Archaic Revival*. New York: Harper Collins, 1991.

———. *Food of the Gods*. New York: Bantam Books, 1992.

Moore, Michael. *Medicinal Plants of the Mountain West*. Santa Fe: Museum of New Mexico Press, 1979.

Moring, Stephen E. Monograph in *Echinacea: The Immune Herb* by Christopher Hobbs, 1–3. Santa Cruz, CA: Botanica Press, 1990.

Mother, The. *Flowers and Their Messages.* Auroville, India: Sri Aurobindo Ashram, 1984.

Mowrey, Daniel B. *The Scientific Validation of Herbal Medicine*, 191. New Canaan, CT: Keats, 1986.

Myss, Caroline. *Anatomy of the Spirit.* New York: Harmony Books, 1996.

Nader, Tony. *Human Physiology: Expression of Veda and the Vedic Literature.* Vlodrop, Holland: Maharishi Vedic University, 1995.

Newall, C.A., L. A. Anderson, and J. D. Phillipson. *Herbal Medicines.* London: Pharmaceutical Press, 1996.

Potterton, David. *Culpeper's Color Herbal.* New York: Sterling, 1983.

Priest, A. W. and L. R. *Herbal Medication.* London: L. N. Fowler, 1982.

Puri, and D. C. Bagchi. "Herb Report: Gota Kola." *American Herb Association* 8, no. 1 (1991).

Ratsch, Christian. *The Gateway to Inner Space: A Festschrift in Honor of Albert Hoffmann.* Dorset, UK: Prism, 1989.

Rendel, Peter. *Introduction to the Chakras.* Wellingborough, UK: Chaucer, 1979.

Ryan, Glen. *Conference Proceedings*, 1988.

Saha, N. N. *Stellar Healing: Cure and Control of Diseases through Gems.* New Delhi, India: Sagar, 1976.

Santillo, Humberto. *Natural Healing with Herbs.* Prescott Valley, AZ: Hohm, 1984.

Schneider, Michael S. *Constructing the Universe.* New York: Harper-Perennial, 1995.

Schultes, Richard Evans, and Albert Hoffman. *Plants of the Gods.* Rochester, VT: Healing Arts Press, 1992.

Shealy, Norman. "The Reality of EEG and Neurochemical Responses to Photostimulation—Part II." In *Light Years Ahead*, 185. Berkeley, CA: Light Years Ahead Productions, 1996.

Shook, Edward F. *Advanced Treatise in Herbology.* Beaumont, CA: Trinity Center, 1978.

Smith, Ed. *The Herbal Magazine* (February 1986): 10.

Somé, Malidoma Patrice. *Of Water and the Spirit: Ritual, Magic, and Initiation in the Life of an African Shaman*. New York: Putnam, 1994.

Spoerke, David G. Jr. *Herbal Medications*. Santa Barbara, CA: Woodbridge, 1980.

Steiner, Rudolf. *Discussions with Teachers*. Hudson, NY: Anthroposophic Press, 1997.

———. *Spiritual Science and Medicine*. London: Anthroposophic Press, 1948.

Stone, Randolph. *Energy: The Vital Polarity in the Healing Arts*. Orange, CA: Pierre Pannetier, 1954.

Stuart, Malcolm, ed. *The Encyclopedia of Herbs and Herbalism*. London: Orbis, 1979.

Sun Bear. *Self-Reliance Book*. Spokane, WA: Bear Tribe, 1977.

Sussman, Janet. *Chakra and Energy Body* seminar series, 1999.

———. *Reality of Time* lecture series, 2007.

———. *Timeshift: The Experience of Dimensional Change*. Fairfield, IA: Time Portal, 1996.

Svoboda, Robert. *The Hidden Secret of Ayurveda*. Weed, CA: Trishula, 1980.

———. *Prakruti: Your Ayurvedic Constitution*. Albuquerque, NM: Geocom, 1988.

Swedish Herbal Institute. "Public Information Document" (1990): 1–3.

Swerdlow, Stewart. *The Healer's Handbook: A Journey into Hyperspace*. Westbury, NY: Skybooks, 1999.

Tansley, David V. *Radionics & the Subtle Anatomy of Man*. Essex, UK: C.W. Daniel, 1985.

ten Dam, Max. *Consciousness and Matter*. Lelystad, Holland: Soma Scientific, 1985.

Tierra, Michael. *Planetary Herbology*. Santa Fe, NM: Lotus, 1989.

Treben, Maria. *Health Through God's Pharmacy*. Steyr, Austria: Wilhelm Ennstahaler, 1982.

Vlamis, Gregory. *Flowers to the Rescue*. New York: Thorsons, 1986.

Vogel, Virgil J. *American Indian Medicine*. Norman: University of Oklahoma Press, 1970.

Wagner, H. L., L. Horhammer, and R. Munster. "The Chemistry of Silymarin (Silybin), the Active Principle of the Fruits of *Silybum marianum* (L.) Gaertn. (*Carduus marianus* L.)," *Arzneim Forsch* 18 (1968): 688–696.

Walker, Barbara G. *The Book of Sacred Stones.* San Francisco: Harper & Row, 1989.

Wallace, Robert Keith. *The Neurophysiology of Enlightenment.* Fairfield, IA: Maharishi International University Press, 1991.

Webster, R. *Gems.* Cornwall, UK: Butterworth, 1983.

Weed, Susun. *Healing Wise.* Woodstock, NY: Ash Tree, 1989.

Weil, Andrew. *The Marriage of the Sun and the Moon.* Boston: Houghton Mifflin, 1980.

Weiss, Rudolf F. *Herbal Medicine*, 1988.

Whitmont, C. Edward. *Psyche and Substance.* Berkeley, CA: North Atlantic Books, 1991.

White, John. *Kundalini: Evolution and Enlightenment.* New York: Anchor Books/Doubleday, 1979.

Wickes-Felter, Harvey. *The Eclectic Materia Medica, Pharmacology & Therapeutic.* Portland, OR: Eclectic Medical, 1985.

Willard, Terry. *The Wild Rose Scientific Herbal.* Calgary, AB: Wild Rose College of Natural Healing, 1991.

Winter, Dan. *Alphabet of the Heart.* New York: Author, 1992.

Wood, Matthew. *The Magical Staff.* Berkeley, CA: North Atlantic Books, 1992.

———. *Seven Herbs: Plants as Teachers.* Berkeley, CA: North Atlantic Books, 1986.

Wren, R. C. *Potter's New Cyclopedia of Botanical Drugs and Preparations.* Essex, UK: C. W. Daniel, 1988.

Wright, Machaelle Small. *Flower Essences.* Jeffersonton, VA: Perelandra, 1988.

INDEX

ABOUT THE AUTHOR

Elizabeth "Lilli" Botchis, PhD, holds a doctorate in Health and Human Services and master's degrees in Herbology and in Health Education and Counseling. She also holds multiple certifications in natural healing therapies, including polarity therapy, color puncture, flower essence therapy, and Reiki. In 2008, she was inducted into the Sovereign Order of the Knights Hospitaller of St. John of Jerusalem, founder of the world's first hospital.

Lilli is a highly sensitive and inspiring educator in the fields of advanced wellness and awakening of the soul's potential. With more than thirty-five years' experience as a holistic health practitioner, teacher, and natural-product developer, she has been a guiding light for thousands seeking a natural alchemical path to elevating mind/body consciousness. Her expertise includes the fields of botanicals, gem and color therapies, bio-energy therapies, flower essence therapy, and natural DNA-gene solutions. She is deeply devoted to helping people unlock their innate and spontaneous healing processes.

A native of Massachusetts, Lilli lives in Vero Beach, Florida, where she enjoys the beauty of the natural world and the rejuvenating influences of sun and ocean.

To contact Lilli Botchis:
lillibotchis@gmail.com
www.earthspectrum.com